Sixth Edition

# International Typewriting

MW01480447

# By the Same Author

GREEK TYPEWRITING Textbook approved for high schools by the Ministry of Education in Greece and Cyprus.

EFFICIENT TYPING Television film produced by the author at the University of Leeds TV Studios

POLITICAL ECONOMY (Co-author with son Nelson). Textbook approved for high schools by the Ministry of Education in Greece and Cyprus.

EDUCATION IN YORKSHIRE A study of Yorkshire educational establishments (approved by the Republic of Cyprus for public libraries).

SCHOOL PULSES An anthology from the author's educational speeches (approved by the Republic of Cyprus for public libraries).

GOLDEN KEY Classical wisdom made comprehensible (approved by the Republic of Cyprus for public libraries).

THE HEADMASTER IN CYPRUS A three-dimensional perspective of the Headmaster (approved by the Republic of Cyprus for public libraries)-Library of Congress Catalogue Card No. 73-170996 (USA).

Sixth Edition

# International Typewriting

**C NEOCLEUS FRSA FSCT FBSC**
**Headmaster, the Nicosia Economic Lycée**
**State Examiner (Cyprus) in Typewriting**

First published by C Neocleus

Sixth Edition published by Stanley Thornes (Publishers) Ltd, Old Station Drive, Leckhampton, CHELTENHAM, GL53 0DN

Reprinted 1986
Reprinted 1987
Reprinted 1988

British Library Cataloguing in Publication Data

Neocleus, C.
International typewriting.—6th ed.
1. Typewriting
I. Title
652.3 Z49

ISBN 0-85950-138-8

ISBN 085950-143-4 PbK

Printed in Hong Kong by Wing King Tong Co. Ltd.

# Contents

## Preliminary Pages (i-x)



## Part 1 (Pages 1-32)



## Part 2 (Pages 34-61)



## Part 3 (Pages 63-71)



## Part 4 (Pages 73-103)



## Part 5 (Pages 105-59)



## Part 6 (Pages 161-220)



## Part 7 (Pages 222-58)




Contents in detail
precede each part of the book

# Acknowledgements

Acknowledgements are due to the *London Chamber of Commerce and Industry (CES)* for kindly permitting me to reproduce selected material from past examination papers.

We are grateful to the LCCI for their permission to use the company name COMLON: the name given by the LCCI to various fictitious companies used in their examinations.

Especial gratitude, however, is owed to the Assistant Director of the LCCI (CES), Mr. B. W. Hurn, and the Chief Examiners in Typewriting, Mr. F. L. P. Thorne, ACP, FFTCom, FSCT, and Mrs. M. Medlyn, FFTCom, FSCT, for reading the manuscripts of this text and offering invaluable suggestions.

Indebtedness is also expressed for a number of speed test passages that have been extracted from *Office Management* (MacDonald & Evans) and the British science journal *Spectrum.*

# Preface

This sixth edition of the 'International Typewriting', produced by Stanley Thornes (Publishers) Ltd, has been made necessary because of the author's desire to update its contents to meet the latest requirements of the various examining bodies.

As has been universally acknowledged this manual offers instruction in a clear and methodical manner and, in addition, it introduces a very effective method of keyboard teaching whereby:

i The strongest fingers are used first and the weakest last - a technique which gives the beginner a feeling of confidence and satisfaction.

ii Complete words are used right from the first lesson, with meaningful phrases and sentences as early as the third - a feature which evokes and maintains the students' interest.

iii Location exercises are supplemented with more drills (common-word, one-hand, alternate-hand, etc) - a prerequisite for the achievement of considerable accuracy and speed by the time the keyboard is fully covered.

Moreover, this edition provides:

1. A wider variety of consolidation and supplementary exercises for the faster students.
2. A careful and progressive introduction to manuscripts.
3. More emphasis on open punctuation and the fully-blocked style.
4. New material (commercial, legal, technical, etc) based on modern requirements.
5. Many LCCI examination assignments on letters, memorandums, tabulations etc, and
6. Ample data on all aspects of the art of typewriting, useful both to the office typist and the examination candidate.

**September 1983** **C Neocleus**

# Index

# To the teacher

As typewriting courses differ in time span and emphasis, it is important that students who do not require the highest level of proficiency should know which exercises of this book are essential to them and those which may be omitted. Thus:

1. To those who are taking up typing to meet only their personal needs, and others who wish to gain a pass at 'elementary' level, I would suggest that they give priority to exercises in Table 'A' below, ignoring those in Table 'D' if time is limited.

2. For those who wish to attain a more advanced level leading to success at the 'intermediate' stage it is imperative that they work on exercises in Table 'B', omitting those in Table 'C', if they must.

3. And, for those who seek perfection in the art of typewriting, and look forward to a 'higher' stage certificate as a key to a professional career, I believe that a comprehensive use of this textbook will enable them to achieve these goals.

---

**TABLE 'A' - Elementary Stage**

**Exercises: 1-142, 144-53, 157-210, 219-25, 228-31, 234, 238-39, 244, 251, 256, 260-67, 274-75, 277-80, 285-98, 305, 355, 363.**

**TABLE 'B' - Intermediate Stage**

**Exercises: 143, 154-56, 211-15, 232-33, 235-37, 240-43, 245-48, 254, 257-58, 268, 271-72, 281-84, 299, 302, 306-9, 317-18, 321-22, 325-28, 331-32, 342, 345-46, 354, 356, 361-62, 365.**

**TABLE 'C' - Higher Stage**

**Exercises: 216-18, 226-27, 249-50, 252-53, 255, 259, 269-70, 273, 276, 300, 303-4, 310-16, 319-20, 323-24, 329-30, 333-41, 343-44, 347-53, 357-60, 364.**

**TABLE 'D' - Exercises that may be omitted through lack of time**

**Exercises: 10, 15, 19, 24, 26, 31, 35, 38, 41, 44, 45, 49, 51, 54, 58, 62, 66, 68, 76-7, 79, 82, 83, 85, 88-90, 98, 103-5, 109, 115, 117, 123, 129, 133-40, 172-80, 182-86, 204, 207, 210, 214-15, 222-25, 229, 232, 239, 241, 243, 245, 249, 252-53, 255, 259, 268, 270, 273, 298, 300, 302, 304, 307, 309-14, 316, 318-20, 323-25, 328, 333-41, 346-53, 357-60, 364-65.**

# Part 1

## Contents

rotated, the copy paper - dampened with spirit - is pressed against the master copy which thus leaves the impression on the paper.

A spirit duplicator can reproduce up to seven colours simultaneously; these, however, fade with time, and the clarity of the image becomes progressively weaker.

## The stencil duplicator

The stencil duplicator can produce as many as five thousand copies from a single well-cut stencil of good quality, provided that the duplicator is operated efficiently.

The stencil is a thin fibre sheet covered on one side with a plastic coating. It is 'cut' either with a typewriter or a hand stylus and then wrapped around an inked drum. As the

drum is rotated the copy paper is fed between it and an impression roller, when the ink is forced through the stencil on to the paper producing the image.

### Cutting a stencil - correcting errors

To cut a stencil effectively: 1. Clean the typebar characters; 2. disengage the ribbon (optional on electric typewriters); 3. type with an even touch; 4. pull the paper-release lever occasionally to avoid wrinkles on

stencil. To correct errors: Separate stencil from its carbon sheet with a pen; brush error over with correcting fluid; wait for a few seconds until fluid has dried; re-type carefully.

### The electronic stencil

An advanced method of reproducing printed matter, line drawings or halftone photographs. The document to be copied is placed around a roller and it is electronically scanned, while 500 perforations to the inch give a faithful reproduction of the stencil which is produced on another cylinder in the machine.

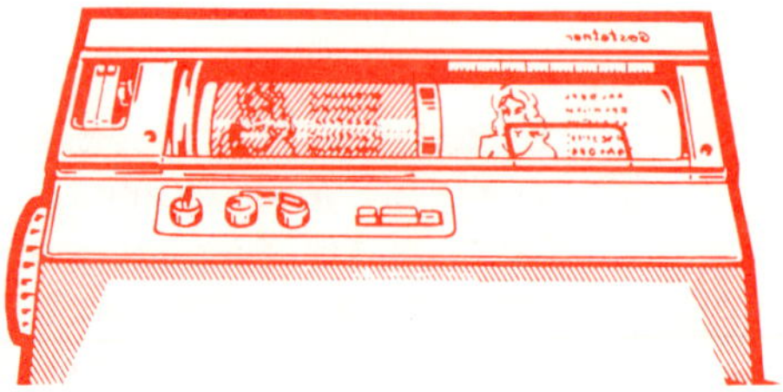

### The Thermal Process

The thermal stencil is processed in a dry heat machine. This method takes only a few seconds in comparison with the electronic which takes about five minutes. The thermal machine, however, cannot reproduce coloured originals and the copies are not of the same high quality as those of the electronic process.

## The photo copier

The photocopying machine can give very clear copies in black and white – some machines even give copies in full colour. They use either special or ordinary paper and run at speeds of up to 30 copies a minute. They can produce enlarged or reduced copies from books, graphs, charts, maps, computer printouts and even three dimensional objects.

The photo copier can often replace the duplicator and the offset lithography process.

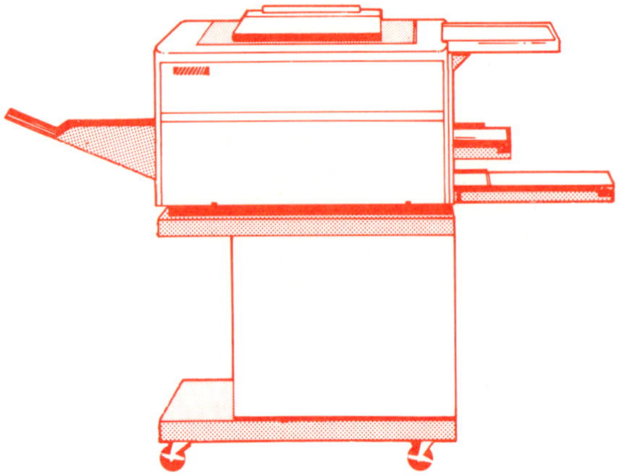

# THE EVOLUTION OF THE TYPEWRITER

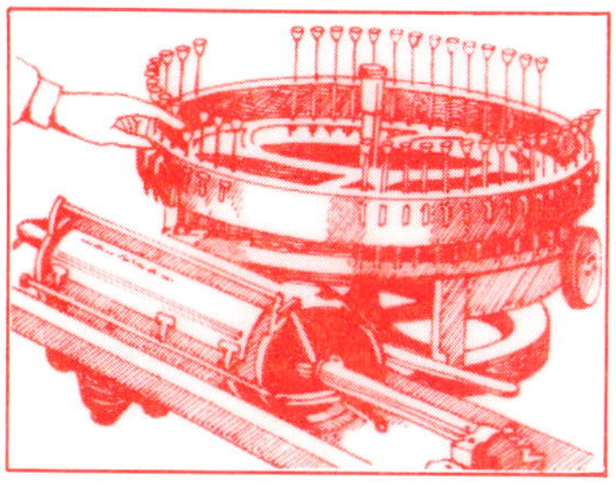

**1843**

**1857**

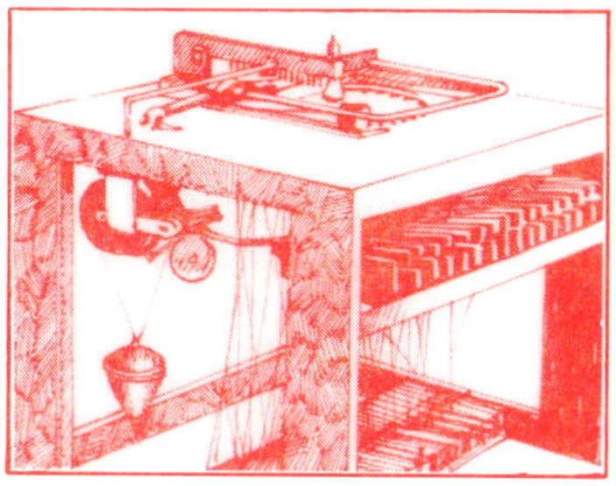

**1868**

The first attempt to produce a writing machine was made by the English inventor Henry Mill who obtained a patent from Queen Anne in 1714. The second patent was granted to the American inventor William Burt in 1829; and in 1833 a third one was given to the French inventor Xavier Progin.

In 1856 a machine was developed by Alfred Beach, USA, which resembled modern typewriters in arrangement of its keys but printed its letters on a narrow strip instead of a sheet. A similar machine patented by the American Samuel Francis in 1856 had a circular arrangement of type bars, a moving paper holder, and a warning bell to ring at the end of the typing line.

**1874**

During the 1850s and 1860s a number of inventors tried to produce a workable typewriter, but none succeeded until 1868 when three Americans, Sholes, Glidden and Soulè, patented an experimental writing machine and finally marketed the first practical typewriter in 1873.

In early typewriters the type bars struck at the bottom of the platen and so the typing line was not visible. In 1883 this disadvantage was removed by E. Horton who introduced the first typewriter with fully visible typing.

Between 1890 and 1905 more than a hundred new typewriter designs were marketed but few of them proved successful. Since then, however, developments of the typewriter have greatly extended its usefulness. As far as the businessman is concerned, the most important advance has been the development of the book-keeping machine.

Electric typewriters have been in extensive use since the late 1930s. In these machines a motor-driven mechanism performs the actual work of lifting the type bars and striking them against the ribbon and also of returning the carriage at the end of the line.

**1914**

**1938**

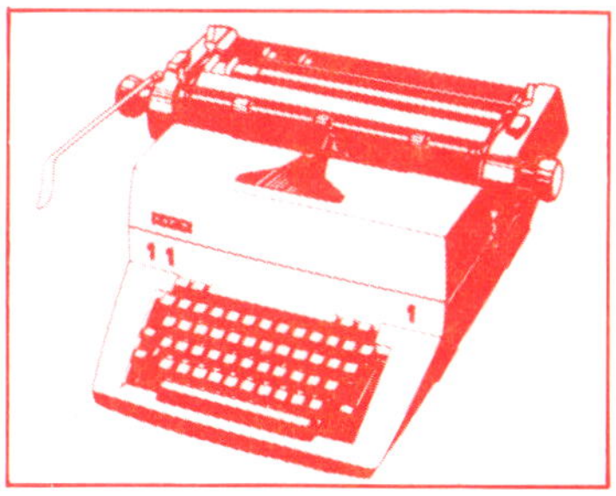

**A modern design**

# Typing for Reproducing Machines

The vast amount of routine and repetitive work in the modern business office has necessitated the development of a variety of duplicating machines, such as the electronic typewriter, the word processor, the traditional spirit and stencil duplicators, etc.

It is worth noting that the use of the conventional carbon sheet makes the ordinary typewriter the simplest form of duplicating machine. Normally, an electric typewriter will produce up to eighteen copies, while a standard one up to eight, depending on the thickness of the copy paper, the condition of the carbon paper, the ribbon (preferably silk or nylon) and the touch of the typist.

## The electronic typewriter with memory

This can store in its memory up to four pages of frequently used words, sentences or paragraphs, ready to be printed whenever required. The electronic typewriter offers many time-saving features: removal of words and/or replacement by others, automatic correction, centring, underlining, tabulation, justification, pitch selection, etc.

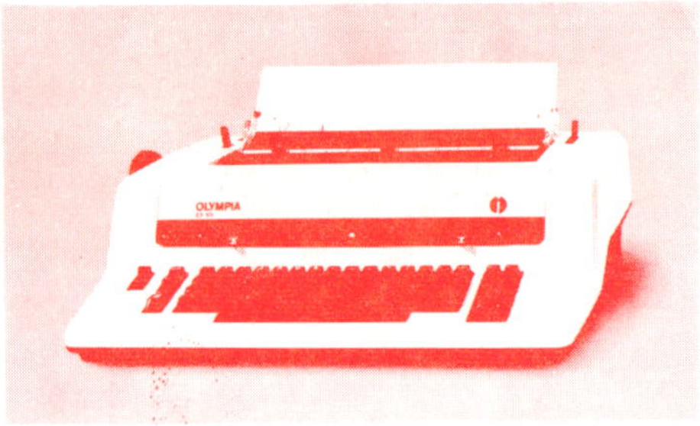

## The word processor

A word processor is an intelligent typewriter based on microelectronic technology and offering a large number of different facilities to increase the productivity of typing operation. A typical word processor consists of a keyboard, a visual display unit, a printer and some form of storage medium (usually magnetic discs), together with a central processing unit which gives the system «intelligence». It can store in its memory about 80 pages of printed text and type them when required at a speed of about 500 words a minute.

The 'Financial Times Review' (16.6.81) described the word processor as a computer which handles words, text and data. The words typed appear on a video screen like a television set in front of the typist; this makes it possible to see what is being typed and to make modification before a word is set in hard copy, and also to review material held in memory. The spelling of about 50,000 words can be automatically corrected, words added or deleted and blocks of text moved from one part of the document to another.

All the material typed can be stored in the computer's memory and retrieved at will. It therefore becomes possible to set up standard documents or create letters from standard paragraphs. When the typescript is considered perfect it can be printed out at the touch of a button.

Training for word processors is offered both by their manufacturers and an increasing number of secretarial colleges and business schools. The qualities needed for a good word processing operator include:

1. Fast and accurate typing: this will enable the typist to exploit in full the machine's capabilities.
2. Interest in machinery: an operator with this interest is likely to use the machine as efficiently as possible.
3. A logical mind to solve particular problems and perform tasks.
4. A high degree of concentration, to cope with the noise and distractions in a large word-processing installation.
5. Transcribing ability: an operator needs to be able to transcribe from longhand or audio with accuracy.
6. Good language skills: the operator needs a good vocabulary, an ability to spell correctly, to punctuate, and to recognise grammatical errors.

## The spirit duplicator (hectograph)

A simple method of reproducing about 150 copies. The master copy consists of a sheet of art paper on which typing is done with a special carbon paper behind it and which is then fastened to a drum. When the drum is

# THE TYPEWRITER

*«A machine which prints characters in sequence, performing the work of writing at a speed far greater than is possible with the pen.»*

*ENCYCLOPAEDIA BRITANNICA*

## The manual typewriter

It has 45 keys which give 90 characters.

Its horizontal spacing (pitch) is either pica, which means typing of 10 characters to an inch; or elite, which means typing of 12 characters to an inch.

Its vertical spacing is normally 6 lines to an inch. On most typewriters, there is also half-spacing, which gives 11 lines to an inch.

*A manual typewriter*

## The electric typewriter

This offers:

More even and more rapid typing, because of ease of operation;

Electrical operation of shift keys, hyphen / underscore, space-bar, backspacer, line spacing, margin setting, tabulator, and carriage return;

Clear impression and uniform density of copies; better quality of stencil work; and a greater number of legible carbon copies;

Perfect alignment, i.e. all letters, whether capital or small, appear on a straight line;

Use of different type faces (with some models only), such as: Courier, Delegate, ORATOR, Advocate, Scribe, Gothic, *Italic*, *Script*, etc.

*An electric typewriter*

In the section on keyboard learning, the sign ϟ will indicate differences in electric typewriter operation.

## The electronic typewriter

In addition to the features of the electric one, this provides:

Automatic centring, underscoring and justification of right-hand margin.

Proportional spacing and use of heavy type for emphasizing words or phrases.

Storing in its memory of frequently used words, sentences or whole paragraphs ready to print whenever required.

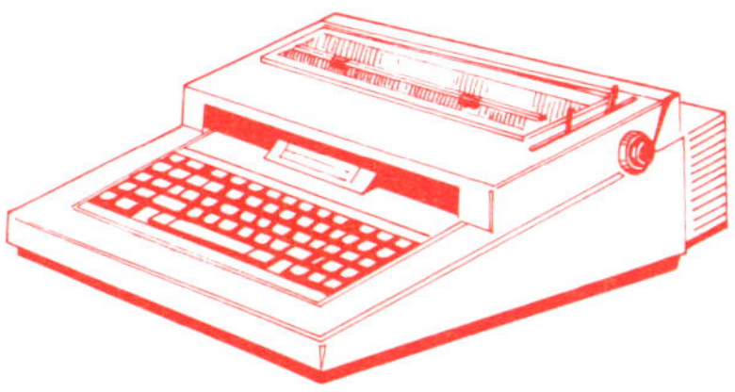

*An electronic typewriter*

# Composition Skill on the Typewriter — Creative typing

**Now that you have learnt to type what you see, try to type what you think; i.e. try to develop a composition skill on the typewriter by recording your own ideas.**

**FIRST STEP: Ask questions which require *word* answers, e.g. «What is my teacher's name?» (type the answer); «What is the weather like today?» (type the answer) and so on. For this stage you can allocate two or three minutes at the beginning or the end of the day's lesson - for two or three consecutive lessons.**

**SECOND STEP: Ask questions which require *sentence* answers, e.g. «What will you do in the school library?» (type the answer in a complete sentence). For this stage you can spend about five minutes at the beginning or the end of the lesson - for three or four consecutive lessons.**

**THIRD STEP: Ask questions that require *short paragraph* answers; e.g. «Preparing for an outing with friends» (type the opening paragraph.) For this stage give a quarter of an hour for, say, five consecutive lessons.**

**PROCEDURE: Type your answer in double-line spacing crossing out any material which you would like to change. When you finish, take your work out of the typewriter and give it more thought: improve your wording and your ideas, and correct grammar, spelling, punctuation and sentence structure. In making corrections, use the official signs - repeated here for your convenience - and give your typescript to your teacher for a final check. Re-type your work clearly in single spacing and put it in your file.**

**LATER STAGES: After you feel you have had sufficient practice in composing, find subject ideas and develop them on the typewriter. These can be impromptu subjects, but occasionally they can be subjects requiring reading and preparation in advance; i.e. «Working in my garden», «The film I saw last night», «Plans for my next holiday», etc. You will type such subjects as though you were talking to someone.**

## Exercise 365

**Type a short essay on a subject of your own choice, read, correct (in the manner shown in the example below); then re-type a clean copy in single-line spacing.**

who had been also invited

A FANCY DRESS PARTY

I had been invited to a fancy dress party and as Iam not very keen on ~~those~~ that sort of part~~ies~~y I did not realy want to go. Most of my friends feel ~~like~~ as I do and beleive that they are ~~alright~~ all right for childrens' parties. Any way we decided to go ~~altogether~~ all together. Each of us ~~were~~ was representing well-known members of parliament. in a group.

At the begining the band played very slow and the people were quite but soon ~~everyone was~~ all were enjoying themselves.It was a different sort of party ~~to~~ from the ones we usualy go to and we had only gone because the girl giving the party ~~because the girl giving the party~~ was a good friend of ~~us.~~ ours. However I must say I enjoyed ~~it very much~~ immensely.

**CORRECTIONS SIGNS** insert apostrophe, insert quotation marks, stet let it stand, insert hyphen, insert dash, insert colon, run on; no new paragraph, two lines under a word: use closed capitals, three lines under a word: use spaced caps, insert, take out, close up, insert space, transpose, indent, N.P. new paragraph, U.C. upper case, l.c. small letter, insert full stop.

## PARTS OF THE TYPEWRITER

**Examine the following parts of the typewriter; identify their location on your machine with the help of the illustrations and learn to operate them. (The location of some parts varies with different makes of typewriters.)**

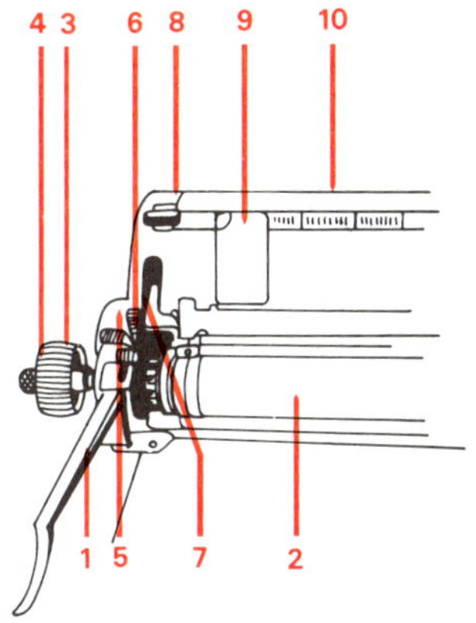


CARRIAGE: The top part of the typewriter that travels from right to left each time you strike a key or the space bar. (More advanced electric machines have no carriage but instead a segment that moves as it types.)

CARRIAGE-RETURN LEVER: The lever on the top left-hand side of the machine; used to return carriage to left margin and to move paper up. (1)

PLATEN (CYLINDER): The roller in the carriage, around which the typing paper is curved. (2)

PLATEN TURNING KNOBS: Situated at each end of the platen, they are turned to move the paper forwards or backwards. (3)

CARRIAGE-RELEASE LEVERS: Situated at each end of carriage. When either of these is pressed, carriage moves freely to any position. (5)

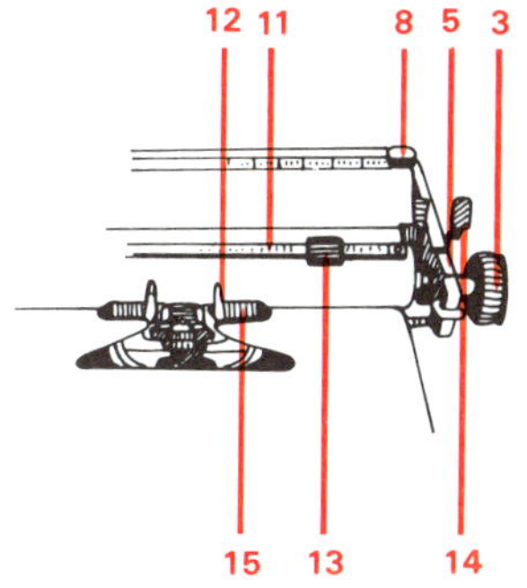


PAPER BAIL: A movable arm, marked with a paper scale, used to hold paper against platen. (11)

PAPER GRIPS: Movable rollers fitted to the paper bail, used to hold paper firmly against platen. (13)

PAPER GUIDE: An adjustable plate against which the paper is positioned as it is inserted into the typewriter. (9)

PAPER-RELEASE LEVER: Used to allow paper to be removed or aligned.(14)

LINE-SPACE SELECTOR: Used to move paper 1, 2 or 3 lines for single, double or treble spacing. (6)

MARGIN STOPS: These are fixed to the points where you wish your lines to begin and end. (8)

CARD GUIDE: Small metal sheet above printing point, used to hold firm thick envelopes, cards, labels etc. against platen. (15)

LINE FINDER: A lever used to change line spacing temporarily. When re-engaged, it brings platen to the original typing line. (7)

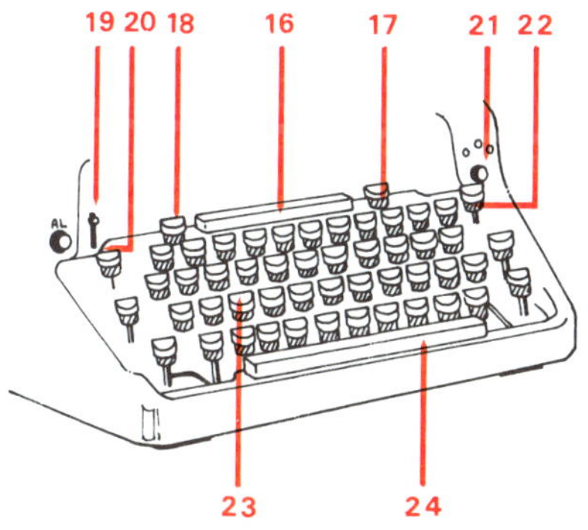


VARIABLE LINE SPACER: Situated at end of left platen turning knob; used to change writing line setting permanently. (4)

SCALES: Used to help in the planning of displayed work. They are known as paper scale (10), bail-bar scale (11) and writing-line scale (15).

TRANSPARENT PAPER HOLDERS: Small plastic sheets to the right and left of printing point, used to hold firm small paper, cards, or envelopes for typing; also used for speedy ruling. (12)

LINE INDICATORS: A series of vertical marks, used to position the paper correctly after erasing. They can be seen at right and left of ribbon, at printing point. (15)

KEYBOARD: The table of keys consisting of four rows. (23)

SPACE BAR: Used to move the carriage forward, one space at a time. (24)

TOUCH-CONTROL ADJUSTER: (Not provided on all typewriters). Used to adapt the machine to various touch pressures. (19)

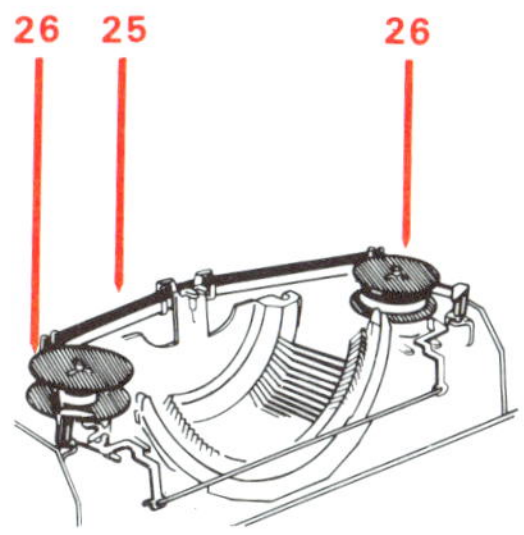


BACKSPACE KEY: Used to move the carriage back, one space at a time. (20)

MARGIN-RELEASE KEY: Used to move carriage beyond margin stops. (22)

TABULATOR BAR, SET and CLEAR KEYS: Usually placed above the rows of keys and used for tabulated display (16, 17, 18)

RIBBON: The tape (cotton, silk, nylon or carbon coated plastic) against which the types strike to leave their impression on the paper (25). It travels from one spool to the other (26); at the end it reverses automatically.

RIBBON POSITION INDICATOR: Used to select ribbon typing position (top half, neutral, bottom half). (21)

# Justification

**Occasionally you might like to give your typescript a better appearance - more or less like that of a printed page. To achieve this you can *justify* the right-hand margin, i.e. make it *even* by lengthening the shorter lines and shortening the longer ones.**

*Procedure*

1. **Type the first line of the passage giving it the required width.**

2. **Type the second line bringing it as near the end of the previous one as possible. If it is shorter by, say, two spaces fill these spaces in by typing two distinctive signs, e.g. two soliduses; (see second line of passage below.)**

3. **Type the third line, again bringing it as near the previous one as possible. If this is longer by, say, one space, underline this *hanging* letter; (see third line of same passage.)**

4. **Continue in like manner completing the shorter lines with soliduses and underscoring the hanging letters.**

This is a passage *before* justification. Note the signs at line ends.

```
1.   Where typists in an organisation are employed on a personal
basis there are always times when some of them are overemployed/
while others are idle.  Mainly in an effort to overcome this, the
typists are usually "pooled" in one room and the work is shared/
among them.  The advantages are so obvious that typing pools have
been set up in all medium and large-scale organisations today.
```

N O W re-type the same passage bearing in mind that:

(a) For each solidus at the end of line you should add an *extra* space between any two words of that line - preferably before relative pronouns and conjunctions or after punctuation marks.

(b) For each underscored hanging letter you should subtract one space from that line. Subtraction is better made from blank spaces that follow punctuation marks. If there are no blank spaces in a line squeeze a word into fewer spaces.

*NOTE: Electronic typewriters and word processors can achieve justification automatically at the push of a button.*

This is the above passage *after* justification.

```
1.   Where typists in an organisation are employed on a personal
basis there are always times  when some of them are overemployed
while others are idle. Mainly in an effort to overcome this, the
typists are usually "pooled" in one room  and the work is shared
among them. The advantages are so obvious that typing pools have
been set up in all medium and large-scale organisations today.
```

## Exercise 364

**Type the following paragraphs - a continuation of the above passage - justifying its right-hand margin. Use the same width of line.**

2. In addition to the more even distribution of work, other advantages of typing pools include the minimising of interruption to work (noise) to other clerks; better training for junior typists; concentration on typing by the typists (junior duties delegated to juniors); ideal working conditions can be provided for the typists; improved supervision of them; and better opportunity to compare the work of different typists.

3. Very few typists prefer to work in typing pools, and the disadvantages appear to be mostly on their side. They lose personal contact with executives and they may lose their continuity. Disadvantages with the management viewpoint are that the work may not be of high quality (different typists dealing with the same work); that there may be delays in getting work done; and that the pool may encourage gossiping.

# CORRECT SITTING POSITION

*Correct position at the typewriter will enable you to work comfortably and efficiently*

* Sit back in chair; body erect
* Keep your eyes fixed on copy
* Shoulders down; chest forward
* Forearms parallel to slope of keyboard; elbows loosely near the sides
* Palms hanging over keyboard; wrists straight; fingers bent; finger-tips vertical to keys
* Legs vertical to floor; preferably, one foot slightly ahead of other
* Relaxed posture; no tension

The desk is about 26″ (66 cm) high. The chair should have a curved back support (to avoid strain on spine); and its height should be adjusted to your own needs.

# Menus

A menu is a list of dishes to be served at a dinner, supper, or the like.

Menus may be displayed in the traditional manner (usually for important occasions) or typed in the blocked method. In either case, the different courses are separated from one another by four or five line spaces with asterisks, hyphens etc., typed along the centre of the space.

Menus are positioned centrally on the page; if displayed in the traditional method, they can be enclosed in a border line.

**EXAMPLES of a displayed and a blocked menu:**

```
            HILTON INTERNATIONAL

                   CYPRUS

               Luncheon  Menu


                Smoked Trout
               Russian Salad

                    ****

     Roast Fillet of Beef  with Mushrooms
             and Natural Gravy
           Croquettes Potatoes
           Seasonal Vegetables

                    ****

              Baked  Alaska

                    ****

                  Coffee

                    ****

                Friandises

                  --00--
```

```
HILTON INTERNATIONAL

CYPRUS

Luncheon Menu


Smoked Trout
Russian Salad

-------------

Roast Fillet of Beef with Mushrooms
  and Natural Gravy
Croquettes Potatoes
Seasonal Vegetables

-----------------------------------

Baked Alaska

------------

Coffee

------

Friandises

__________
```

## Exercise 363

**Lay out the following Menu in both styles - the blocked and the indented - and enclose in simple borders.**

MAJESTIC HOTEL  Menu --- Egg Mayonnaise --- Trout, Escalope, Fresh Garden Peas --- Fruit Salad and Ice Cream --- Chilled White Wine, Spirits, Beer --- Coffee

# KEYBOARD FINGERING CHART

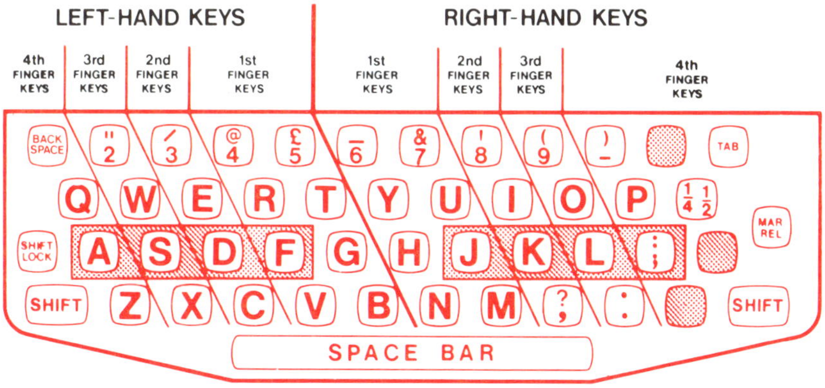


The keyboard is divided into two parts, and each of them is subdivided into four sections. Each finger strikes only the keys which are allocated to it.

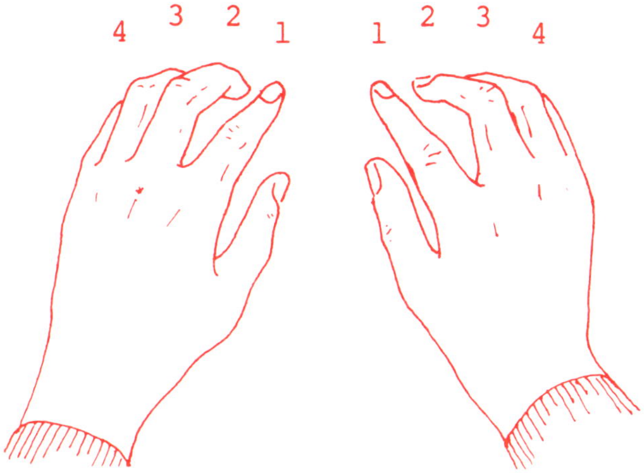


**Left-hand fingers rest on**

**Right-hand fingers rest on**

**The Home Keys**

The above eight keys, located on the middle row of letters, are called home keys, and act as guides for the rest of the keys.

On electric typewriters, the fingers should rest very lightly upon their home keys.

# Ornamentation

**By combining two or more characters of the typewriter you can create a wide variety of ornamental borders which can be used to decorate programmes, menus and other artistic work.**

**Ornamentations should be neat and simple; elaborate ones, which were popular in the past, are now out of fashion and are better avoided.**

**The following specimens will give you an idea of what you can achieve with some imagination. Repeat them once and then make a few borders of your own taste. (***The fifth border uses the colon (:) and the equals (=) sign.***)**

The first wealth is health

THE PRICE OF WISDOM IS ABOVE GOLD

LET JUSTICE BE DONE
THOUGH THE HEAVENS FALL

A good laugh is sunshine in a house

HE WHO SINGS FRIGHTENS AWAY HIS ILLS

Using the IBM 'Alphameric' ball you can make such border lines as the following:

E3E3E3E3E3E3E3E3E3E3E3E3E3E3E3E3E3E3E3E3E3E3E3E3

Using E and 3

2222222222222222222222222222222222222222222222222

Using number 2

525252525252525252525252525252525252525252525252

Using numbers 5 and 2

With the IBM 'Symbol' ball you can create such border lines as the following - using the half spacer:

×

××××××××××××××××××××××××××××××××××××××××××××××××

§

§§§§§§§§§§§§§§§§§§§§§§§§§§§§§§§§§§§§§§§§§§§§§§§§

{ }

{}{}{}{}{}{}{}{}{}{}{}{}{}{}{}{}{}{}{}{}{}{}{}{}

TAILPIECES

Tailpieces are used as decorations at the end of programmes, menus, book chapters, etc. The following are a few examples:

o:o:o:o:o

:-:-:-:-:

--oo0oo--

# Keyboard Learning

## Preliminary Instructions

### Before starting your first typing lesson:

1. See that the front frame of your typewriter is level with the edge of the desk.

2. Place your textbook to the right of the typewriter, raising its top for easy reading.

3. Move your chair slightly to the right so that the centre of your body is opposite to letter 'j' of the keyboard.

4. Insert paper:

   Set the paper guide on number '0' on the scale. Drop paper between platen and feed rollers with its left-hand edge against the paper guide.

   Raise the paper bail.

   Turn the right-hand platen knob until the paper comes to the required position.

   Push the paper bail back to hold the paper against the platen. (If the paper is not straight, pull the paper-release lever to straighten and align it.)

   *To protect the platen from the typing blows, place a sheet of thick paper - «backing sheet» - behind the typing paper.*

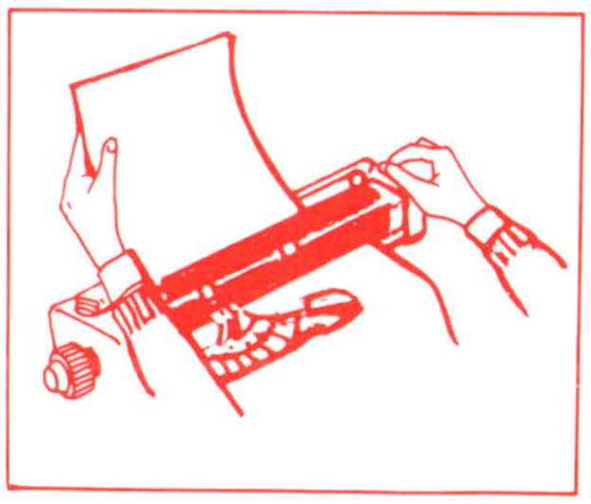

5. Set margin stops:

   Ways of setting margin stops vary according to the type of machine; the commonest, however, is the following:

   Press the left-hand margin key and move to the point where you wish to start your line.

   Press the right-hand margin key and move to the point where you wish your line to finish.

   (On electric typewriters: return carriage to margin stop and hold down the margin set key as you move the carriage to the desired margin point.)

# Itineraries

**An itinerary is a plan of a proposed tour giving a detailed account of a business journey. It is prepared by the secretary in consultation with the employer and it shows precise information on: (1) dates, (2) travel arrangements, (3) booking of accommodation, and (4) names, addresses and telephone numbers of people to be visited at specific times.**
**Short itineraries are usually typed on small-size cards; bigger itineraries, covering a journey of two or more days, are typed on A4 paper.**

## Exercise 361

**Type this one-day itinerary on A6 paper (14.8 x 10.5 cm)**

I T I N E R A R Y

Meeting with Mr N Newman
South-Western Area Manager
Tuesday, September 5

| | | |
|---|---|---|
| Departure: | King's Cross | 0915 hrs |
| Arrival: | Exeter | 1200 hrs |
| | Lunch with Mr Newman | |
| | Visit Plant | 1345 hrs |
| | Visit Office | 1530 hrs |
| Departure: | Exeter | 1800 hrs |
| Arrival: | King's Cross | 2145 hrs |

## Exercise 362

**Copy the following itinerary on A5 paper.**

Three-day tour - Mr R G White

| | | |
|---|---|---|
| Tuesday 13 April | 0810 hrs | Leave Euston for Leicester |
| | 1220 hrs | Lunch at Grand Hotel with Mr D Green |
| | 1400 hrs | Conference at Grand Hotel |
| | Accommodation booked at Imperial Hotel | |
| Wednesday 14 April | 1000 hrs | Leave Leicester for Leeds |
| | 1315 hrs | Meeting with Mr B Bendix in his office (35 Churchill Street) followed by lunch |
| | 1700 hrs | Leave Leeds for Edinburgh |
| | Accommodation booked at Northern Hotel | |
| Thursday 15 April | 0930 hrs | Conference with Scottish dealers at Northern Hotel |
| | 1130 hrs | Leave Edinburgh for Euston |

# Correct Techniques

## 1. FINGERING POSITION

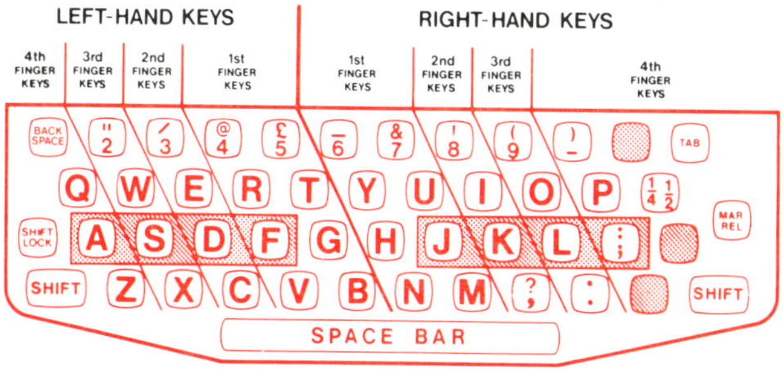


Look at the keyboard chart (opposite) and find the left-hand home keys: **A S D F.** Locate these keys on your typewriter and place your left-hand fingers on them; start with the index finger on F and finish with the little finger on A.

Locate the right-hand home keys: **J K L ;**. Place your right-hand fingers on them, starting with the index finger on J and ending with the little finger on ;.

## 2. HOW TO STRIKE THE KEYS

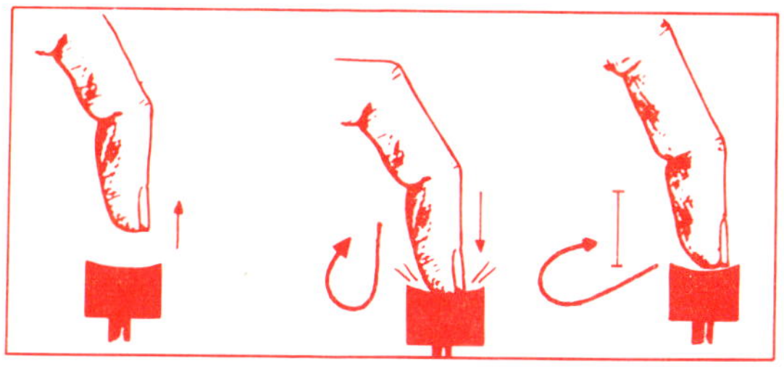

a. Strike keys exactly in their centre.
b. Use a fast, sharp, firm, but light blow.
c. Before striking, raise the finger slightly; this can be followed to some extent by the neighbouring fingers.

With electric typewriters: Do not strike the keys; only touch them lightly.

**Try now to strike the 'f' key**

1. Raise your left-hand index finger slightly (with finger-tip directed vertically on to the key).

2. Move finger down quickly and strike 'f' key *with a lively but gentle blow.*

3. Re-place finger immediately on its home position and get ready for the next blow.

*Repeat the same procedure several times, until you are satisfied that you have achieved the correct striking. Then, continue with the 'j' finger, using the same technique.*

## 3. HOW TO STRIKE THE SPACE BAR

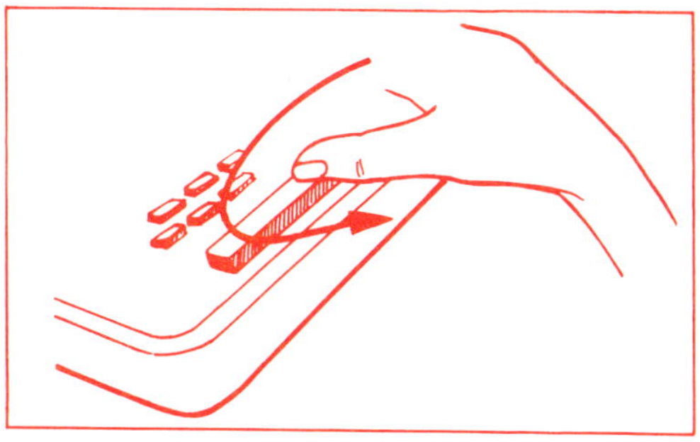

To obtain a space after typing a word you should strike the space bar once. To do so, use only the right thumb, letting the other fingers follow in a natural way. Make a 'downward/inward' sharp movement and return immediately to the home keys.

# Poetry

**In order to give poems a well-balanced and artistic effect observe the following rules:**

1. **Centre them on the page - short poems on A5 paper and longer ones on A4.**
2. **Centre the title over the longest line; use either capitals or lower case with underscore.**
3. **Start every line with a capital letter.**
4. **Use single spacing between lines and double or treble between verses.**
5. **Type the poet's name two line spaces below the end of the poem. This may be preceded by a dash (see poem A), typed in closed capitals (see poem B), in lower case and underscored (see poem C) or enclosed in brackets (see poem D). In all cases, it should line up with the longest line.**

```
A.        UPON WESTMINSTER BRIDGE

Earth has not anything to show more fair;
Dull would he be of soul who could pass by
A sight so touching in its majesty:
This City now doth like a garment wear
The beauty of the morning: silent, bare,
Ships, towers, domes, theatres and temples
                                     (lie
Open unto the fields and to the sky;
All bright and glittering in the smokeless
                                     (air.

                            - Wordsworth
```

**Where successive lines rhyme - as in the above poem - or where there is no rhyming at all, all lines should start at the same point.**
**Where a word or phrase extends outside the normal line it is 'hooked in', i.e. it is carried to the end of the succeeding line after a bracket sign.**

```
B.            THE PRINCESS

Sweet and low, sweet and low,
  Wind of the western sea,
Low, low, breathe and blow,
  Wind of the western sea!
Over the rolling waters go,
Come from the dying moon, and blow,
  Blow him again to me;
While my little one, while my pretty
                          (one sleeps.

                              TENNYSON
```

**In the above poem, rhyming lines begin at the same point. Thus, lines 1,3,5,6 and 8 start at the margin, while lines 2, 4 and 7 are indented two, or even three, spaces.**

*NOTE:*
*In modern style all lines, whether rhyming or not, may begin at the same point.*

## Exercise 359

**Copy the following two poems, noting in each the relationship between indentation and rhyming.**

```
C.        BABY BYE

Baby bye
Here's a fly,
Let us watch him, you and I,
  How he crawls
  Up the walls
  Yet he never falls.

          Theodore Tilton
```

(with "Theodore Tilton" underscored)

```
D.            Hyperion

The swallow is come!
The swallow is come!
  O, fair are the seasons, and light
Are the days that she brings,
With her dusky wings,
  And her bosom snowy white!

                        (Longfellow)
```

(with "Hyperion" underscored)

## Exercise 360

**Display the following poems typing the titles and the poets' names in any one of the accepted styles.** *(The bracket indicates a 'hooking in'; while the solidus a change of line.)*

**(a)** *'Venus and Adonis' by Shakespeare* **Lo! here the gentle lark, weary of (rest, / From his moist cabinet mounts up (on high, And wakes the morning, from whose (silver breast / The sun ariseth in his majesty.**

**(b)** *'Song' by Lowell* **Violet! sweet violet! / Thine eyes are full of tears; / Are they wet / Even yet / With the thought of other years.**

## 4. HOW TO RETURN THE CARRIAGE

When the typing line is nearing the right-hand margin stop, the typewriter bell will ring. This is a warning that you must change the line, provided that you have finished or hyphenated the word which you may have started.

To begin a new line you should return the carriage to the left-hand margin stop, as follows:

1. Keeping the right-hand fingers motionless on their home keys, move the left hand to the carriage-return lever, and bring back the carriage with a quick motion *without removing your eyes from the book.*

2. Re-place your hand on its home position as follows: Let your left-hand index finger feel its way to the right-hand index finger, move it to the left three keys and stay there - this being the correct position. *(In time you will not need to count the in-between keys; your fingers will find their home position automatically.)*

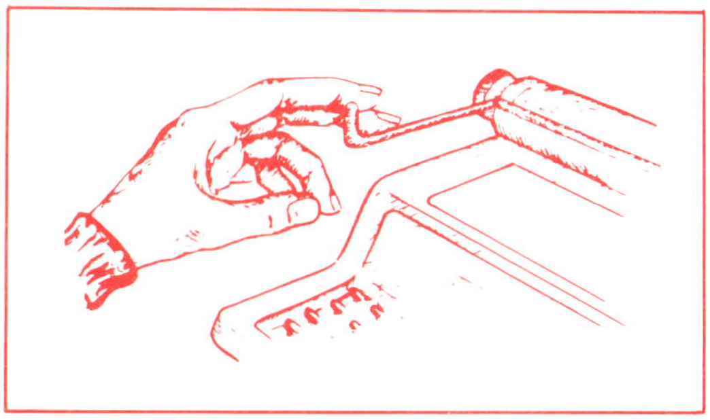

*Return carriage with a quick wrist-and-hand motion, without too much pressure on the margin*

On electric typewriters: To return the carriage, reach the finger of the right hand to return key, tap it and release it quickly. Return immediately to the home position.

* * *

## Exercise 358

**Repeat the following first page of a play. If you are using a pica machine make the necessary margin adjustments.**

MERRY WIVES OF WINDSOR

ACT I

SCENE 1

SCENE: The Street

Enter Mrs. Page, Mrs. Quickly, and William

MRS. PAGE Is he at Master Ford's already, think'st thou?

QUICKLY Sure he is by this; or will be presently: but truly he is very courageous mad about his throwing into the water. Mistress Ford desires you to come suddenly.

MRS. PAGE I'll be with her by and by; I'll but bring my young man here to school. Look, where his master comes; 'tis a playing day, I see. (Enter Sir Hugh Evans) How now, Sir Hugh? no school to-day?

EVANS No; Master Slender is let the boys leave to play.

QUICKLY Blessing of his heart!

MRS. PAGE Sir Hugh, my husband says my son profits nothing in the world at his book; I pray you ask him some questions in his accidence.

EVANS Come hither, William; hold up your head; come.

MRS. PAGE Come on, sirrah: hold up your head; answer your master; be not afraid.

EVANS William, how many numbers is in nouns?

WILLIAM Two.

QUICKLY Truly, I thought there had been one number more; because they say od's nouns.

EVANS Peace your tattlings. What is fair, William?

WILLIAM Pulcher.

QUICKLY Polecats! there are fairer things than polecats, sure.

EVANS You are a very simplicity, 'oman; I pray you, peace. What is

/lapis, William?

# Lesson 1

## Starting with F and J

1. Look at the chart below and find the left-hand home keys: **a s d f**. Locate these keys on your typewriter and place your left-hand fingers on them; start with the index finger on **f** and finish with the little finger on **a**.

2. Locate the right-hand home keys: **j k l ;** Place your right-hand fingers on them, starting with the index on **j** and ending with the little finger on **;**

3. Now, remove your hands from the home keys and set left-hand margin stop at 20 (for pica letters) or 24 (for elite). The right-hand margin stop is not at present required; therefore, set it at the end of the scale.

4. Check your sitting position, place your hands on on the home keys again and start typing the exercise below, applying strictly the technique described on pages 8-9.

5. Strike **f** key with your left-hand index; strike **j** with your right-hand index.

## Exercise 1

**Location drill**

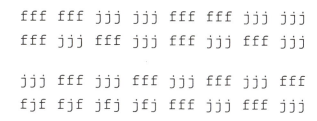

```
fff fff jjj jjj fff fff jjj jjj
fff jjj fff jjj fff jjj fff jjj

jjj fff jjj fff jjj fff jjj fff
fjf fjf jfj jfj fff jjj fff jjj
```

**Silently say each letter as you type it.**

*Sit in an erect position*

Repeat the above exercise twice, taking care to:

1. Type at a slow but steady speed.
2. Use rhythmic beats both for the keys and the space bar.
3. Avoid looking at the keyboard or your typing paper.
4. Examine your typing line only after it is finished.

*Keep elbows loosely near your sides*

**On electric typewriters**

1. Let your fingers hover lightly over the home keys; not rest on them.
2. Do not strike the keys; only touch them slightly.
3. Return the carriage with a light strike of the carriage-return key. Use your right-hand little finger.

## Exercise 357 **Type a copy of the following second prefatory page of a play.**

Justify the right-hand margin; i.e. bring the last letter of each line to form a straight line. (See detailed instructions on page 255.)

SYNOPSIS OF ACTS AND SCENERY

ACT I

| | | |
|---|---|---|
| Scene I | .. .. .. | Windsor. Before Page's House |
| Scene II | .. .. .. .. .. .. .. | The same |
| Scene III | .. .. .. .. | A Room in the Garter Inn |
| Scene IV | .. .. .. | A Room in Dr. Caius's House |

ACT II

| | | |
|---|---|---|
| Scene I | .. .. .. .. .. | Before Page's House |
| Scene II | .. .. .. .. | A Room in the Garter Inn |
| Scene III | .. .. .. .. .. .. | Windsor Park |

ACT III

| | | |
|---|---|---|
| Scene I | .. .. .. .. | A Field near Frogmore |
| Scene II | .. .. .. .. | The Street in Windsor |
| Scene III | .. .. .. .. | A Room in Ford's House |
| Scene IV | .. .. .. .. | A Room in Page's House |

ACT IV

| | | |
|---|---|---|
| Scene I | .. .. .. .. .. .. | The Street |
| Scene II | .. .. .. .. | A Room in Ford's House |
| Scene III | .. .. .. .. | A Room in the Garter Inn |
| Scene IV | .. .. .. .. | A Room in Ford's House |
| Scene V | .. .. .. .. | A Room in the Garter Inn |

ACT V

| | | |
|---|---|---|
| Scene I | .. .. .. .. | A Room in the Garter Inn |
| Scene II | .. .. .. .. .. .. | Windsor Park |
| Scene III | .. .. .. .. | The Street in Windsor |
| Scene IV | .. .. .. .. .. .. | Windsor Park |
| Scene V | .. .. .. .. | Another part of the Park |

## Introducing R and U

1. Locate the new keys **r** and **u** on the keyboard chart below.

2. Then locate the same keys on your typewriter keyboard.

3. Strike **r** with the *f* finger, and **u** with the *j* finger.

*Set left-hand margin stop at 15 (pica) or 20 (elite) and type each line three times. Double space before the next line.*

### *HOW TO STRIKE THE NEW KEYS*

1. Move the *f* finger to **r**, raising the neighbouring fingers as little as possible.

2. Strike **r** sharply, lightly and firmly, and return quickly to the home position.

3. Follow the same technique to strike **u** with the *j* finger.

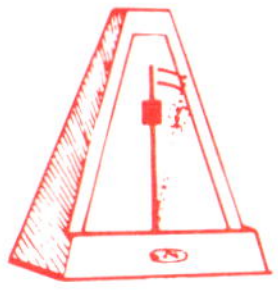

*Use rhythmic beats*

## Exercise 2

**Location drill**

```
jjj jjj fff fff jjj jjj fff fff
fff jjj fff frf frf jjj juj juj

jjj juj juj fff frf fur fur frf
fur fur fff frf jjj juj fur fur
```

*Strike keys lightly but firmly*

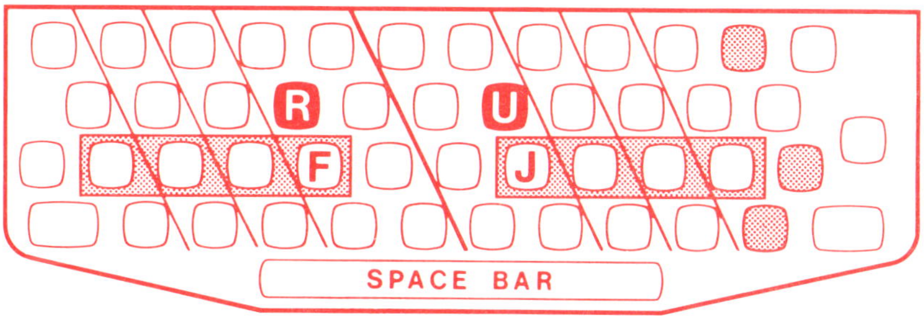


## When You Have Finished the Day's Lesson

1. **Remove paper from the typewriter.** Raise the paper bail, pull forward the paper-release lever with your right hand, remove paper with your left hand, and return paper bail and paper-release lever to their normal positions.

2. **Centre the carriage.** Depress the right-hand carriage-release lever, hold the platen knob firmly, and centre (approximately) the carriage.

3. **Cover the typewriter** to protect it from its great enemy - dust.

# Plays

In typing a play you should consider the following points:

1. The size of paper generally used is A4, the left-hand margin at least 3.5 cm and the line spacing single.

2. The first sheet, called 'the title page', contains (a) the title of the play, (b) the type of the play (whether tragedy, comedy etc.), (c) the number of acts, and (d) the author's name (see 'a' below).

3. The second sheet contains a synopsis of the acts and the scenes (see next page).

4. The third page shows the 'Persons Represented' in the play. The names of the actors are usually typed opposite the persons whose roles they play (see 'b' below).

5. On the main sheets of the play the names of the speakers are typed in capital letters in the left-hand margin opposite their respective parts. They should be underscored, unless typed in colour.

6. Stage directions and cues which are not actually spoken should also be underscored, unless some other colour is used.

7. The first line of each speaking part is indented.

PREFATORY PAGES

In reduced size

M E R R Y   W I V E S   O F   W I N D S O R

A   C O M E D Y

I N   F I V E   A C T S

- b y -

WILLIAM SHAKESPEARE

(a) Title page

PERSONS REPRESENTED

| | |
|---|---|
| SIR JOHN FALSTAFF | |
| FENTON | |
| SHALLOW .. .. .. .. .. .. .. | A Country Justice |
| SLENDER .. .. .. .. .. .. .. | Cousin to Shallow |
| MR. FORD)<br>MR. PAGE) .. .. .. .. | Two Gentlemen dwelling at Windsor |
| WILLIAM PAGE .. .. .. .. .. | A boy, Son to Mr. Page |
| SIR HUGH EVANS .. .. .. .. .. .. | A Welsh Parson |
| DR. CAIUS .. .. | A French Physician, Host of the Garter Inn |
| BARDOLPH)<br>PISTOL )<br>NYM ) .. .. .. .. .. .. | Followers of Falstaff |
| ROBIN .. .. .. .. .. .. .. | Page to Falstaff |
| SIMPLE .. .. .. .. .. .. .. | Servant to Slender |
| RUGBY .. .. .. .. .. .. | Servant to Dr. Caius |
| MRS. FORD | |
| MRS. PAGE | |
| MRS. ANNE PAGE .. .. .. | Her Daughter, in love with Fenton |
| MRS. QUICKLY .. .. .. .. .. | Servant to Dr. Caius |
| Servants to Page, Ford, etc. | |

(b) Third page

# Lesson 2

## Introducing D and E

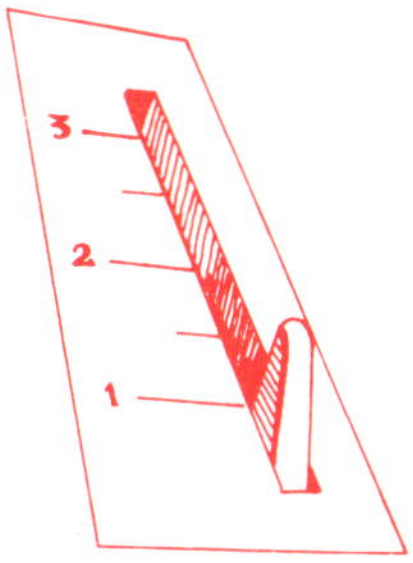


*Set line-space selector for single spacing*

*Strike space bar sharply, using right-hand thumb*

*Raise top of book for easy reading*

1. Align machine with edge of desk; insert paper and straighten it; adjust the paper bail.

2. Sit properly; set line-space selector on '1' for single spacing; set left-hand margin at 20 (pica) or 25 (elite) and type each line three times, double spacing before the next line.

3. Strike letter **d** with left-hand middle finger. With same finger strike letter **e** which is above *d* and slightly to its left.

4. Place fingers on home keys and get ready for the exercise below.

## Exercise 3

**Location drill**

**Strike the keys sharply and release them quickly.**

```
fff ddd fff frf frf ddd ded ded
fff frf fee fee fff fur fur fff
fur fur fee fee fed fed red red
```

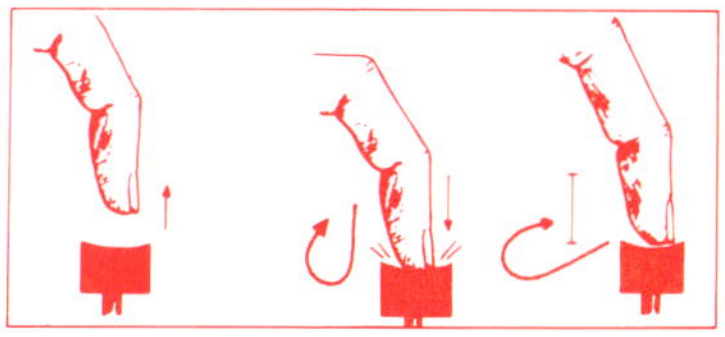

*Correct stroking*

## Exercise 4

**Location drill**

**Raise your fingers just enough to make quick, sharp strokes.**

```
fff jjj fee fee fed fed ere ere
fur fur red red rue rue fur fur
due deed deed due feed feed due
due free free due jeer jeer due
```

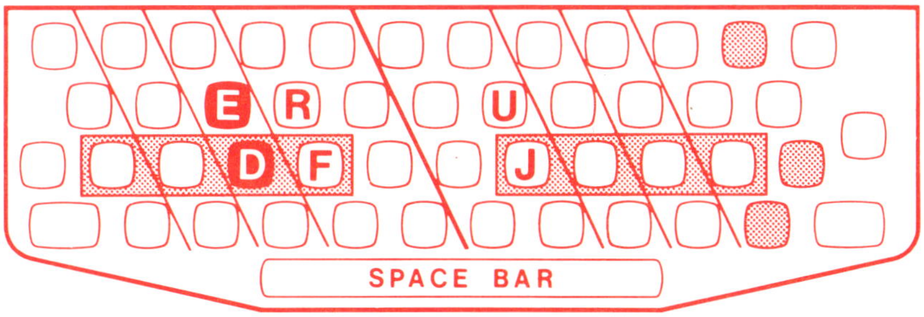

## Exercise 356 Copy the following table of contents, taken from an International Labour Office publication.

Leader dots should be vertically aligned.

T A B L E  O F  C O N T E N T S

## Introducing K and I

Strike letter **k** with your right-hand middle finger. With the same finger strike also letter **i** which is located above *k* and slightly to its left (see chart below).

When fingers are not operating they rest gently on their home keys ie, A S D F, and J K L ; .

Set left-hand margin at 25(30) and type each line three times in single space; double space before the next line. *Figure in brackets applies to elite type.*

*Raise book for easy reading*

### Exercise 5

**With electric typewriters tap keys lightly.**

```
jjj kkk kik kik jjj kkk kik kik
fff ddd did did did uuu rrr fur
fur fir fir die die fur fur fir
```

### Exercise 6

**Type without pauses between the strokes.**

```
rid rid ride ride rider rider fir fir fire fire
did did jerk jerk fired fired fur fur feed feed
die die died died refer refer did did jerk jerk
```

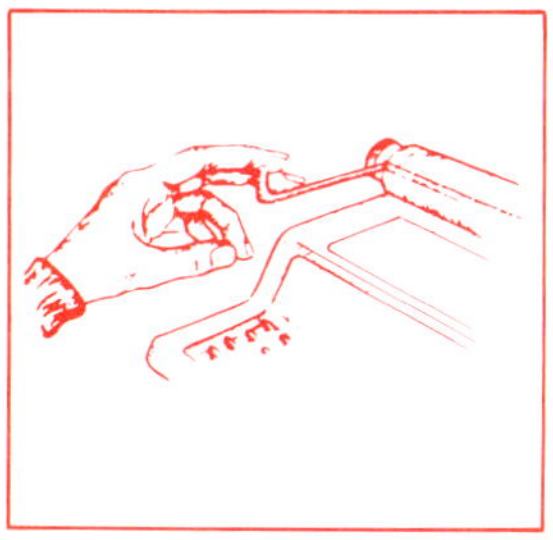

*Return carriage quickly, gently, and without looking up*

### Exercise 7

*Return carriage at each colour divider.*

```
feed / if fed / did jerk / did ride / did refer
dried fur / if dried / fur dried / if fur dried
if died / if fired / red fur / if red fur dried
```

# Roman Numerals

Roman numerals are different from the Arabic numbers we use today. They are based on the letters of the alphabet and are not very easy to read or write. However, as they are used in typewriting for a number of purposes it is important that the typist should understand their usage.

The following table shows the Arabic numbers and their corresponding Roman ones - both large and small. Repeat it carefully, using two columns instead of three.

| Arabic | Large Roman | Small Roman | Arabic | Large Roman | Small Roman | Arabic | Large Roman | Small Roman |
|---|---|---|---|---|---|---|---|---|
| 1 | I | i | 11 | XI | xi | 30 | XXX | xxx |
| 2 | II | ii | 12 | XII | xii | 40 | XL | xl |
| 3 | III | iii | 13 | XIII | xiii | 50 | L | l |
| 4 | IV | iv | 14 | XIV | xiv | 60 | LX | lx |
| 5 | V | v | 15 | XV | xv | 70 | LXX | lxx |
| 6 | VI | vi | 16 | XVI | xvi | 80 | LXXX | lxxx |
| 7 | VII | vii | 17 | XVII | xvii | 90 | XC | xc |
| 8 | VIII | viii | 18 | XVIII | xviii | 100 | C | c |
| 9 | IX | ix | 19 | XIX | xix | 500 | D | d |
| 10 | X | x | 20 | XX | xx | 1000 | M | m |

A line over a Roman numeral multiplies it by one thousand, e.g. $\overline{V}$ = 5,000

To form a Roman number, take each figure separately and add all of them together, e.g.

| | |
|---|---|
| 67 = 60 + 7 | LX (60) + VII (7) = LXVII |
| 542 = 500 + 40 + 2 | D (500) + XL (40) + II (2) = DXLII |
| 736 = 700 + 30 + 6 | DCC (700) + XXX (30) + VI (6) = DCCXXXVI |
| 1981 = 1000 + 900 + 80 + 1 | M (1000) + CM (900) + LXXX (80) + I(1) = MCMLXXXI |

Note that when a numeral is followed by another of equal or less value the whole expression denotes the sum of those numbers, e.g. CC = 200, XV = 15. Conversely, when a number is preceded by another of less value, the whole expression denotes the difference between the value of the two numbers, e.g. IX = 9, XC = 90. (When subtracting, only one symbol can be placed in front of another, e.g. CM, XL.)

USE OF ROMAN NUMERALS Large Roman numerals are used: (a) For chapter headings, e.g. CHAPTER XII; (b) in numbering paragraphs; (c) in plays, to number acts, e.g. «TEMPEST» ACT II; (d) in the titles of monarchs, e.g. King Edward VII; (e) in school classes, e.g. Form Lower VI; (f) in examination stages, e.g. Royal Society of Arts Stage III; (g) over buildings to show year of construction, e.g. MDCCLX.

Small Roman numerals are not followed by a full stop except in the numbering of paragraphs.

## Exercise 355

Type the following exercise paying particular attention to the inset matter. You will note that Roman numerals are so arranged that at least 1.5 cm are left between margin and longest group of numerals.

. . . Salaries were frozen for those earning more than $16,000. Allowances and perquisites were also frozen, with some exceptions to cater for hardships imposed by health and medical reasons and pensions, . . . In March 1976 the guidelines were modified to restrict pay increases to $10 per week with the following exceptions:

(i) where the cost-of-living adjustment exceeded $10;

(ii) to ensure comparability with similar workers in other enterprises;

(iii) special improvements in skills.

# Lesson 3

## Introducing T and Y

Letter **t** is located one place to the right of ***r*** and it is struck with the ***f*** finger. Letter **y** is one place to the left of ***u*** and it is struck with the ***j*** finger (see chart below).

Set left-hand margin at 15(20) and type each line three times in single space; double space before the next line.

When you make a mistake, ignore it; leave a space and repeat the word.

*Keep your eyes on copy*

## Exercise 8

**Hold both hands directly over the keys: type with quick, sharp strokes.**

```
fff frf frf ftf ftf fff frf ftf
jjj juj juj jyj jyj jjj juj jyj
fff ftf jjj jyj frf juj fty jyj
```

## Exercise 9

**Keep your eyes on the copy; return the carriage without looking up.**

```
tie tie jet jet fit fit tree tree true true tried
key key yet yet dry dry tide tide jury jury tried
kit kit rye rye dye dye dury duty feet feet fifty
```

## Exercise 10

*Return carriage at each colour divider.*

```
it tried / it tried it / it fitted / it fitted it
try it / if it did try it / if it did try it free
it fed it / if it fed it / it fed fifty free deer
```

each 4 times
whole 2 times

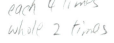

*Set paper grips at equal distances*

# Footnotes

**Footnote signs are introduced in the text with Arabic numbers or letters of the alphabet, enclosed in brackets. The sign is raised half a space above the line, with no space preceding. In the actual footnote, however, the sign is not necessarily raised and is separated from the text of the footnote by one space.**

**To avoid confusion, footnote signs in technical and mathematical scripts are shown by an asterisk * for the first reference, a dagger † for the second, a double dagger ‡ for the third, and a section sign § for the last. If there are more than four footnotes on the same page, these signs are repeated by duplication, e.g. ** , †† etc.**

**Footnotes are separated from the text by a continuous line extending from margin to margin. This line is typed one-and-a-half spaces below the text while footnotes start two lines below the dividing line.**

**Footnotes may begin at the margin or be inset about five spaces. They are typed in single-line spacing, in blocked form, and with a line of space between them. The last footnote should be about six lines from the bottom of the page.**

*NOTES:*

*(1) If you are using an electric typewriter that can change pitch and typestyle, it is in better taste to type the footnotes with different letters (see example below).*

*(2) If you are preparing work for the printer, type footnotes separately below the words to which they refer. Each footnote - typed in double spacing - should be separated by the text both above and below by a line of underscore running from margin to margin.*

## Exercise 354

Outside Parliament, party control is exercised by national and local organisations,(1) while inside Parliament it is exercised by officers known as 'Whips'.(2) The Opposition Whips have no official position, although the Opposition Chief Whip in both Houses receive a salary: £7,500 in the House of Commons and £2,500 in the House of Lords, and two other Opposition Whips in the Commons are paid £4,000 a year. On the Government side in the House of Commons the Chief Whip receives a salary of £9,500; the Deputy Chief Whip receives £5,000 a year; the other Government Whips (who include five Lords Commissioners of the Treasury(3) and the Comptroller and Vice-Chamberlain of the Household) are paid £4,000 a year.(4)

---

(1) For information about party political organisation, see 'The Organisation of Political Parties in Britain'.

(2) There are Government and Opposition Whips in both Houses of Parliament, but the Whips in the House of Lords are less exclusively concerned with party matters.

(3) Junior Lords of the Treasury devote their whole time to Parliament.

(4) These salaries are additional to their parliamentary allowances.

## Introducing G, H, and (,)

Locate the new keys on the keyboard chart below.

Then strike **g** with the *f* finger; **h** with the *j* finger, and the **comma**, with the *k* finger.

Set left margin at 15(20) and type each line twice; double space before the new line.

### Exercise 11

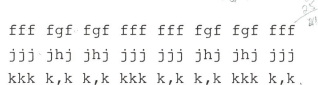

**The comma can pierce the paper; strike it lightly.**

```
fff fgf fgf fff fff fgf fgf fff
jjj jhj jhj jjj jjj jhj jhj jjj
kkk k,k k,k kkk k,k k,k kkk k,k
```

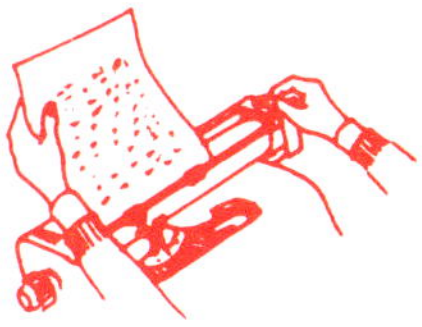

*Remove paper from machine by pulling paper-release lever*

### Exercise 12

**Develop a well-controlled, quick and rhythmic stroke.**

```
get get, rug rug, dig dig, gift gift, hurt hurt
dug dug, fig fig, the the, they they, hide hide
hit hit, hut hut, her her, here here, huge huge
```

### Exercise 13

**After a comma leave one space.**

```
the tie, get the tie, try the tie, hide the tie
the jet, get the jet, try the jet, hide the jet
the key, get the key, try the key, hide the key
```

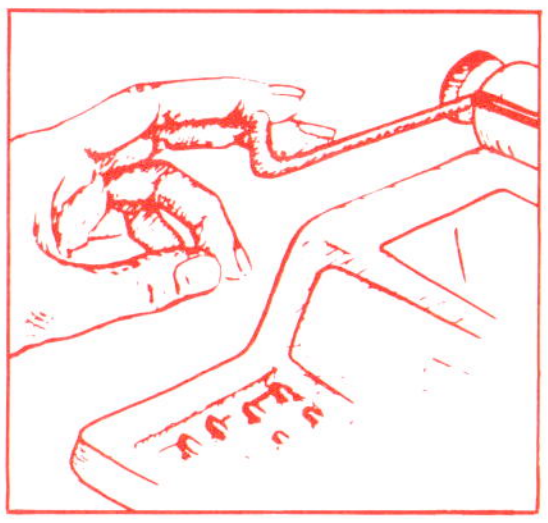

*Throw carriage quickly and firmly*

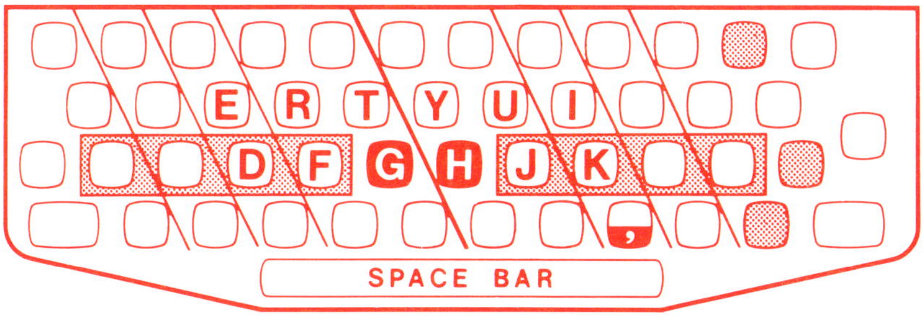


If you are using an electric typewriter switch it off at the end of your work - especially at the end of the day. This will prevent unnecessary wear on the motor.

**Exercise 353** **Type the following page from a specification, taking a carbon copy. Begin marginal headings at 10(12) and the body of the specification at 25(30). Type it in a solely indented or blocked style.**

Specification for Electrical Installation

Schematic diagrams showing all equipment as fitted complete with electrical main and sub-main circuits and their connections thereto.

The Contractor shall commence the preparation of the record drawings referred herein prior to the completion of the Works.

Tender Measurements — The tender shall be submitted on the basis of true and net measurements and no extra to the Nominated Sub-Contracts Sum shall be allowed on account of any dimensional or clerical errors or omissions on the Drawings or in the Specification.

Schedule of Prices — The prices contained in the Schedule of Prices shall form the basis of any adjustment of the Nominated Sub-Contract Sum which may be necessary in respect of variations duly authorised ~~in~~ by the Architect.

Workshop and Store — The Sub-Contractor shall provide and maintain watertight temporary huts, sheds etc., for workshops and for the storage of his materials, goods, tools etc.

Contingency Sum — The Sub-Contractor shall include in the Tender any sum described in Analysis of Tender as Contingency Sum to be expended or deducted as a whole or in part as shall be directed by the Architect.

Cleanliness of Site — The Sub-Contractor shall at all times keep the site free from obstruction and rubbish and he shall remove from the Site at his own expense all surplus materials and temporary works as soon as they are no longer required on Site.

Builders' Work Drawings — The Sub-Contractor shall provide the main Contractor with drawings illustrating the positions and dimensions of all bases, supports, holes and chases to be formed or left in doors, roofs and walls.

Check Relevant Builders' Work — Where preformed holes and slots are provided at given locations, the Sub-Contractor must satisfy himself that such slots and holes are suitable for their intended purposes, and in the correct position, before proceeding with the Works.

Type slowly but steadily. Concentrate on correct key-striking. Good habits and techniques are the foundations for high speed.

*Strike keys in the centre using quick and firm stokes*

## Exercise 14

**Double-letter drill**

Strike double letters evenly but directly; i.e. without returning finger to home key.

```
deed feet deed feet deed feet deed feet
free deer free deer free deer free deer
deed free deer feet deed free deer feet
```

## Exercise 15

**Phrases — Sentences**

Disregard errors at this stage. Do not cross them out and do not overtype correction.

```
the tree, the fir tree, he hit the huge fir tree
they tried the key, they tried the dirty hut key
he, the tired guide, tied the greedy tiger there
```

## Exercise 16

**Balanced-hand drill**

*Type each line twice at a slow pace; then repeat the whole exercise quickly.*

```
if he, if he did, if he did it, if they did, if they did it
if the fur, if the eye, if the fur, if the eye, if the fire
if they fit, if they fit it, if they fire, if they fired it
```

# Care of the Typewriter

**Dust is the greatest enemy of the typewriter. To keep your machine clean:**

1. Twice a week remove frame cover and brush dirt out with a brush.
2. Brush towards you - not sideways.
3. Clean type faces regularly with a brush and a little spirit.
4. Once a week remove all dirt from carriage rails with a soft duster. Lightly oil part of a cloth and wipe the rails.
5. Cover machine with a dust-cover at the end of the work.

## Exercise 352

**The same specification with that on previous page but set out in the blocked style. This method of layout requires the word 'specification' to be typed in closed capitals, and the date level with the last line of main heading. Type the exercise in duplicate.**

SPECIFICATION of Electrical Installations to be executed

at 122 Park Avenue, Winchester, for A Richardson Esq to

the satisfaction of

Messrs J White & Co
Architects & Surveyors
49-53 High Buildings
Winchester WH5 6UJ

FEBRUARY 1982

CHARACTER OF WORK

The whole of the work is to be completed in the best possible manner and in the style, character, and finish of first-class work.

MAKE GOOD

The Contractor shall at his own cost make good and reinstate all injury from failure or breakdown in service equipment, carelessness or any other cause arising.

INTENT

It is the intention of these specifications and drawings to call for complete systems, tested and operational. The Contractor shall assume full responsibility for the compatibility of the equipment provided and for the satisfactory operation of the integrated systems. Where the word "provide" is used it shall mean "furnish and install and make ready for use."

INFORMATION AND DRAWINGS

The Contractor shall acquaint himself fully with the provisions of these specifications and associated drawings as well as for the provisions of the specifications of other trades affecting the work of this trade. The Contractor shall seek clarifications where he considers necessary for the satisfactory completion of the systems, regarding possible inconsistencies in the specifications.

Unless otherwise indicated, the drawings for Electrical Trades show the general arrangement and approximate location of the fittings or equipment. The Contractor shall follow these drawings in carrying out his work and shall consult architectural, structural, mechanical and siting drawings to verify all conditions and spaces affecting this installation.

CODES, REGULATIONS AND STANDARDS

The Contractor shall include in his tender all labour, materials, services, drawings etc., necessary for the compliance of the installation . . . .

# Lesson 4

## Introducing M and V

These two letters are located in the first (lowest) row of the keyboard.

The striking fingers will now move downwards, will strike sharply, and return immediately to their home row.

Strike **m** with the *j* finger, and **v** with *f* finger.
Set left margin at 12(15) and type each line twice; if you are not satisfied repeat each exercise once more.

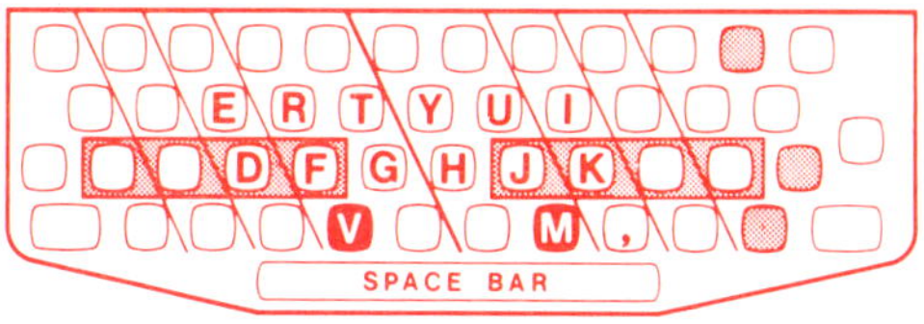


## Exercise 17

```
jjj juj jjj jmj jmj jjj jmj jmj
fff frf fff fvf fvf fff fvf fvf
fff fgf fvf fff jjj jhj jjj jmj
```

## Exercise 18

**Type with minimum hand or arm motion. Use short snappy strokes.**

```
me met meet merry might, they might meet her here
my yet very drive vivid, he hit the fir tree here
the tree, the fig tree, they tried every fig tree
```

*Develop a rhythmic stroke*

## Exercise 19

**Common-word drill**

**You are now building up an automatic vocabulary.**

```
if he did it, if he met them here, they get them there
they fired it, if they meet there, he hid my tie there
he met her here, they get them there, if they hit them
```

## Exercise 20

**Sentences**

**Type at a steady pace without pausing between strokes, words or lines.**

```
he met the third guide, he met the third guide
get the dirty mug here, get the dirty mug here
the merry guide met the huge tired driver here
```

*Keep your body erect; concentrate on what you are typing*

**ERRORS** When you make an error leave a space and start the word from the beginning. Do not type the correct letter over the faulty one. On pages 21, 28 and 36 you will learn how to erase errors properly.

## Exercise 351

**Type one copy of the following technical specification using the indented style of layout. Note that the word 'specification' is typed in spaced capitals and it overhangs the other lines by 5(6) spaces.**

S P E C I F I C A T I O N of Electrical Installations

to be executed at 122 Park Avenue, Winchester,

for A. Richardson, Esq., to the satisfaction of

Messrs. J. White & Co.,
Architects & Surveyors,
49-53 High Buildings,
Winchester WH5 6UJ.

FEBRUARY, 1982

CHARACTER OF WORK

The whole of the work is to be completed in the best possible manner and in the style, character, and finish of first-class work.

MAKE GOOD

The Contractor shall at his own cost make good and reinstate all injury from failure or breakdown in service equipment, carelessness or any other cause arising.

INTENT

It is the intention of these specifications and drawings to call for complete systems, tested and operational. The Contractor shall assume responsibility for the compatibility of the equipment provided and for the satisfactory operation of the integrated systems. Where the word "provide" is used it shall mean "furnish and install and make ready for use".

INFORMATION AND DRAWINGS

The Contractor shall acquaint himself fully with the provisions of these specifications and associated drawings as well as for the provisions of the specifications of other trades affecting the work of this trade. The Contractor shall seek clarifications where he considers necessary for the satisfactory completion of the systems, regarding possible inconsistencies in the specifications.

Unless otherwise indicated, the drawings for Electrical Trades show the general arrangement and approximate location of the fittings or equipment. The Contractor shall follow these drawings in carrying out his work and shall consult architectural, structural, mechanical and siting drawings to verify all conditions and spaces affecting this installation.

CODES, REGULATIONS AND STANDARDS

The Contractor shall include in his tender all labour, materials, services etc., necessary for the compliance of the installation with all applicable local rules, codes and regulations. In particular, the electrical installation shall comply with the regulations of the Electricity Authority and it is the responsibility of the Contractor to obtain the approval of the Authority for all materials used as well as for the complete installation.

## Introducing S, W, L and O

Letter **S** - a home key - is struck with the left-hand ring finger. This finger also strikes **W** which is located above *S* and slightly to the left.

Letter **l** - another home key - is struck with the right-hand ring finger. This finger also strikes **O** which is above *l* and slightly to the left.

Set left margin at 15(20) and type each line twice.

## Exercise 21

**Strike space bar in rhythm with the typing of letters.**

```
fff ddd sss fff ddd sss ddd sss
fff ddd sss sws sws sss sws sws
jjj kkk lll jjj kkk lll kkk lll
jjj kkk lll lol lol lll lol lol
```

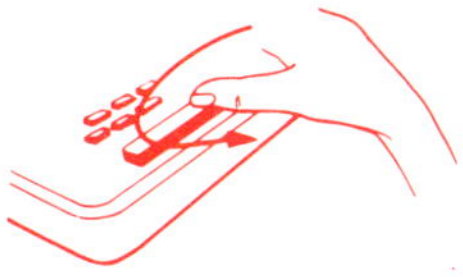

*Strike space bar with downward - inward movement*

## Exercise 22

```
sir sir sum sum see see set set his his why why
few few wet wet sew sew led led let let lie lie
lit lit its its low low our our out out how how
```

## Exercise 23

**Double-letter drill**

**Electric: Allow time for key to return to position before striking it again.**

```
tell roof merry tell roof merry tell roof merry
foot meet stuff foot meet stuff foot meet stuff
tree took hurry tree took hurry tree took hurry
```

## Exercise 24

**Two-letter easy words typed with balanced hands**

*Type three times; the third time as fast as you can.*

*The striking finger can now be followed freely by remaining fingers*

```
to it, to do it, if he, if he is, if he is to do it
or me, me or it, it or me, if he or it, if me or it
to go, or go, if it is, if it is to, if it is to go
```

# Technical Specifications

A technical specification is a document which sets out in detail the work to be carried out by a contractor on a particular job (builder's specification, engineer's specification and so on).

Specifications are usually typed on A4 paper with black ribbon. Line spacing may be double, one-and-a-half, or single, depending on the length of the document. The body of a specification usually begins at about 6.3 cm (23 pica or 28 elite spaces) on the scale, and marginal headings - if used - at 2.5 cm (10 pica or 12 elite). The pages, after the first one, are numbered at the bottom of each sheet in the centre.

A specification consists of:

1. THE MAIN HEADING

This is introduced with the word 'specification', and describes in brief the nature of the work; this short paragraph is always typed in double-line spacing. Below that follows the name and address of the architect, the builder or the customer for whom the specification is written; this information is indented a few spaces to the right and is typed in single-line spacing. The date follows two spaces below and starts at the left-hand margin.

2. TRADE AND SUB-HEADINGS

The heading is followed by detailed paragraphs for each item involved (e.g. excavation work, concrete work, etc.) with headings in capitals (often underlined). Headings may preferably be at the side, either in capitals or in lower case with underscore.

3. THE BODY OR PARAGRAPHS

As with all other documents, specifications may be typed in the blocked or the indented style.

NOTE The layout of technical specifications varies widely from office to office; there is no one style that can be accepted universally as the correct one. Therefore, in typing such documents adopt the method your employer prefers.

ENDORSEMENT

An endorsement gives a brief description of the specification, i.e. place where work is to be carried out, name of customer as well as name and address of architect etc. This information will help to identify the document after it has been folded.

Long specifications, when completed, are bound in book form with pages flat; if they are short, they are folded (and creased) in two from left to right and the endorsement typed in the centre of the upper surface.

EXAMPLE OF A SPECIFICATION ENDORSEMENT

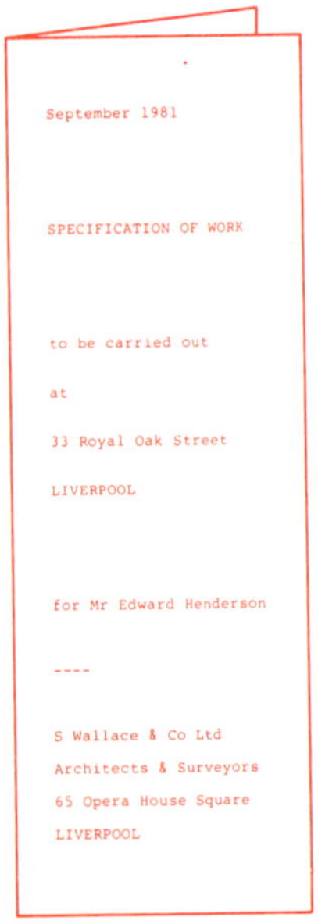
September 1981
SPECIFICATION OF WORK
to be carried out
at
33 Royal Oak Street
LIVERPOOL
for Mr Edward Henderson
----
S Wallace & Co Ltd
Architects & Surveyors
65 Opera House Square
LIVERPOOL

**Blocked Style**

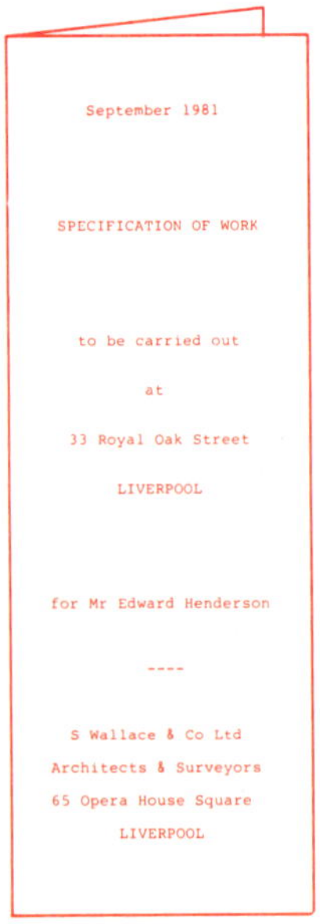
September 1981
SPECIFICATION OF WORK
to be carried out
at
33 Royal Oak Street
LIVERPOOL
for Mr Edward Henderson
----
S Wallace & Co Ltd
Architects & Surveyors
65 Opera House Square
LIVERPOOL

**Indented Style**

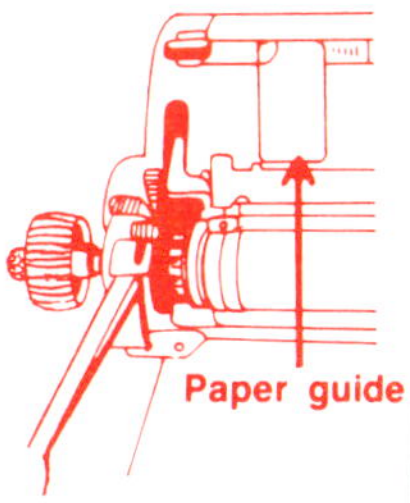


## Uniform Left-hand Margin

To keep a uniform left-hand margin on successive sheets:
1. Insert paper with left edge on 0.
2. Set margin stop at the desired margin, say 15(20).
3. Move paper guide to the right until it touches the left edge of the paper.

Insert subsequent sheets with edge against the paper guide.

## Exercise 25

**Fluency practice**

*Type each line three times; the third time as fast as you can.*

```
if he lets her out, if he lets him out, if they do let us out
if they wish they will go, he will go there to work with them
he will let her go to the firm to get the forms he likes most
```

Sit erect

## Exercise 26

**Strike keys slowly and rhythmically.**

```
sight shift sheet serve sweet white where width
worth world write limit light still style smell
grill lower other ought short offer order outer
```

## Exercise 27

**Fluency sentences**

*Type each line three times; then the whole exercise once more.*

```
she will lift the lid, she will do so with my very good wishes
the lost mug, the girls of the west seem to like the good show
they left the wire there, her sister looks for the short lists
she sold the west side of the house to these workers this week
```

Shoulders down chest forward

## Clashing of Typebars

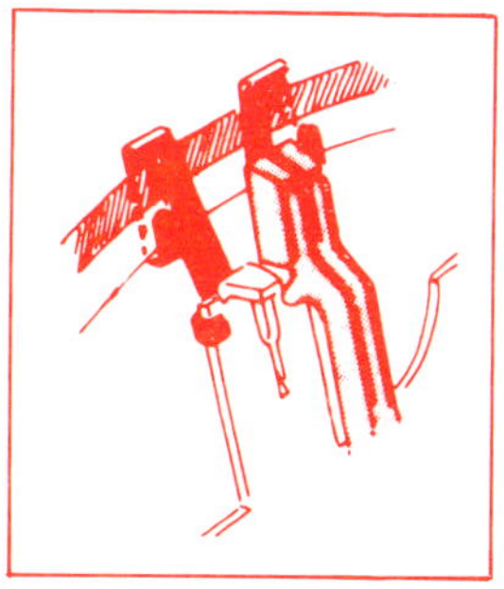

If you strike two keys simultaneously, their typebars will clash and jam near the printing point. To overcome this, separate the typebars by releasing them with the fingers.

Some machines are fitted with a special button which frees the jammed typebars.

## Exercise 350

**Type a copy of the following Lease paying attention to the style of layout, the use of capitals and the underscoring. The document has been shortened so that it can be confined to one page.**

T H I S   L E A S E made the THIRTY-FIRST day of OCTOBER One thousand nine hundred and eighty-one BETWEEN EDWARD HENRY COOPER of 55 Rotary Avenue Kingston in the County of Surrey (hereinafter called 'the landlord' which expression shall where the context so admits include the person for the time being entitled to the reversion immediately expectant on the determination of the term hereby created) of the one part and ANTHONY WEBSTER of 39 Highgate Terrace Kingston in the County of Surrey (hereinafter called 'the tenant' which expression shall where the context so admits include his successors in title) of the other part——

W I T N E S S E T H as follows——

1. The landlord demises unto the tenant the premises described in the first part of the schedule hereto (hereinafter called 'the demised premises') subject to the exceptions and reservations specified in the second part of the said schedule TO HOLD the same unto the tenant from the first day of January . . .——

2. The tenant covenants with the landlord as follows——

   (1) To pay the reserved rents on the days and in manner aforesaid——

   (2) To pay all existing and future rates taxes assessments . . . except only such as the owner is by law bound to pay notwithstanding any contract to the contrary——

   (3) To keep the demised premises including the drains and sanitary apparatus and all fixtures and additions thereto in good tenantable repair and condition throughout the term and to yield up the same in such repair and condition at the determination of the tenancy——

   (4) Not to make any alterations or additions to the demised premises or erect any new buildings thereon without the written consent of the landlord——

IN WITNESS whereof the parties hereto have hereunto set their hands and seals the day and year first hereinbefore written——

SIGNED SEALED AND DELIVERED )<br>
by the said EDWARD HENRY COOPER) Edward Henry Cooper (L.S.)<br>
in the presence of )<br>
John Smith<br>
Peter Brown

SIGNED SEALED AND DELIVERED )<br>
by the said ANTHONY WEBSTER ) Anthony Webster (L.S.)<br>
in the presence of )<br>
John Smith<br>
Peter Brown

## Lesson 5

### Introducing A, B, and N

Letter **a** - the weakest of the home keys - is struck with the left-hand little finger. Letter **b**, which is next to *v* in the first row of keys, is struck with the *f* finger. Letter **n**, next to *m* in the first row, is struck with the *j* finger.

Set left margin at 20(25) and type each line twice.

*Keep eyes constantly on copy*

**Keep your eyes fixed on the copy; return carriage without looking up.**

## Exercise 28

sss aaa aaa sss aaa sss aaa aaa

fvf fbf fbf fvf fbf fvf fbf fbf

jmj jnj jnj jmj jnj jmj jnj jnj

## Exercise 29

air aim all ago are arm art ask fat lad sat

but bus bit big boy buy bad beg ebb rib bob

new not now nor one ink and any ant tin ten

## Exercise 30

**Balanced-hand drill**

*Type the whole exercise three times; the third time as fast as you can.*

but he, but they, and they, and their own, but their own

and is the, and are the forms, and is the right big form

and he may lend them the, but he may lend them the forms

*Have front frame of machine level with edge of desk*

## Exercise 31

**Type slowly and rhythmically.**

also half make fare mail large after alike agree madam

bill blow bear bell able birth board brief above about

name near note into only night north enjoy enter under

## Exercise 349 **Display the following Will typing also an endorsement on the back of the sheet.**

W I L L   A N D   T E S T A M E N T

I JOHN LIONEL BURTON of 25 Lowther Hill Ashford in the County of Kent do hereby make and DECLARE this to be my last WILL-----

1. I HEREBY REVOKE all former testamentary dispositions made by me heretofore-----------------------------------------

2. I APPOINT my wife Anna Maria Burton of 25 Lowther Hill Ashford aforesaid to be the executrix of this my WILL----------

3. I GIVE DEVISE AND BEQUEATH the real property known as Number two Main Street in Forest Hill Ashford in the County of Kent now occupied by me as my residence unto my beloved wife Anna Maria Burton absolutely and forever-----------------------

4. I GIVE DEVISE AND BEQUEATH all the rest residue and remainder of my estate both real and personal of every kind and nature and wheresoever situated unto my son Alexander Burton of 25 Lowther Hill Ashford in the County of Kent and I DIRECT him to pay thereout all my just debts and funeral and testamentary expenses-----------------------------------------------

IN WITNESS whereof I have hereunto set my hand this Fifth day of JUNE One thousand nine hundred and eighty-one---------------

SIGNED by the said JOHN LIONEL BURTON )<br>
the Testator therein named as and for )<br>
his last Will in the presence of us )<br>
and of each of us who at his request )<br>
in his presence and in the presence )<br>
of each other have hereunto subscribed)<br>
our names as witnesses )

______________________ residing at Forest Hill<br>
Ashford County of Kent

______________________ residing at Forest Hill<br>
Ashford County of Kent

## HOW TO ERASE ERRORS WITH A RUBBER ERASER

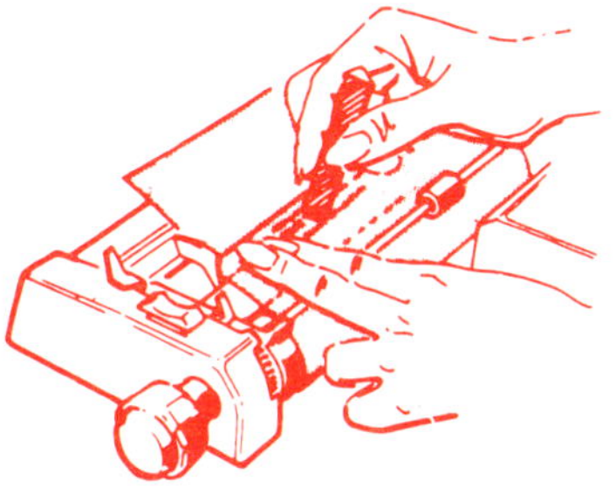

Move the carriage to the extreme left or right to allow erasure dirt to fall out of the machine.

Turn up platen so that the error lies on the erasure table. (If the error is on the lower part of the page turn paper backwards.)

Rub the error away, using first a soft eraser and then a hard one. Rub gently to avoid damaging the paper and see that you do not erase any neighbouring letters.

Return paper to position and type.

## Exercise 32

**Common-phrase drill**

**Building up automatic phraseology.**

and if he is, and if they wish, and if you will be
of this year, in the same way, and in all his life
and if you are, and if you will, and if you should

## Exercise 33

**Easy sentences**

*Type each line three times. Check sentences only at the ends of lines; correct errors of third typing.*

now is the time for her and all of them to do it
all of them were out at that time but she was in
she will do it now not only for them but for all

## Exercise 34

**Double-letter drill**

soon look asset agree dinner soon look asset agree
free miss error green little free miss error green
week foot allow offer letter week foot allow offer

*To prevent neighbouring letters from being erased you can use an erasure shield.*

## Exercise 35

**Fluency practice**

**After a comma leave one space.**

*Type each line twice, as fast as you can.*

but he may, but he may be, but he may be there in good time
if they find the money, if they find the right sum of money
we think he, we think he will be the right man for this job

**Exercise 348** **Type a copy of the following Memorandum of Agreement.**

M E M O R A N D U M   O F   A G R E E M E N T

T H I S   A G R E E M E N T   made this SIXTEENTH day of APRIL in the year One thousand nine hundred and eighty-one BETWEEN VICTORIA JOHNSON of 12 Palmer Avenue Winchester in the County of Hampshire (hereinafter called "the Employee") of the one part and BENJAMIN STEVENS of City Palace Winchester in the County of Hampshire (hereinafter called "the Employer") of the other part WHEREBY IT IS AGREED THAT——————————

1. THE Employer hereby appoints the Employee (who hereby accepts the appointment) as a full-time Shorthand-Typist at City Palace Winchester in the County of Hampshire on and from the FIRST day of SEPTEMBER One thousand nine hundred and eighty-one——————

2. THE commencing salary to be Eighty Pounds (£80) per week———

3. EXCEPT in respect of a period during which the Employee is absent from work owing to illness or injury the Employer shall pay to the Employee as from the date of her appointment a salary payable under and in accordance with the scale applicable to the appointment hereby made——————————

4. IF the Employee gives or is given notice to terminate her employment in accordance with the provisions of this Agreement then the said notice becomes effective at the end of four clear weeks——————————

AS WITNESS THE HANDS OF THE PARTIES the said VICTORIA JOHNSON and the said BENJAMIN STEVENS the day and year first above written—————— in the presence of

...................... Witness ...................... Employer's Signature

...................... Witness ...................... Employee's Signature

# Lesson 6

## Shifting for Right-Hand Capitals

### SHIFTING FOR RIGHT-HAND CAPITALS

To type a capital letter (or *upper case*) with the right hand you must depress the shift key placed at the left-hand of the first row of the keyboard.

To strike, say, capital J, you will use the following three-step method:

1. Remove your *left* hand from its home keys and hold down the shift key with the little finger.
2. Strike letter J.
3. Release the shift key and return to home position.

*To find your home position: Bring the index of the moving hand to feel the other index and from there move back by three keys.*

**The shift key is depressed only with the small finger, always supported by the full weight of the hand.**

## Exercise 36

**Technique drill**

*Type very slowly and rhythmically repeating each line three times.*

```
Jj Jj Kk Kk Jj Jj Ll Ll Kk Kk Ll Ll
He He It It On On Us Us Me Me No No
If it, In it, On it, On us, On them
```

## SHIFTING TECHNIQUE

Hold the shift key down firmly until you have typed the capital: if you do not, the capital letter will be out of line with the other letters: e.g. Depress.

If you strike *a lower case* letter (not capital) before you release the shift key fully, that letter will appear out of line with the others: e.g. Depress.

With electric typewriters there is no danger of making such errors.

## Exercise 37

**Technique drill**

**On manual typewriters capital letters require a slightly stronger blow.**

```
James saw Henry, Helen and Lilian in the Hall
John gave Linda a silver gift on her birthday
Mary and Nora offered Jimmy their good wishes
```

*Keep a relaxed posture without tension or nervousness*

## Exercise 38

**Fluency sentences**

**Type quickly and accurately.**

```
Of the, in the, for the, will be, for your, thank you
If you, by the, that we, and the, that the, letter of
On the, of our, of your, of this, with the, have been
```

# Legal Documents

Legal documents, such as Agreements, Leases, Conveyances, Wills etc are typed on draft size paper (40.6 x 33.0 cm), although in class and the examinations room A4 may be used. The style preferred is the blocked, and the ribbon should be black record.

The various stages in the typing of legal documents are:

1. THE DRAFT This is the rough copy of a document, typed in treble spacing so that alterations and insertions can be made easily. The word «Draft» should be typed at the head of each page.

2. THE FAIR COPY This is the corrected draft typed in double or one-and-a-half spacing. If corrections on draft are insignificant typing of fair copy may be omitted.

3. THE ENGROSSMENT This is the final copy of the document prepared for signature; it is typed either from the fair copy or directly from the draft. Line spacing may be double or one-and-a-half.

### IN TYPING AN ENGROSSMENT

(a) Type on both sides of the paper and omit page numbers. On the 1st, 3rd, 5th etc pages leave a left-hand margin of 3.5 cm (15 pica or 18 elite spaces) and a right-hand margin of 1 cm (5 pica or 6 elite spaces). On the 2nd, 4th, 6th pages etc margins are reversed: wide on right-hand and narrow on left-hand.

Note: Many legal offices use specially ruled paper so that typing is done within the ruling.

(b) Avoid punctuation marks, abbreviations, alterations or division of words at the ends of lines.

(c) Type sums of money, dates and any other figures in words, except numbers of paragraphs, property numbers and dates of Acts of Parliament.

(d) Do not erase or correct errors; if you make a mistake, re-type the work.

(e) When a clause does not finish at the end of a line complete it with a line in ink or with hyphens. This is to avoid any additions after signature.

(f) Use capitals (closed or spaced) with/without underscore for such words and phrases as: AGREEMENT, ALL THAT, APPOINT, HEREBY ASSIGN, ASSIGNMENT, BETWEEN, IT IS HEREBY CERTIFIED, IN CONSIDERATION, THIS CONVEYANCE, HEREBY COVENANTS, DECLARE, I GIVE DEVISE AND BEQUEATH, HEREBY CONVEYS, TO HOLD, THIS LEASE, NOW THIS DEED WITNESSETH, I HEREBY REVOKE, SIGNED SEALED AND DELIVERED, SWORN, THIS IS THE LAST WILL AND TESTAMENT, WHEREAS, IN WITNESS. Follow the same procedure for the day and the name of the month as well as the names of the parties concerned.

(g) Start the attestation clause about half an inch to the left of the left-hand margin.

(h) Where there is a continuation sheet place a catchword at the foot of the previous page using the solidus (or the dash on either side) followed by the first word on the following page.

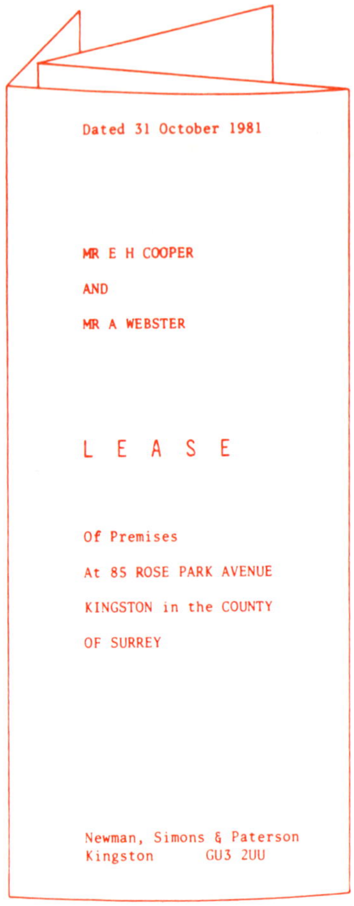


## Endorsement

An Endorsement describes briefly the purpose of a legal document, the parties concerned and the name of the solicitor. This information is typed for easy identification of the document after it has been folded.

The folding of a document is done in four equal sections by bringing the lower edge to meet the upper edge and then doubling the paper again. The text is typed on the outside backsheet of the second section from the top of the document (see diagram).

## The Line-space Selector

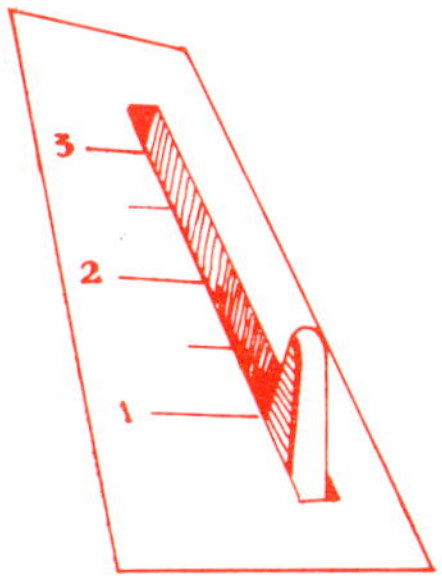


This is a lever - usually near the left platen turning knob - which controls the depth of spacing between the lines. You can adjust this lever for single, one-and-a-half, double, two-and-a-half and treble line spacing.

In typing the following exercise set the line-space selector to: single-line spacing for (a), one-and-a-half for (b), double for (c), two-and-a-half for (d), and treble spacing for (e).

## Exercise 39

**Fluency sentences**

(a)

It is a good thing to learn from the errors of others
It is a good thing to learn from the errors of others
It is a good thing to learn from the errors of others

*Single-line spacing (Two half spaces)*

(b)

He who lives in a glass house should not throw stones

He who lives in a glass house should not throw stones

He who lives in a glass house should not throw stones

*One-and-a-half-line spacing (Three half spaces)*

(c)

You may enjoy doing those tasks that others find hard

You may enjoy doing those tasks that others find hard

You may enjoy doing those tasks that others find hard

*Double-line spacing (Four half spaces)*

(d)

My duty towards my neighbour is to love him as myself

My duty towards my neighbour is to love him as myself

My duty towards my neighbour is to love him as myself

*Two-and-a-half line spacing (Five half spaces)*

(e)

Let not your left hand know what your right hand does

Let not your left hand know what your right hand does

Let not your left hand know what your right hand does

*Treble-line spacing (Six half spaces)*

## Exercise 347

**Make a copy of the following report.**

Additional abbreviations used: Sholders = Shareholders, subsidy = subsidiary, satisfy = satisfactory, tax'n = taxation, imprvmt = improvement, contd = continued, presentg = presenting, wd = would, wh = which, trdg = trading, providg = providing, deprec'n = depreciation, expressg = expressing

HOUSEHOLD WARES LIMITED

Annual Report to Sholders

| | |
|---|---|
| Fifteenth Annual Report | The Drs. of Household Wares Ltd have ~~the~~ pleasure ~~to~~ in presentg to the Sholders the fifteenth annual report. |
| Acquisition of Subsidy Cos. | Two yrs ago I stressed that we wd continue to extend our interests by the further acquisition of subsidy cos. This has bn implemented during the present yr in wh we have expended over £900,000 for this purpose. |
| Results for the past year | Results for the past year must be considered satisfy, the trdg profit of the group after providg for deprec'n being £520,000. |
| Net Profit | After providg for tax'n the net profit for the yr was £195,600 & from this sum it is proposed to appropriate the sum of £41,000 being the total cost of past service pensions. |
| Future Prospects | It is not expected that our main export products will show much imprvmt, as the economic conditions in our main export market are not expected to improve ~~shortly~~. in the near future. |
| Resignation of Manager | I regret to report that one of our Mngrs, Mr. A. Smith, will tender his resignation owing to ill health. I take this opportunity of expressg my apprec'n of Mr. Smith's valuable work over the long period of his service. |
| Thanks to staff | I wd like to thank the staff of this co. at ~~all~~ all our ~~over~~ branches ~~the country~~ for their contd loyalty & devotion to duty. |

# Lesson 7

Letter **C** is below **d** and is struck with the **d** finger. The **full stop** is below *L* and is struck with the *L* finger.

Note: Full stops and commas should be struck very lightly; for they can damage the platen and also pierce the paper - thus giving your page an untidy impression.

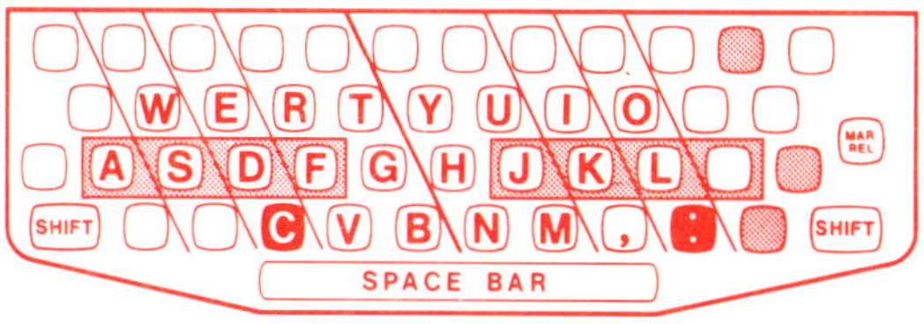


## Introducing C and (.)

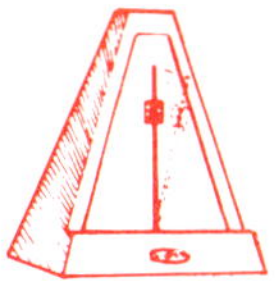

*For location drills use absolute rhythm.*

## Exercise 40

**Location drill**

**Use small L for numeral «one» (l). Use capital o for «zero» (O).**

```
ddd ded dcd dcd lll lOl l.l l.l
cut cow ice cry act can car cat
Henry carried lO cases of coal.
```

## Exercise 41

**Type at an easy, controlled pace.**

```
clock dock close sick trace touch change charge action
clear much clerk each carry cover choose client credit
check luck chief fact court could common cancel costly
```

## Shifting for Left-Hand Capitals

### SHIFTING FOR LEFT-HAND CAPITALS

To type a capital with the left hand you must depress the shift key which is placed at the right-hand end of the first row of the keyboard.

To strike, say, capital F, you will:

1. Remove your *right* hand from its home keys and hold down the shift key with the little finger.
2. Strike letter F.
3. Release the shift key and return to home position.

## Exercise 42a)

```
Ff Ff Jj Jj Dd Dd Kk Kk Ss Ss Ll Ll Aa Aa
Go Go Do Do So So At At To To We We Be Be
Do it, To us, At it, We go, So is, By her

Simon, Betty and Robert met in the College Library.
Tom led the way while John, Anne and Mary followed.
The term C.O.D. or COD stands for Cash on Delivery.
```

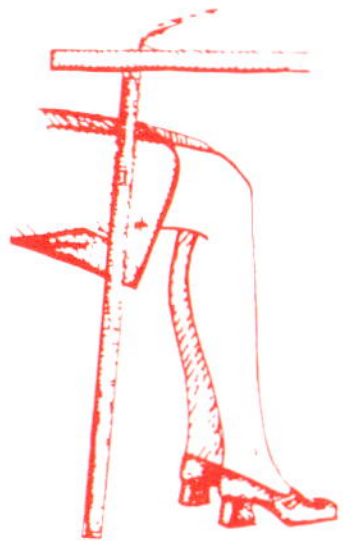

*Keep legs vertical to floor*

## Exercise 42b)

```
The Smiths came back.  They will join you.
I enjoy work.  I can look at it for hours.
```

*Two spaces after (.) at end of sentence.*

```
Jim sold all the goods to Mr. A. S. Shore.
Your note of lOth inst. has been received.
```

*One space after (.) after abbreviations or initials of first names.*

```
Miss Farlow, B.A., arrived here at lO a.m.
Mary Anderson left the U.K. for the U.S.A.
```

*No space after (.) within other initials.*

**Exercise 346** **Type the following report on A4 paper. (Part of examination paper set by the East Midland and Educational Union Examination.)**

Additional abbreviations used: ref = reference, + = and, Rd = road, apptd = appointed

REPORT FOR THE DEVELOPMENT MANAGER

<u>Development of land at Windsor Rd., Duffield</u>

With ref. to the discussions we have had with you recently relative to the design of the above project, we shall be pleased to act for you subject to yr. agreeing the fllwg. terms of appointment:-

2 ~~1~~. All statutory regulations are complied w. + necessary consents obtained.

1 ~~2~~. You will give an assurance that no other architects, surveyors or consultants have bn. instructed or are working on this scheme.

4 ~~3~~. You will agree the draft programme for the works prepared by us + submitted to you.

5 ~~4~~. You agree to the work being carried out in ⁄ (accordance) w. the RIBA Conditions of Engagement + Scale of Professional Charges.

3 ~~5~~. A Clerk of Works is apptd. to supervise work on the site.

(Insert today's date) Signed ......................

## Exercise 43

**One-hand drill**

**Type one-hand words by letter response; i.e. think each letter, and pass from one letter to the next quickly.**

*Words that are not one-hand are shown in italics.*

See you, see him, you were, were ever, as you saw, we look on.
In fact, as we agreed, as you are aware, we refer *to* my cases.
Only John saw my estate.  In fact, you gave *the* federal rates.

## Exercise 44

**Common-phrase drill**

*Type each line three times; the third time very quickly.*

so that, so that the, so that they will be there
this is known, it has been made, it will be made
all of them, there have been, she will not be so

## Exercise 45

**Double-letter drill**

**Keep your mind on the words you are copying.**

He usually collects all sorts of buttons, bottles and glasses.
Miss Keeler will get four assignments in the office this week.
A letter followed the offer of a free book on Current Affairs.

## Exercise 46

**Prefix/suffix drill on con-, sub- and -ful**

control confirm concern contain control confirm concern contain
subsist sublime subject subside subsist sublime subject subside
lawful grateful joyful thankful lawful grateful joyful thankful

## Exercise 47

**Accuracy drill**

**After a full stop leave two spaces.**

When you cannot act as you wish, you must act as you can.
Be wise to correct your errors from the errors of others.
Kindness is the oil which takes the friction out of life.
I enjoy work.  I can look at it for hours.  This is true.

*One space after (,)*

*Two spaces after (.)*

**Exercise 345** **Type the following report in double-line spacing. (Part of LCCI examination paper LC/54/Sp78 - Intermediate.)**

R E P O R T ON VISIT TO ALLIED HOLDINGS LIMITED - ~~19 to 20 MARCH~~ 1928 26 TO 28 April

To Assistant Promotions Manager

From Promotions Manager

After our conversation yesterday, I thought it might be helpful if I put down on paper some of the advantages the above firm will ~~have~~ gain if they use our agency.

Allied Holdings have said that the reason they have looked after their own sales promotion ~~because~~ is that their distribution is mainly through department stores and mail order catalogues. They claim that the sales promotion companies are unfamiliar with these, being mostly geared to groceries.

run on

We do not agree with this and find that most major users of promotions prefer to work with a consultancy, such as ours, ~~the main reason being~~ mainly because of the higher standard of work that comes from a specialist.

We are dealing with promotion work most of the day. We see the effects of hundreds of promotions in different situations and we have discovered most of the problems at the same time. We can say with reasonable certainty what the effect of doing a thing a ~~certain~~ particular way will be.

Perhaps the ~~main~~ most important reason for using a consultancy is the fact that there are only a few really good creative sales promotion experts and they ~~like~~ prefer to work in the freer and more stimulating environment of a consultancy rather than within a big company.

Although the consultant obviously does not know as much as the client about his business he does make it his business to learn a great deal about it.

# Shift Lock

When you want a whole word, phrase, or sentence in capital letters, lock the shift key of your typewriter.

To lock, depress the shift lock key with your left-hand little finger; the typewriter mechanism will then be in position to type continuous capitals.

To unlock, press lightly the left-hand shift key.

Note: The shift lock key is placed only on the left-hand side of the keyboard.

## Exercise 48

**Technique drill**

*Repeat the same line until you have completed a correct typing.*

Dr Jane B Richard works with UNESCO in the city of New York.
BEA is a member of IATA.  So is TWA, SAS and other airlines.
ILO, NATO, YMCA, NASA and RAF are a few well known acronyms.

## Exercise 49

**One-hand drill**

*Words that are not one-hand are shown in italics.*

I saw only Stewart in *the* street.  Join him at *the* great base.
We gave him *the* best case.  You are regarded as great traders.
We saw *the* great state base.  In fact, Jim traced a few seats.

## Exercise 50

**Balanced-hand drill**

**Leave two spaces after a full stop but only one after a comma.**

By the lake.  Both he and she did the work for them by the lake.
It is the duty.  It is the BIG DUTY and the WISH of men to work.
VIC AND LEO own the field of corn and the land by the city lake.

## Exercise 51

**Speed drill**

**Type as quickly and accurately as you can. Double-space between paragraphs.**

They think they will call on you in four or five days.
I think he will be in your own town today or tomorrow.

We have just seen your letter and thank you very much.
He will try to be at your new office at an early date.

I thank you for your letter which came to me just now.
I am sure you will settle the bill as soon as you can.

**Exercise 344** **Type the following report, taking two carbon copies.** *(Courtesy: 'The Institute of Linguists', London.)*

| | |
|---|---|
| The Institute<br>of<br>Linguists | Report of the Sub-Committee<br>set up to consider the Procedural Resolution<br>arising from the Annual General Meeting<br>of February 19th 19-- |

| | |
|---|---|
| Members of the Sub-Committee: | B. Gomes da Costa (in the Chair)<br>Miss J. Gadsby<br>Miss B. M. Snell<br>W. O. Harris<br>Dr. J. B. Sykes |
| In attendance: | M. D. Payne |

MANDATE:

To consider the election of Council members and the machinery thereof:

The following recommendations of the Sub-Committee have been considered by the Council of the Institute and approved.

1. The Editor and Secretary shall prepare descriptions of Council work (partly objective facts, partly various personal views) to increase awareness among members of the Institute of the work of Council to appear in the spring issue of the "Incorporated Linguist".
2. Nomination papers to be available to qualified members by 1st August and shall be sent separately if the "Incorporated Linguist" is not ready for despatch in time for this date. If papers are sent with the "Incorporated Linguist" there shall be some clear external communication of their presence.
3. Article 61 to be amended to read "the Vice-Presidents and not more than 15 Councillors elected from the Fellows . . ."
4. The Committee draws the attention of Council to the need to form relatively small ad-hoc working parties to solve particular problems. Such working parties to report to Council, but their members should not necessarily be members of Council. The Chairman of such working parties to be a member of Council.
5. If the size of Council is reduced it shall be arranged that the number of vacancies is one fewer than the number of retiring members of Council for three successive years until the reduced number is reached.
6. Council should have the right to co-opt qualified members of the Institute until the next Annual General Meeting provided that . . .

MICHAEL D. PAYNE
Secretary

February 24th 19--

## Lesson 8

**Introducing**

**; P and Q**

The **semi-colon** and the letter **p** are struck with the right-hand little finger, while the letter **q** is struck with the left-hand little finger.

Note: Strike the combinations (**;p**) and (**aq**) very carefully until your little fingers acquire sufficient strength.

# Exercise 52

**Location drill**

juj kik lol ;;; ;p; ;p; lol ;p;
frf ded sws aqa aqa sws aqa aqa
jùj frf kik ded lol sws ;p; aqa

**When erasing, move carriage to the extreme left or right of the printing point.**

# Exercise 53

pen pay put pin pot map dip cup tip top
pair pack ship shop pass past rope open
upon play pure tape type pull port post

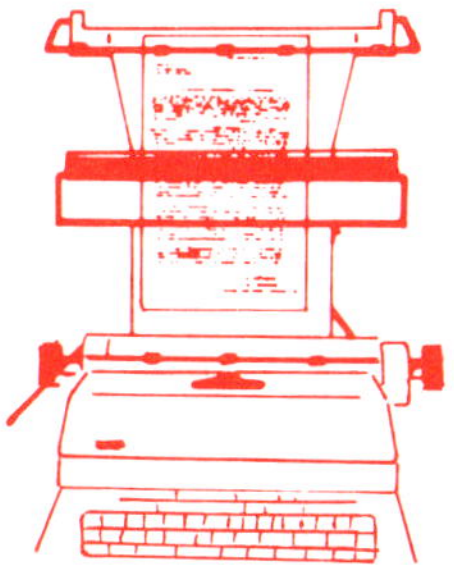

*One of many stands for holding text in front of eyes*

# Exercise 54

**Common-phrase drill**

can be, may be, this is, in your, would be, the above
do not, you to, to have, you are, has been, which you
in our, one of, like to, able to, from the, very much
and we, with a, in this, to make, for this, a copy of

# Exercise 55

spend price prime print group party penny
quest queen quote quota quite quiet quick
apply piece place speed point pound press

*Clean your typewriter regularly for better results*

# Exercise 56

**Suffix drill on -ness, -less and -ible**

goodness fairness holiness fineness goodness fairness
stainless endless blameless sinless stainless endless
invisible legible impossible edible invisible legible

**Exercise 343** **Type the following informal report written in the form of a letter.** *(Courtesy: 'Office Management' - J. C. Denyer.)*

5 February 1982

The Board of Directors

Gentlemen

<u>Works Accident, 5.2.1982</u>

I deeply regret that a serious accident occurred in the Company's works at 3.35 pm this afternoon. The floor of the warehouse at present used for jar storage suddenly collapsed, and unfortunately two employees:

Eric Fawcett (single, aged 29), warehouse clerk, and
Robert Brown (married, aged 52), packer,

who were in the building at the time were both killed instantly.

| | |
|---|---|
| ACTION TAKEN | (1) The police were called in immediately.<br>(2) The relatives of the deceased employees have been notified, and have been visited to ascertain what help can be given them.<br>(3) Temporary shorings are being erected to prevent any further collapse of the building.<br>(4) Formal notification has been given to the Factory Inspector.<br>(5) The Western Insurance Company has been notified, and a claim under the Company's insurance policy will be made in due course. |
| ESTIMATE OF DAMAGE | While it is too early to give a precise figure of the damage, it is probable that the building will have to be rebuilt. Its cost was £2,000 in 1938, and is likely to be not less than £60,000 today. |
| DECEASED EMPLOYEES | The date of the inquest on the two employees has not yet been fixed, but I will let the Board know as soon as possible, to enable arrangements to be made for the Company's representation thereat. |
| INQUIRY INTO CAUSE | The Works Manager has been instructed by the Chairman to institute an immediate inquiry into the reasons for the accident, and his report will be presented within seven days from the date of this report. |

I M GREEN
Secretary

## Abbreviations and Full Stops

Modern tendency requires abbreviations without punctuation marks - open punctuation.
Examples: eg ie etc am pm No (number) Mr R M Smith.

### Exercise 57a)

*(a) Open punctuation*

Mrs B R Williams MBE BA has just returned from a long tour.
She arrived at the New Station at 10.10 am and went straight
to the BBC for a recital programme.

The traditional method - which is being abandoned - requires full stops after all abbreviations.
Examples: e.g. i.e. etc. a.m. p.m. (no space after the full stop) No. (number) Mr. R. M. Smith (one space after the full stop).

### Exercise 57b)

*(b) Traditional method*

Mrs. B. R. Williams, M.B.E., B.A., has just returned from a
long tour.  She arrived at the New Station at 10.10 a.m. and
went straight to the B.B.C. for a recital programme.

### Exercise 58

**Sentence drill**

*Type each line three times; then the whole exercise once more.*

It is really tragic to have talent and not use it properly.

In fact there are many ways to do a job; use the right one.

She can see our superb antique clocks at our downtown shop.

### Exercise 59

**Accuracy**

**After a semi-colon allow one space.**

I regret often that I have spoken; never that I have
been silent.

Hear one side and you will be in the dark; hear both
sides and all will be clear.

The more we do, the more we can do; the more busy we
are, the more leisure we have.

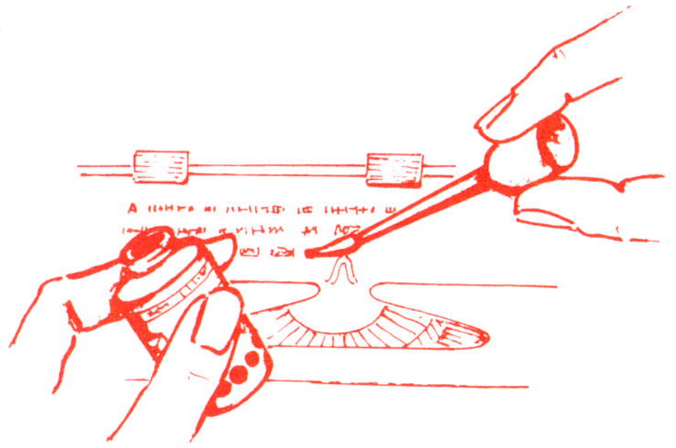

## A Second Method for Correcting Errors

Besides the use of the rubber eraser, described on page 21, you can correct an error using a special liquid (available in several colours to match your paper).

Procedure: Paint over the error with the brush provided, wait for a few seconds until it is completely dry, and make the correction.

# Reports

**Reports are official statements of facts which have been investigated by means of inspection, research or experiment.**

**Reports are of several kinds: business, economic, scientific, educational, government etc; and they may be formal or informal. Basically, however, they fall into two categories: *Ordinary* and *special*. Ordinary reports are those dealing mainly with Company meetings or reports to shareholders. Special reports are those which, in addition to the recording of facts, include the writer's conclusions and recommendations.**

**Headings in the paragraphs of a report should be typed in the margin, either in closed capitals or in lower case with underscore.**

## Exercise 342

**Type the following report on A4 paper, taking one carbon copy.**

THE CYPRUS ANTI-CANCER SOCIETY

REPORT OF THE COUNCIL OF MANAGEMENT

The Council of Management has pleasure in submitting its Ninth Report, together with the Society's Balance Sheet and Income and Expenditure Account for the year ended 31 December 1980.

The excess of income over expenditure for the year was C£16,612 as against C£13,265 for the year 1979. Net receipts from the Christo's March amounted to C£38,655 as compared with C£26,184 in 1979; donations totalled C£20,340 as against C£12,964 in the previous year, while the Government subvention was C£6,000. The accumulated fund amounted to C£174,313 as at 31 December 1980 compared to C£157,478 at the end of 1979.

The total cost of the building, equipment and furniture as at 31 December 1980 was C£117,058 and the aggregate provision for depreciation amounted to C£24,292.

The Council wishes to express its gratitude for the continuing support and generous help it receives from the Government, the United Nations High Commission for Refugees, the Cyprus Red Cross Society and all the other private benefactors of the Society. On 31 December 1980 the Society's paid-up membership was . . . .

A PATSALIDES
President

20 May 1981

## Backspace key

Use the backspace key to fill in an omitted letter. Reach this key with the appropriate finger; depress it firmly and release it quickly.

On electric typewriters, reach the backspace key with the little finger (right or left depending upon key location); tap and release it quickly as this is a repeater key.

## Exercise 60

*Type the first incomplete word as shown in black; backspace and type in the missing letter (shown in colour). Type the remaining words one by one in the same way.*

```
The eco omic l w of sup ly a d de and
       n       a       p    n    m
```

## Exercise 61

**Prefix/suffix drill on com-, in- and -der**

common commit comply compel common commit comply compel

income indeed invite inward income indeed invite inward

sender render leader ponder sender render leader ponder

## Exercise 62

**Speed sentences**

**Correct mistakes with a rubber eraser or with correcting fluid.**

She is sorry indeed that you will soon be leaving her.
He very much looks forward to meeting them personally.

I am afraid I shall not be able to manage it this time.
We look forward to hearing that you will come tomorrow.

We are very sorry to miss you and hope you will be back.
Thanks all the same; we look forward to seeing you soon.

## Changing the Ribbon

To change a worn out or faded ribbon follow these steps:

1. Wind the ribbon on the right-hand spool.
2. Raise and lock the **ribbon carrier** as follows:
   a. Depress the shift lock.
   b. Set the *ribbon indicator lever* for typing on the lower part of the ribbon.
   c. Depress simultaneously any two central keys, say **h** and **g** to lock them together.
3. Remove the ribbon from the carrier; then remove both spools from the machine.
4. Hook the new ribbon on the empty spool and wind a few inches on to it.
5. Place both spools on their holders. Thread the ribbon through the ribbon carrier.
6. Release the shift lock. Return the ribbon indicator lever to type on the upper part of the ribbon. Unlock the two keys.

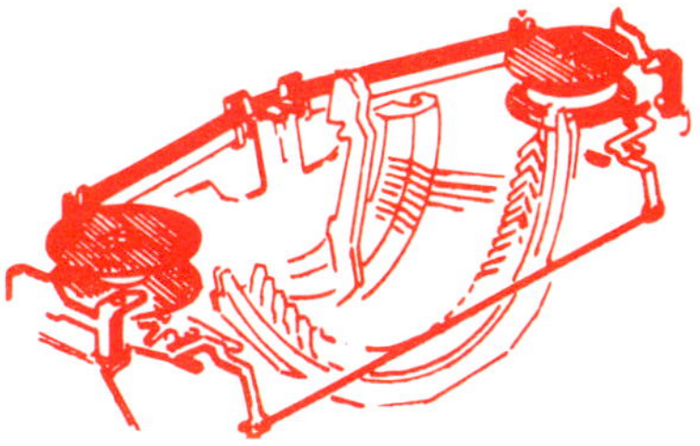

**Raise and lock ribbon carrier**

**Three types of ribbon carrier**

**Exercise 341** **Type the following Minutes on a sheet of A4 paper, using any acceptable style.**

Additional abbreviations used: Mon = Monday, w = with, Co = Company, Drs = Directors, bn = been, Mngr = Manager, apprec'n = appreciation, fllwg or folg = following.

(Typist: Arrange in 2 columns in the order shown; omit numbers)

Minutes of a Mtg of the Board of Drs of the Household Wares Ltd held in the ~~Ball~~ Boardroom on 16th Sept. 1982 at 5.00 p.m.

Present: (1) R. Jameson (Chairman) (6) ~~2~~ B. Lancaster (2) ~~3~~ T Sullivan (3) ~~4~~ F. Simons (8) ~~5~~ A. Richards (4) ~~6~~ L. Taylor (5) ~~7~~ H Wallace (7) ~~8~~ C. Newman (9) D. Harrison (Secy.) (10) W. Stevens (Treasurer)

Previous Minutes — The minutes of the previous mtg which had bn circulated to all members, were taken as read, approved and signed by the Chairman.

Matters Arising — There were no matters arising out of the minutes.

Apologies — Mr Harrison read a letter from Mr Williamson regretting his inability to be present owing to illness.

Retirements — The Drs reported the retirement of Mr B. Whitehead who ~~has~~ had served the Co for ~~twenty five~~ 25 years. They ~~asked to~~ recorded their sincere apprec'n of the valuable work he ~~has~~ had done.

Purchase of New Van — Mr. Taylor submitted a report advising the purchase of an additional delivery van to cope w. the increased volume of sales. It was RESOLVED that:

The Transport Mngr. be instructed to purchase for ~~cash~~ cash a suitable vehicle for local delivery.

Accounts — The fllwg A/cs were sanctioned for payment:

| | | |
|---|---|---|
| Electrical Equipment Ltd | (Installations) | £ 140.00 |
| R. Browning & Co | (Stationery) | 25.00 |

Next Meeting — The next mtg. of the Board of Drs was fixed for Mon. 19 October in the Boardroom at 6.30 p.m.

# «Squeezing» and «Expanding» Words

In correcting errors on manual typewriters, it is often possible to insert an omitted letter in a word or to remove from it an unwanted one.

### A. To insert a letter

Suppose you have to insert an omitted **t** in the phrase **for beter results:** Erase the incorrect word (beter); position the carriage at the space after the word **for;** depress and hold the space bar; strike **b,** release the space bar and repeat the process for each remaining letter of **better.**

ERROR: `for beter results`

CORRECTION `for better results`

### B. To remove a letter

Follow the above procedure but start the correction one space to the right; i.e. having positioned the carriage at the space after **for** allow an additional space before starting **better.**

ERROR: `for bettter results`

CORRECTION `for better results`

Some electric typewriters are equipped with a half backspace lever; this is a great help for squeezing or expanding words as it permits typing half-way between characters or spaces.

## Exercise 63

**Suffix drill on -ment, -lity and -able**

```
movement lodgement pavement allotment movement lodgement
docility inability fidelity hostility docility inability
reliable desirable amicable advisable reliable desirable
```

## Introducing X, Z, ? and :

Letter **X** is struck with the *s* finger, and **Z** with the *a* finger. (These new key reaches are a little awkward and require more practice.) The **question mark** (**?**) is, in most cases, the shift of the comma, while the **colon** (**:**) is the shift of the semi-colon.

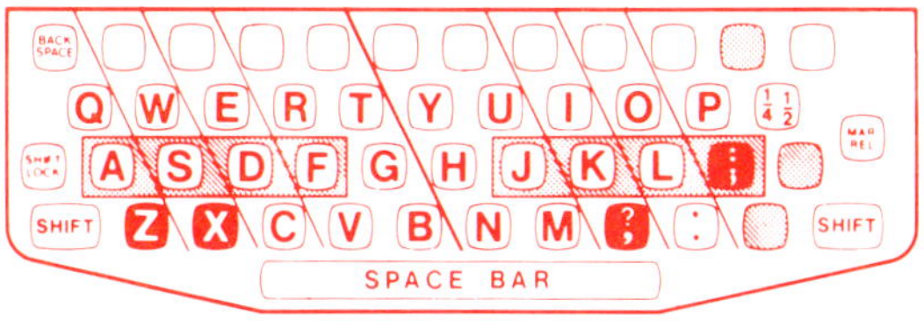


## Exercise 64

**Location drill**

```
ded dcd sws sxs sxs sws sxs sxs
fvf dcd sxs sxs aza aza sxs aza
k,k k?k k?k lll ;:; ;:; lll ;:;
```

*Type these combinations slowly and very carefully.*

*Do not remove eyes from copy*

## Exercise 65

```
box six next text exact extra zip zeal dozen frozen
fix fox luxe axle exert index viz zero prize puzzle
mix tax taxi flux exist proxy axe lazy razor zigzag
```

## Exercise 340

**An alternative method of setting out Minutes. Compare it with that on previous page, and type it in duplicate.**

WORLD TRADING SERVICES LIMITED

Minutes of Meeting held on Wednesday 6 January 1982 in the Board Room, Head Office.

<u>Present</u>

Mr. R. Jameson (in the Chair)
Mr. F. Short (Managing Director)
Mrs. Constance S. Ellams
Mrs. Julia D. Riley
Mr. T. Singleton
Mr. W. Sullivan

<u>In attendance</u>

Mr. R. Warren (Secretary)

| | |
|---|---|
| Apologies | Mr. B. Dennison, Mr. S. Hutchinson and Mr. S. Hamilton sent their apologies. |
| Chairman's Welcome | The Chairman gave a welcome to Mr. W. Sullivan who was attending his first Meeting of the Board. |
| Minutes of Last Meeting | The Minutes of the Meeting of 15 December were read, adopted and signed by the Chairman. |
| Matters Arising | It was reported that (a) discussions on technical developments were still taking place, and (b) interviews for the Personnel Officer vacancy had now been held and subject to the Board's approval, the position would be offered to Mr. Edward Goodwin. Approval was given. |
| Sales | The Chairman informed the Board that the figures for the year were double those of the previous year. |
| Estimates for Expansion Projects | The Managing Director reported that he had recommended that Turner & Co should be awarded the contract. This decision was ratified by the Board. |
| Date of Next Meeting | It was decided to hold the next meeting of the Committee on Wednesday, 3 February 1982. |

Chairman
8 January 1982

## Exercise 66

The fox changes his skin but not his habits.
It is said that blind zeal can only do harm.
Take the middle route; excess gives trouble.

## Exercise 67

**Accuracy/Speed**

After a question mark allow two spaces; after a colon and a semi-colon allow one space.

Do you wish men to speak well of you?  Then never speak well of yourself.

Each needs the other: capital cannot do without labour, nor labour without capital.

*From now on you will often be required to type from text that has been written by hand.*

## Exercise 68

**Balanced-hand drill**

Clean the typewriter keys often in order to have sharp copies.

bit box six map bit box six map bit box six map box
man may pay men man may pay men man may pay men pay
Did she pay the Firm for the work by the city dock?

**PUNCTUATION MARKS**

*Type any punctuation mark close up to the preceding word or punctuation mark.*
*Leave one space after a comma, semi-colon or colon.*
*Leave two spaces after the end of a sentence, whether it ends with full stop, question mark or exclamation mark.*

## Exercise 69

**Accuracy drill**

If you want enemies, excel others; if you want friends, let others excel you.

The excesses of our youth are drafts upon our old age, payable with interest, about thirty years after date.

I daily examine myself on three points: In planning for others, have I failed to be honest?  In my dealing with friends, have I failed to be sincere?  In my teachings, have I failed to practise what I have taught?

## Exercise 339 **Type a copy of the following Minutes on A4 paper.**

M I N U T E S   O F   M E E T I N G

A meeting of the Committee Management of the Nicosia Race Club was held at the Race Club Offices on Monday 21 December 1981 at 1800 hrs.

PRESENT

Mr G W Portsmouth (Chairman)
Mr A N Druce
Dr D Everton
Mr R Johnson (Secretary)

1  APOLOGIES

Mr Stewart regretted his inability to attend as he was out of the country on important personal business.

2  MINUTES

The minutes of the previous meeting held on 3 November 1981 were read, approved and signed by the Chairman.

3  MATTERS ARISING

The Secretary reported that the Sub-Committee agreed on a suggestion to dismantle the shelter in the old Enclosure and erect it behind the Main Stand.  This would give space for eight additional boards.

4  CYPRUS GOVERNMENT BONDS

Dr Everton said he had disposed of all the Cyprus Government Bonds and deposited the sum of C£3,750 with the Club.

5  AUDITORS' FEES

The Chairman read a letter from the auditors whereby they accepted the fees of C£900 for 1980.  They agree to accept the same fees for 1981 on condition that for any meetings in excess of 24 they would be paid an additional fee of C£40 per meeting.

6  ANY OTHER BUSINESS

There being no other business the Chairman declared the meeting closed at 1950 hrs.

7  DATE OF NEXT MEETING

The date of the next meeting was fixed for 10 February 1982.

G W PORTSMOUTH
Chairman

28 December 1981

## Exercise 70

**Speed sentences**

**When erasing do not let erasure grit fall into mechanism of your typewriter.**

I think this would be useful for all of them.
Perhaps he will give her another opportunity.

He will be calling on you some day next week.
We will call at your office within two weeks.

*Text written by hand, i.e. neither typed nor printed, is called manuscript. This is a word of Latin origin.*

## Exercise 71

**Shift key drill on all letters of the alphabet**

**Depress shift keys fully; faulty timing will result in a raised capital letter.**

Adams Brown Clark Davis Eliot Foster Gordon Henry Irving

Jerome Knight Lennox Miller Nelson Oxford Patrick Quinby

Roger Smith Thomas Ursula Venus Wells Xavier Young Zweig

## Exercise 72

**Space bar drill**

**Strike space bar quickly, gently, and in rhythm with letter keys.**

a b c a b c a b c d e f d e f d e f g h i g h i

g h i j k l j k l j k l m n o m n o m n o p q r

p q r s t u s t u s t u v w x y z v w x y z y z

## Exercise 73

**Alphabetic sentences**

*Each of these sentences contains all letters of the alphabet. Copy them out occasionally, sticking to correct techniques: i.e. eyes on copy, position at typewriter, correct fingering, absolute rhythm etc.*

The quick brown fox jumps right over the lazy dog.

He mixed quickly a very big jar of soap for the new prize.

The boy realized very quickly that jumping was excellent for him.

## Exercise 338

**This is an example of a Chairman's Agenda. Note the wide right-hand margin which is needed by the Chairman to record his remarks.**

THE BRITANNIA BISCUIT COMPANY LIMITED

ANNUAL GENERAL MEETING

To be held at Lion House, Thatchford, on Friday 5 March 1982 at 1400 hrs.

A G E N D A

1 The Secretary to read the notice convening the meeting.

2 The Secretary to read the Minutes of the previous meeting.

3 The Auditors' report to be read.

4 The Chairman to ask the meeting whether the Directors' Report and Accounts as printed and submitted shall be taken as read.

5 The Chairman to:

(a) Address the meeting on the Company's position and prospects.

(b) Move: 'That the Report and Accounts . . . be and are hereby approved and adopted.'

(c) Call on Mr. S. Wilkins to second the motion.

(d) Invite the shareholders to discuss any points arising out of the motion.

(e) Put motion to meeting and declare result.

6 The Chairman to move: 'That the dividend . . . be approved and . . . be paid . . . to the shareholders.'

7 The Chairman to declare the proceedings at an end.

The vertical line may be substituted by the brace, as )

**Part 2**

# Contents

## Exercise 336

**Set out the following notice of meeting and agenda in correct style. Leave a wide right-hand margin for notes.**

Abbreviations used: Mtg = Meeting, Cttee = Committee, Tues. = Tuesday, Sec. or Secy = Secretary, Feb = February.

'VENICE' GLASSWARE LTD

A Mtg of the Board of Directors will be held in the Cttee Room A at 1800 hours on Tues. 16 Feb. 1982.

Agenda

(1) Minutes of last Mtg (2) Apologies for absence, if any (3) Matters arising from the Minutes (4) Correspondence (5) Selling policy (6) Secy's Report (7) Appointment of new Auditors (8) Any other appropriate business (8) Date and time of next mtg.

S. Larsen
Secy

2 Feb. 1982

## Exercise 337

**Type a copy of the following notice of meeting and agenda issued by Mr E. Xenophon, Hon. Treasurer, on 20th May 1982.**

Abbreviations used: Rpt = Report, A/cs = Accounts, B/S = Balance Sheet, yr = year, Dec. = December, a.o.b. = Any other business, Gen. = General.

THE CYPRUS ANTI-CANCER SOCIETY

Notice is hereby given that the Ninth Annual General Meeting will be held at the "ARODAPHNOUSA" Nursing Home at 5.00 p.m. on Wednesday 17 June 1982.

A G E N D A

1 To receive and consider the Rpt of the Council and the statement of A/cs and the B/S for the yr ended 31 Dec 1981.

2 To elect new members of the Council.

3 To fix the remunaration of the Auditors.

4 To transact a.o.b. which may properly be transacted at an Annual Gen. Mtg.

# Common-Phrase Exercises for Increased Accuracy and Speed

Set a left-hand margin of 15 pica (20 elite) and type each line three times; then repeat the whole exercise at your highest speed.

Use higher speed for easy words that are typed with alternate hands; use lower speed for difficult words that are typed with one hand.

*Always keep a balanced position*

## Exercise 74

In this country, at your leisure, at your service.
I think you are, I think you may, I have only one.
I am very sorry, when we are not, it will only be.
Let us remember, long before you, to let you have.
For the present, there are times, for some reason.

## Exercise 75

**Depress shift keys fully.**

I have been, I have some, I have your, I think the.
I have just, I know this, we shall be, first prize.
On his part, all you can, in this way, zero number.
The size of, it is known, let us know, at the time.
It is right, extra sizes, bad quality, you will do.

## Exercise 76

**Type speedily and accurately.**

And as it may be, as we know it is, for his own good.
For which we are, you will be glad, see me next week.
All these things, all these places, it is quite easy.
To which you can, it is impossible, quite impossible.
Wherever you are, he should not be, this will not be.

*Chest forward, shoulders down*

## Exercise 77

**Strike full stops and commas very lightly.**

And I have, that has never been, that is not the case.
And I only, I am not interested, as long as necessary.
And I want, shall be considered, there is no question.
And I must, there are those who, there is no occasion.
And I will, you will some times, all over the country.

# Notice of Meeting – Agenda – Minutes

## Notice of Meeting

A Notice of Meeting is prepared by the secretary of a company and sent to all persons who are entitled to attend the meeting. This states the day, time, place and purpose of a meeting.

## Agenda

An Agenda is a programme of the business to be done at a meeting. It is drawn up by the secretary in consultation with the chairman and contains the items for discussion in the order in which they will be dealt with.

Agendas are typed in the fully-blocked style, although some organisations still use the traditional method. In either case a wide right-hand margin should be allowed for the taking of notes during the meeting.

## Chairman's Agenda

This is not to be confused with the Meeting Agenda; for it is specially prepared for the use of the chairman only as it includes special notes under each item to facilitate his conduct of the meeting. The right-hand side of the paper is left blank for his personal notes.

## Minutes

Minutes are the official record of the business transacted at a meeting. They should be brief, accurate and clear.

Minutes are first typed in draft on A4 paper in double or treble spacing, and are checked for omissions or inaccuracies against the agenda and the notes taken during the meeting. After their approval by the chairman they are typed in single spacing.

Minutes usually contain the following information:

(1) Description of meeting, place, date and time. (2) Names of those present (Chairman's name first, Secretary's last). In a general meeting where the members present are many, only their number is mentioned. (3) Reading, if required, and confirmation of the Minutes of last meeting. (4) Matters arising from the Minutes. (5) Apologies for absence. (6) Correspondence. (7) Other business. (8) Date of next meeting.

The Minutes are signed by the Chairman at the next meeting. Below his signature follows his name and his designation. The date may be typed or inserted in ink at the time of signing.

## Exercise 335

**Type on A5 paper**

**Notice of Meeting and Agenda in the blocked style:**

THE NICOSIA RACE CLUB

A meeting of the Committee of Management of the Nicosia Race Club will be held at the Club premises, Room 3, on Monday 21 December 1981 at 1800 hrs.

A G E N D A

1 Apologies for absence
2 Minutes of previous meeting
3 Matters arising therefrom
4 Cyprus Government Bonds
5 Auditors' fees
6 Any other business

R JOHNSON
Hon Secretary

30 November 1981

# Additional Accuracy–Speed Exercises

Type each paragraph once; then repeat the exercise as fast as you can. Do not type line for line. Set margins for a 55-space line, say 15 and 70 (20 and 75). *Figures in brackets refer to elite type.*

**Allow 2.5 cm (six line spaces) from top of paper and type your name.**

## Exercise 78

We will be in the town next month and will most certainly give you a ring.

She looks forward to being of service to you and I am sure you will like her.

We are sure you will wish to see them shortly and talk to them on the matter.

### Setting the right-hand margin

If you require equal side margins, set the right-hand margin stop three spaces to the right of where you aim to end your line. For example, if you wish to end your line at 70, set the margin stop at 73; this will prevent your right-hand margin from tending to become wider than your left-hand one.

If the carriage has locked before you have completed the word depress the Margin Release Key.

## Exercise 79

It is better for a city to be governed by good rulers than by good laws.

Throw a lucky man into the sea and he will come up with a fish in his mouth.

The only person who can never make a mistake is the person who never does anything.

## Exercise 80

*Any help you might be able to give us in this respect would be very much appreciated.*

*I have just heard from my sales manager that you are planning to be in town next week.*

*Please let us know if ever there is anything we can do to make our service even better.*

## Exercise 333

**Type a fair copy of the following invoice. Complete the missing amounts and total the final column.**

Messrs Smith & Traxler, Inc.,
1630 Ashland Avenue,
EVANSTON, Illinois.

Today's date

| Quantity | Particulars | @ | Amount |
|---|---|---|---|
| | | | £ |
| 12 sets | Medium teaspoon set, 6 pieces | 9.15 | 109.80 |
| 12 " | Large teaspoon set, 6 pieces | 9.75 | 117.00 |
| 24 " | Fruit Knife set, 6 pieces in box | 8.25 | |
| 24 " | Fruit Fork set, 6 pieces in box | 8.25 | |
| 12 " | Coffee spoon set, 6 pieces | 6.80 | |
| 12 " | Dessert set, 24 pieces in box | 40.25 | |
| 24 " | Dinner set, 24 pieces in box | 45.00 | |
| 12 " | Salad servers, 2 pieces | 6.80 | |
| | Less: 5% cash discount | | |
| | | | £ |
| E & OE | (VAT included in prices) | | |

## Exercise 334

**Display the following invoice completing all missing sums and totalling the final column. Rule with a ball point pen.**

To: Messrs D Baker & Sons Ltd, 117c Bevis Marks, London EC3A 7JB. 14 July 198- 5 dozen assorted biscuits 'Rose Drum' @ £14.15 per doz., 10 doz. assorted biscuits 'Banquet Drum' @ £14.15 per doz., 5 doz. ATC Petit Beurre @ 2.90 per doz., 5 doz. ATC Cream Cracker @ £2.90 per doz., 10 doz. ATC Golden Puff @ £2.95 per doz., 6 doz. ATC Ginger Nut @ £2.95 per doz., 12 doz. ATC Digestive @ £2.90 per doz., 12 doz. ATC Cottage Cream @ £2.80 per dozen. E&OE (All prices include VAT)

## A Third Method for Correcting Errors

The use of the rubber eraser and the correcting fluid is already known to you. Besides these methods you can correct an error using specially coated correcting paper strips.

Procedure: Place the strip over the error; re-strike same error through strip; remove strip, backspace to original position, and re-type the letter or word correctly.

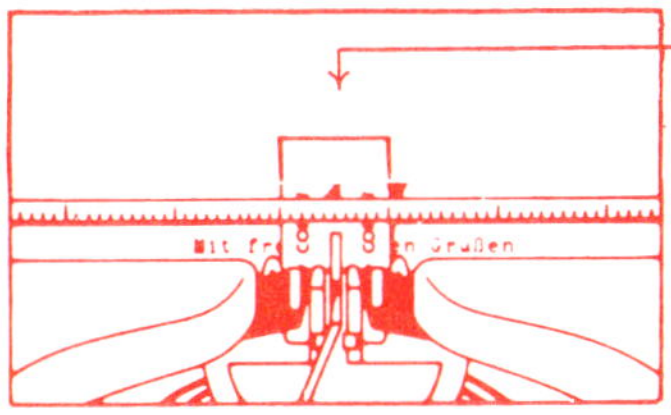


## Exercise 81

He is leaving our company for personal reasons and we are very sorry indeed to lose him.

I would be most grateful if you would do what you can for them during their stay in your city.

If you will kindly let us know when and where we might call on you we should be most grateful.

## Exercise 82

**Depress shift keys fully.**

It has been said that the battle for success is half won when one gains the habit of work.

We have two ears and only one tongue in order that we may hear more and speak less.

That which is unjust, can really profit no one; that which is just, can really harm no one.

## Exercise 83

It was good to hear from you and I shall be pleased to let you have the information you need.

Thank you for visiting us yesterday and for making your first purchase on your credit account.

His standing is very high indeed and he has put in a good deal of work in the general interest.

## Exercise 84

*Before typing read the sentences through carefully.*

We are writing to thank you for the business you have given us during the past years.

We are very pleased to learn that you have decided at last to come and see our plant for yourself.

**Exercise 332** **Type the following invoice on paper 2/3 A4. Draw all lines in ink except those above and below the total sum.**

# *S & R LEISURE LIMITED*

*Mercury Way, Warren Industrial Estate, COVENTRY CO42 11L*

VAT Reg No.: 365 7084 15

The Porto Novo Import Co
P O Box 6234
PORTO NOVO
Dahomey

Invoice No. ..6345.....

Date: 15 September 1982

| Quantity | Description of Goods | Unit Price | Amount |
|---|---|---|---|
| | | £ | £ |
| 2 doz | Front-driven children's tricycles | 93.55 | 187.10 |
| 4 doz | Pedal-driven children's autos | 120.00 | 480.00 |
| 2 doz | Chain-driven children's bicycles | 135.00 | 270.00 |
| 4 doz | Front-driven children's tricycles | 105.00 | 420.00 |
| | | | £1,357.10 |

PRICES: CIF Dahomey, net, including packing, in Sterling currency

PAYMENT: Irrevocable Letter of Credit

PACKING: In export carton box

SHIPMENT: Thirty days after receipt of L/C

E & O E

Purchaser's name and address starts over the first vertical ruled line.

The lines above and below the total sum cover the whole width of column.

## Exercise 85

He who waits to do a great deal of good at once, will never do anything in his life.

Old wood best to burn, old wine to drink, old friends to trust and old authors to read.

Do not buy what you want, but what you have need of; what you do not want is dear at a penny.

## Exercise 86

I am sure you will want to come in and see it, even though you have not been our way for quite a while.

I am sure you will understand my position and ~~that~~ thank you again most sincerely for your kind invitation.

I have known Miss Brown for about seven years, during which we were working together in the same office.

**When making errors never type the correct letter over the faulty one. In all Typewriting examinations overtyping and crossing out mistakes are penalized severely.**

## Exercise 87

He has been calling on us for over five years and, needless to say, he is well known to all of us.

Once a month you would get our bill and you would pay for all your purchases with one single cheque.

He has been calling on us for almost ten years and during that time we have become very good friends.

## Exercise 88

In youth the days are short and the years are long; in old age the years are short and the days long.

We judge ourselves by what we feel capable of doing, while all others judge us by what we have already done.

I have found that the great thing in this world is not so much where we stand as in what direction we are moving.

# Invoices

**Invoices are documents that give full details of the goods sold to purchasers; they are typed on paper A4, 2/3 A4 or A5 depending on their length.**

**The printed information on invoices includes: 1. Name and address of seller, 2. Date, 3. Invoice number, 4. Ruled columns, 5. Terms of payment, and 6. The initials E&OE (meaning** *Errors and Omissions Excepted***).**

**The typewritten particulars include: 1. Name and address of purchaser, 2. Date of purchase, 3. Quantity of goods supplied, 4. Description of goods, 5. Unit price** *(per kilo, per metre, per dozen, etc.)*, **6. VAT** *(Value Added Tax)*, **7. Total price, 8. Discount** *(if any)*, **9. Carriage or postal charges, and 10. Method of despatch. For export invoices, name of vessel, details of cargo marks and cargo charges should also be added.**

## TYPING INVOICES

1. Invoices are typed in single-line spacing; if, however, the items are not more than three or four you may use 1.5 or double spacing.
2. Set left-hand margin stop at the point where the first column will commence; set tab stops for each following column.
3. The first column and the purchaser's address start at the same point.
4. Begin the items in the description column about two spaces below the ruled line.
5. When an item takes more than one line, indent the second and succeeding lines 2 or 3 spaces.

*NOTE: The above rules also apply to the setting out of Debit and Credit Notes.*

## Exercise 331

**Type this invoice on A5 paper (landscape). Allow 6 lines from top for the printed heading. Do not rule.**

# WILKINSON PLASTICS LTD

REGENCY HOUSE
JUNIPER ROAD
GUILDFORD GU44 12Q

INVOICE

Mr John Alexander
12 Pallas Street
ATHENS 125
Greece

26 June 1982

| | £ | £ |
|---|---|---|
| 250 wallets No 3456-8 | 1.10 | 275.00 |
| 100 school sets No 22 | 2.30 | 230.00 |
| 100 brush cases No 33 | 2.50 | 250.00 |
| 200 brush cases No 66 | 3.10 | 620.00 |
| 150 frame purses No 7 | 1.00 | 150.00 |
| (Prices include VAT) | | £1,525.00 |

## Exercise 89

If you will kindly complete and return the enclosed card in the envelope provided, it will help us with our records.

We are really pleased to hear that everything is going so well with you.  If we can help in any other way, do let us know.

If there is anything I can do to make your charge account with us even more useful to you, please do not hesitate to tell me.

## Exercise 90

Who is the happiest of men?  He who values the merits of other people and in their pleasure takes joy, even as though it were his own.

No man ever sank under the burden of the day.  It is when the burden of tomorrow is added to that of today that the weight is more than a man can bear.

You should never be ashamed to admit that you have been in the wrong, which is but saying, in other words, that you are wiser today than you were yesterday.

**Correction should be neat, whether mistakes are erased or corrected by some other method, eg by the use of correcting fluid or chemical strip. Use these methods for small errors only, but retype if a more extensive correction is needed.**

## Exercise 91

You can fool some of the people all of the time and all of the people some of the time, but you cannot fool all of the people all the time.

If you are unable to keep that which is small, who will entrust you with that which is great?  For he that is faithful in very little, is also faithful in much.

Tell me, is there anyone who is able for one whole day to apply the energy of his mind to virtue?  It may be that there exists such, but I have never met him.

## Exercise 92

*Read the passage carefully before typing it.*

In many retail businesses sales are made on a cash basis. However, in most wholesale businesses sales are made on a credit or charge basis. For this reason it is necessary to keep an account with each customer.

# Part 7

# Contents

Lesson 9

# THE TABULATOR

**The tabulator (or tab) is a device which allows the carriage to be automatically moved (tabulated) to any pre-determined position.**

## The tabulator consists of:

1. A tab-set key which fixes the tab stops.
2. A tab-clear key which clears a previously-set tab position.
3. A lever which clears all set tab stops with a single depression.
4. A tab bar which is depressed to move the carriage to each tab position.

Note: The tab bar is not struck in the way you strike keys; it is pushed down and held until the carriage reaches the pre-set position.

## Tabulating on manual typewriters

Depress the **tab bar** with the right-hand index finger (or the **key** with the little finger) and hold it down until the carriage has stopped.

## Tabulating on electric typewriters

Tab the **tab key** with the little finger (or the **bar** with the index finger) very lightly. Remove the finger immediately.

## How to use the tabulator

To set a tab stop, move to the desired point on the writing line and depress the tab-set key. Repeat this for any desired settings.

To clear one or more tab stops, move the carriage to the points where the stops were set and depress the tab-clear key.

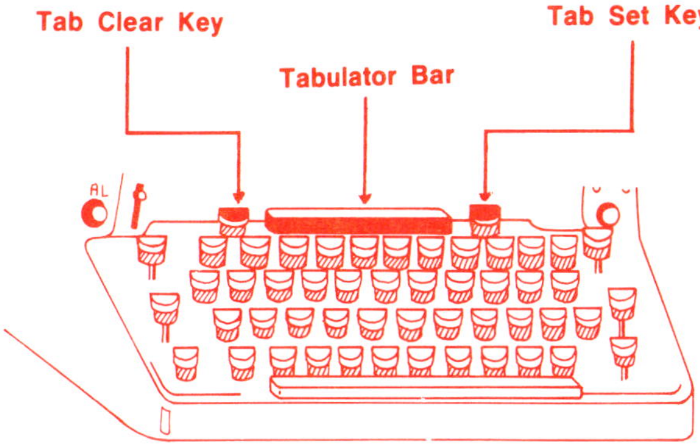


## Exercise 93

*Left margin at 15; set first tab stop at 20, second at 25, and third at 30. Start first line at the left margin. Use the tab key (or bar) to type the remaining three lines.*

```
It is hard for an empty bag to stand upright.
```

*Tab once* →

```
     The early morning has gold in its mouth.
```

*Tab twice* →

```
          Small boats should keep near shore.
```

*Tab three times* →

```
               Of two evils choose the least.
```

**Tab, release, and type steadily.**

## Exercise 330

**Type as fast as you can. However, do not sacrifice accuracy for speed.**

Strokes

The market for motor homes is only now starting to find its feet again, 72
although the market for used vehicles is approaching boom 130
proportions. There are plenty of keen buyers around willing to pay the 203
quite high prices being demanded in a successful market. Dealers feel 275
that the good months for trading will probably last well into the end of 348
December next and the optimists expect that the market will hold up 417
until September of next year. There is no doubt that devaluation has 489
made a foreign holiday an even more expensive proposition; this has 557
meant that more and more people have been turning back to the 619
motorised caravan. The most marked demand is now coming from 682
many hire companies who are finding it difficult to meet requirements 752
with the rise in the number of people looking for a motor home as the 822
most economical way of taking a touring holiday in Britain. Much of 892
this demand is now coming from foreign tourists. 941

For the motor home manufacturers that survived the recession—and 1010
several on the fringes of the industry did not—the future prospects 1080
must now look far more encouraging. One firm is now looking to 1145
future investment again after a period of retrenchment and 1204
re-organisation. It sees a particularly bright prospect in the export field, 1284
where it has been working hard to build up a business. About 1347
one-third of their production is now going into the export field and so 1419
successful has the export rush generally been that in one recent 1484
quarterly period exports were 70 per cent up on the same period last 1553
year. Next year it expects great improvements in both the export and 1624
the domestic markets and one particular company is already quoting 1691
December delivery dates to dealers and importers for certain models. 1761

The motor home market has always had a rather cyclical pattern with 1830
buyers appearing most keen in the spring and summer months, but in 1897
recent years there have been several artificial booms caused by 1961
Government action in the taxation field. The rush to buy before the 2032
introduction of car tax 18 months ago caused most dealers to sell out 2102
but this was followed by a desperate lull as the recession deepened. 2171
Imminent price rises from the main manufacturers have caused similar 2240
artificial movements in the market, but now with apparent public 2305
acceptance of higher petrol prices and the help received in the Budget 2377
in the form of HP relaxations, motor home builders seem set for a 2444
period of gradual sustained recovery. One expert in this field thinks 2517
that the industry over-reacted after the boom at the beginning of the 2587
decade, which meant that they were hit particularly hard in the 2651
recession. He considers that growth will never be so fast again and 2721
that there will not be such great peaks and troughs in the industry. In 2795
his view there will be a steady growth rate with an annual output of 2864
about 9,000 vehicles by the end of the decade. Vehicles like the 2931
Sherpa are due for large-scale conversion and the spokesman in 2995
question considers that the pace of this new activity will gather 3061
momentum within three months. *(LCCI Higher)* 3091

WORDS: 618

# Use of the Tabulator

**To indent a paragraph means to allow five spaces to the right of the margin before starting the first line.**

## A. TO INDENT QUICKLY THE FIRST LINE OF EACH PARAGRAPH

### Exercise 94

*Set margin at 10(15) and a tab stop at 15(21). Indent the first line by depressing the tab key.*

**(a)**

*Tab* → Mr. Smith will be speaking at the next meeting of the Club and, as I know how much you would like to hear him, I wonder if you would care to join me there for lunch.

**(b)**

*Tab* → There are three classes of writers: those who think before they write; those who think while they are writing; and those who think after they have written. It is best to belong to the first class.

## B. TO SET OUT WORDS OR FIGURES IN COLUMNAR FORM

### Exercise 95

*Clear all previously-set stops. Set left margin at 13(16) and tab stops at 27(32), 48(58) and 62(74). Start heading at 24(29).*

SIX COUNTRIES WITH THEIR CAPITALS

| | | | | | | |
|---|---|---|---|---|---|---|
| Canada | → | Ottawa | → | Kuwait | → | Kuwait |
| Gambia | *Tab once* | Banjul | *Tab again* | Poland | *And a third time* | Warsaw |
| Greece | | Athens | | Turkey | | Ankara |

### Decimal Tabulation

Some typewriters are equipped with five or six tabulator keys for decimal tabulation: units, tens, hundreds, etc. This is a great help for the typing of tables, invoices, balance sheets and the like.

Look at the sketch. The key marked «1» tabulates the carriage to a certain previously set tab stop (the units); the key marked «10» tabulates it to one space before that tab stop (the tens) and so on.

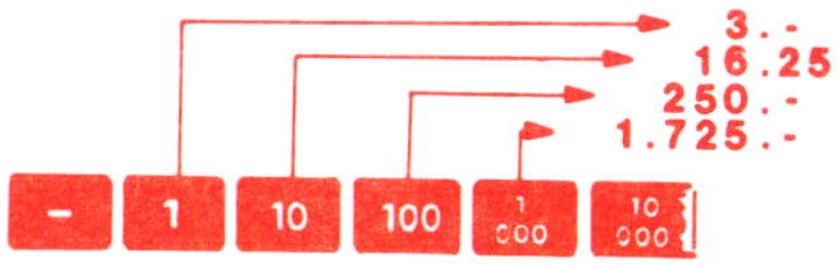


### Exercise 96

*Clear all previously-set stops. Set left margin at 17(20) and tab stops at 34(41), 47(56) and 64(76). Start heading at 26(31).*

METRIC UNITS AND THEIR SYMBOLS

| | | | | | | |
|---|---|---|---|---|---|---|
| Kilometre | → | km | → | Millimetre | → | mm |
| Metre | | m | | Kilogram | | kg |
| Centimetre | | cm | | Gram | | g |

## Exercise 329

**Concentrate on what you are typing; do not let your thoughts wander.**

A greenhouse or glasshouse is a structure made mostly of glass or 66
clear plastic. The sizes and shapes vary a great deal. The most simple 141
of these structures provide protection from the extremes of hot and 209
cold temperatures. The more sophisticated ones are used, generally, by 282
commercial growers who produce fruit and vegetables for sale. The 350
decorative glasshouses, where design has been considered carefully, 418
are used in parks and exhibitions and are more ornamental than 481
functional. 492

When planning a glasshouse, an initial step is to choose the correct 563
location. The land must be level and the placement of the house in 632
relation to the sun is vital. Where a glasshouse has been properly sited 707
the sun will follow a uniform path over the plants. There should be no 780
trees or buildings close to the area as the best results for growing 849
plants are obtained when the light is even with no shadows. A 913
continuous supply of water is essential. In some areas water from lakes 987
or streams can be used, while others may have only well water. A 1055
water sample should be analysed to check that it is chemically 1118
acceptable to the plants to be grown. The next consideration is the 1188
style of the house. The commercial grower generally uses the span 1256
type of house or a modification known as the ridge and furrow house. 1325
The former type is the most common. In this structure the sides of the 1399
roof are of equal length and both side walls of equal height. The 1467
centre height of the roof is from fifteen to twenty feet high. The ridge 1542
and furrow house is really just two or more span houses joined at the 1612
side wall. This latter type is more economical as regards heating costs 1686
than single span houses covering the same growing area. 1742

Nowadays most glasshouse frames are made of different types of alloy. 1814
However, where wood is used, it must be able to withstand high 1878
moisture and humidity. Suitable woods for this use are redwood, cedar 1950
and cypress. In order to avoid rust any screws, nails, pipes and other 2023
metal parts should be coated with zinc or made of aluminium or some 2091
other metal which is resistant to rust. As about eighty per cent of a 2163
glasshouse is constructed of glass, the choice of this material is 2228
important. In some areas where strong winds prevail and where 2292
hailstorms and heavy snowfalls are frequently experienced, it is 2357
necessary to use double weight in preference to single weight glass. In 2432
many instances fibreglass and plastics are used in place of glass. 2499

Benches and growing areas, such as built-up beds or trays, have to be 2571
provided inside the houses. Generally, these are made of wood with 2640
walks from two to three feet wide between the growing areas. Most 2707
owners of glasshouses try to keep these walks to a minimum. Where 2775
benches are built a level growing surface must be provided with 2839
suitable drainage for taking away any excess water. Great attention 2909
needs to be paid to heating. The systems can use either steam or hot 2981
water. The choice will depend on the size of the growing area. Boilers 3055
for steam heat are expensive, so the small glasshouses are usually 3120
fitted with hot water systems which cost considerably less. For either 3193
system pipes are laid throughout the houses for even distribution of 3262
heat. The final important factor is ventilation. Apertures are usually near 3342
the peak of the roof and can be operated automatically by electricity; 3414
they are regulated by fluctuations of temperature. *(LCCI Intermediate)* 3465

# Accuracy Exercises in Indented Form

*Copy each exercise, line for line, two or three times. Indent the first line, i.e. allow five spaces (for elite type allow six) from the left-hand margin. Use the tabulator for each indentation. Type your name at top right.*

## Exercise 97

(a)

No man is rich whose expenses exceed his means; and no one poor whose incomings exceed his outgoings.

(b)

A good deed can never be lost. He who sows courtesy reaps friendship, and he who plants kindness gathers love.

## Exercise 98

**Untidy erasures and holes in the paper will spoil your work.**

(a)

There is no advantage in having a lively mind if it is not accurate; the perfect clock does not go fast, but correctly.

(b)

The greatest fact in life is this, that it never is too late to start again. History is full of startling examples of this truth.

(c)

Refuse to be ill. Never tell people that you are ill; never admit it to yourself. Illness is one of those things which a man should resist on principle at the onset.

## Exercise 99

**If you have difficulty in spelling consult a dictionary.**

(a)

An agent is a person or a firm acting on behalf of another, called a principal. Agents are normally rewarded by a payment of commission.

(b)

Deposit box is a box provided by a Bank for holding valuable documents etc. which can be locked by the customer and stored in the Bank vaults.

(c)

Make it a rule not to bear more than one trouble at a time. Some people bear three kinds of trouble: all they have had, all they have now, and all they expect to have.

## Exercise 327

Strokes

Advertising comes in for a great deal of criticism. Some people claim that 77
poster displays are ugly and spoil the look of the country. Others think advertising 164
tends to manipulate the public. They point to the vast amount of advertising aimed 249
at children, who then ask their parents to buy that product. Most critics feel that 335
advertising is a very costly business and it must add to the price of a product. 416
But under a free-enterprise system, advertising can be a helpful, and even vital, 500
part of business. Many firms feel they have to advertise, for they face strong com- 586
petition. Since most goods are mass produced, to keep their cost to a reasonable 669
level a manufacturer must sell his goods in large amounts to make enough profit, 750
and this will increase as he sells more goods. Outselling his competitors is a condi- 838
tion for the success of any businessman. 879
If the manufacturer can bring his product to the notice of the public, (provided 963
he can explain convincingly why they should buy it), people are more likely to 1043
choose that product than a brand of goods which is unknown. In the same way, a 1124
new manufacturer will want to advertise himself in order to make people interested 1207
and so persuade them to buy something new, which they may like and will continue 1288
to purchase. In all these cases, the advertising, if successful, should pay for itself in 1380
increased sales. 1397

WORDS: 279

**The number of spaces after punctuation marks should not be varied. Always allow two spaces after a full stop, a question mark and an exclamation mark; one space after a comma, a colon, and a semi-colon.**

## Exercise 328

Strokes

Six years ago a large firm let it be known that a few of the films produced by 79
the company were to be released in the form of video cassette. Within six months 162
this tentative venture was proved successful. Three advantages emerged. The 242
copies in cassette form were cheaper to make than the original film prints. Very 325
little damage was caused either in transit or by the users. There had been numer- 409
ous bookings for the new form, particularly from the sector of education. Since the 495
introduction of these cassettes other concerns have released film in this form. It is 583
now the exception rather than the rule for a film library not to offer some film titles 671
on video cassettes. 691
Up to the present manufacturers and users have not been willing to quote pre- 769
cise statistics. This makes it difficult to gauge the impact that cassettes have made 857
in the growth of the distribution of the moving picture to schools, colleges and 938
businesses. However, from the information that has been gleaned, it seems that 1019
companies manufacturing video cassettes account for between an eighth and a 1095
quarter of loans or hiring of films, where the titles of the same film are available 1180
both in tape and film versions. There is room for much increased use of this 1259
medium and it looks as if video recordings are about to command a much larger 1337
portion of that movie market which is not specifically for theatrical presentation. 1422
There could come a time when printing films might be uneconomical. 1490

WORDS: 298

# Correction Signs — 1

You will often be asked to type a fair copy from a corrected typescript or manuscript. It is, therefore, important that you should learn and understand all signs used for correction.

On this page you will study the meaning of four such signs; on pages 45, 48, 55 and 59 you will learn all the remaining ones.

| *Sign in Margin* | *Key to Signs* |
|---|---|
| lc / | Change to lower case; i.e. put in small letter instead of capital. (Under the letter/letters to be changed two lines are drawn.) |
| cap / or uc / | Change from lower to upper case; i.e. use shift key. (Under the letter/letters to be changed two lines are drawn.) |
| word(s) required / | Insert at points indicated any letter, word, punctuation mark etc given in the margin. |
| ∂/ | "d" for 'delete'; take out letter, word, phrase etc which has been crossed out in the text. |

## Exercise 100

*Type a corrected copy of the following exercise. The place where the correction is to be made in the text is indicated by a caret (*⋏*).*

The Trading Account is an account constructed for
the purpose of finding the gross profit. On the debit
∂/ side ~~there~~ are placed the stock at start, i.e. at the
commencement of the period ⋏ which the account relates, to/
the purchases, carriage inwards and wages. On the credit
side are placed the sales and the Closing stock. The lc/
excess of the credit side over the debit side is the
;/ gross profit ⋏ if there is an excess of the debit side over
the credit side, that is a gross loss. This balance is
transferred to the Profit and loss Account. uc/

## Exercise 325

Strokes

Migraine may affect as many as 19 per cent of men and 25 per cent 66
of women throughout the world, and the proportions of sufferers are 134
roughly similar in every country where statistics are available. 199
The average age at which symptoms appear is 19 but much younger 264
people, including young children, are affected. Apart from the 329
unpleasant symptoms, which include headaches, nausea, vomiting and 396
visual disturbances, migraine causes a great deal of mental distress 465
and severe depression; it is also responsible for the loss of a lot 533
of working time. 550

Although many factors which can bring on attacks have been identified, 623
the underlying biochemical causes of the disease have remained 686
mysterious. In the last year or two, however, medical researchers 754
have begun to identify certain biochemical abnormalities in migraine 823
sufferers. Their findings may in the long run lead to the develop- 892
ment of more effective drugs to control attacks or, better still, 958
to prevent them. 975

WORDS: 195

**Return the carriage as soon as possible after the bell rings. Do not look up for line endings, as this will break your typing rhythm and continuity.**

## Exercise 326

Strokes

Charles Darwin is one of those few names, among them Newton, Galileo 71
and Einstein, that are known equally well to the general public and 140
to professional scientists, and which carry a great deal of authority 210
long after their owners have departed. 249

When we think of Darwin it is his work on natural selection and 316
evolution that almost inevitably comes first to mind. Indeed, events 387
rarely let us forget it. Recurrent attempts by certain groups to 454
suppress the teaching of post-darwinian biology are a striking 517
acknowledgement of the intellectual upheaval his writings have helped 587
to bring about, and only recently his theory of evolution was at the 656
centre of some of the most lively debate for years at the annual 721
meeting of the British Association for the Advancement of Science. 792

This emphasis reflects no more than a proper evaluation of Darwin's 864
achievement. But it would be misleading, and unfair to the man 929
himself, to concentrate on that part of his output exclusively. 992

Outwardly, apart from one long episode, his life seems to have been 1062
much like that of many other 19th-century English country gentlemen 1131
of independent means. He was born in Shrewsbury in 1809, the son of 1202
a doctor. After being educated locally he went to Edinburg Univer- 1274
sity in 1825, with the intention of following his father's career. 1342
What he experienced there, in the days before anaesthesia existed, 1410
revolted him, so it was decided that he should become a priest in 1476
the Church of England. For this to be possible he needed an English 1549
degree and accordingly he was sent to Cambridge in 1827. 1606

WORDS: 321

# Common-Phrase Exercises

Strike all keys with equal force, except the full stop and the comma which must be struck lightly.

## Exercise 101

To make sure, it is no use, by all means, for your own.
We cannot be, that is only, please write, not just now.
In this case, it should be, you can have, in all cases.
Till we know, there can be, there may be, we have seen.
Which is now, which is not, when we know, at all times.

## Exercise 102

Keep eyes on copy.

I have the honour, I believe you are, we have the honour.
We shall give you, as far as you can, as it is necessary.
Which is possible, we are very sorry, please let us know.
In all directions, we would not have, I shall be pleased.
That there may be, but we have known, you may have heard.

## Exercise 103

Return carriage firmly.

I hope he may, for some time, in this place, as far as you.
As it will be, more and more, for your sake, in his letter.
As it was not, at first hand, for they were, in some cases.
And they were, to this place, because it is, long time ago.
Which must be, at all events, not more than, and as it may.

## Exercise 104

Keep shoulders down.

I am sorry, I have noticed, everyone of us, here and there.
At present, as I have seen, it is possible, in his own way.
It is said, for some years, we called upon, those who have.
As well as, as if you were, if you will be, for it will be.
We enclose, for the moment, as I have said, which has been.

## Exercise 105

Sit comfortably.

Do we know, throughout the, you should not, it can be seen.
He must be, though we have, because it was, it seems to me.
As good as, I am very glad, I am very sure, I am surprised.
As long as, and some times, they will then, that is to say.
As fast as, which you must, should be said, please enclose.

## Exercise 324

Strokes

In England and Wales arrest may be made with or without a warrant 68
issued by a magistrate. An arrested person is entitled to ask the 136
police to notify a named person, such as a relative or a solicitor, 204
about the arrest. The police may delay notification in the inter- 272
ests of the investigation, prevention of crime or apprehension of 338
offenders and may question an arrested person in custody, so long 404
as he or she has not been charged with the offence or informed 467
that he or she may be prosecuted for it. Answers to such questions 536
are admissible as evidence in any subsequent proceedings, provided 603
that they have been given voluntarily. 642

Guidance on the questioning of arrested persons is contained in 708
the Judges' Rules and Administrative Directions to the Police; 777
although these do not have the force of law, the police are required 846
to comply with them. 867

The Judges' Rules also require the police to caution an arrested 937
person before charging him or her. Once a person has been charged 1005
with an offence, the police may not ask further questions, except 1071
in exceptional circumstances, to prevent or minimise harm or loss 1137
to some other person or to the public or to clear up an ambiguity 1203
in a previous answer or statement. 1238

If the police decide not to charge the arrested person (for example, 1310
because of insufficient evidence) he or she may be released imme- 1377
diately. Alternatively, the police may decide to release the 1440
person and proceed by way of summons, or to issue a caution (repri- 1509
mand). If the police need to make further inquiries they may 1573
release the arrested person on bail to return to the police station, 1642
where he or she may be charged on reappearance. 1690

Anyone arrested without a warrant must be released by the police 1757
on bail if he or she cannot be brought before a magistrates' court 1825
within 24 hours, unless the alleged offence is serious. If 1887
detained in custody, the defendant must be brought before a magis- 1953
trates' court as soon as practicable. On appearance before a 2017
magistrates' court, a defendant charged with an imprisonable offence 2087
may be refused bail in certain specified circumstances only, the 2152
most important being substantial grounds for believing that he or 2218
she might abscond, commit further offence or otherwise interfere 2283
with the course of justice. If bail is refused, the defendant 2347
can apply to a judge of the High Court and, if committed to the 2413
Crown Court, may apply for bail to that court. The majority of 2480
people remanded by magistrates are given bail. 2527

A person who thinks that the grounds for detention are unlawful 2593
may apply to the High Court for a writ of habeas corpus against 2659
the person who detained him or her, requiring the person to appear 2726
before the court to justify the detention. An application for this 2795
writ is normally made by the person detained or by someone acting 2861
on his or her behalf. Similar procedures apply in Northern Ireland. 2933

WORDS: 587

# Lesson 10

## FIGURES AND SYMBOLS

**Introducing**
**4 @**
**8 (')**

Figure **4** is above *r* and is struck with the *f* finger; its shift is the symbol @ which stands for the phrase *at the price of*.

Figure **8** is above *i* and is struck with the *k* finger; its shift is the apostrophe (').

## Exercise 106

**Location drill**

**The apostrophe may pierce the paper; strike it lightly.**

```
frf f4f f4f f4f frf frf f4f f@f f@f f@f
kik k8k k8k k8k kik kik k8k k'k k'k k'k
f4f f@f f4f f@f fff k8k k'k k8k k'k kkk
```

## Exercise 107

**Use small L for numeral 1.**

```
Both goods trains left at 4 o'clock pm.
4, 8, 48, l, 8, l8, 4, l, 4l, 8, 0, 80.
He got the woollen cloth @ 84p a metre.
```

## Exercise 108

**Accuracy**

```
That which is everybody's business, is nobody's business.
I bought 4 pencils @ 8p, 4 pens @ 84p and l0 books @ 88p.
You know you can't be wrong if your life is in the right.
```

## Exercise 109

**Speed**

Many thanks for your note of 4 May which I have just received.

I have your letter of 8 November, asking for information about Mr Peter Brooks and am very happy to comply with your request.

I shall be very happy to let you have the information you need but hope you don't mind waiting for it until my return to Kent early next week.

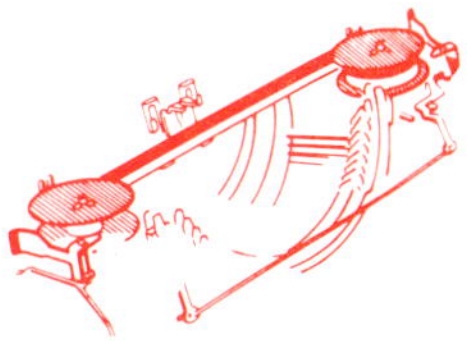

*The ribbon should always be in good condition*

## Exercise 323

Strokes

Man has known about electric fish at least since the ancient Egyp- 68
tians decorated the walls of tombs with fishing scenes that depicted 137
the formidable electric catfish of the Nile, which is capable of 203
delivering a 500 V pulse to stun its prey. But I wonder whether 271
the millions of people in certain states in central Africa know they 341
are eating large numbers of another type of electric fish endowed 407
with a sense unique in the Animal Kingdom. Because their discharges 479
are barely perceptible, they are called 'weakly-electric' fish. 545
Nevertheless, they use their discharges to communicate with each 611
other and find their way about in complete darkness. 664

In contrast to the catfish and other strongly electric species, 730
weakly-electric fish produce electric organ discharges (EODs) of 800
only two to three volts and do so continuously throughout their 864
lives. The discharges were first described by Hans Lissman, who 932
worked at Cambridge in the 1950s. Later, with Kenneth Machin, he 1002
showed that the EOD was the energy source of a unique electro- 1068
sensory system. 1084

Each discharge, emitted by a special electric organ in the fish's 1153
tail, sets up an instantaneous electric field in the surrounding 1218
water. Objects in the near vicinity distort this field in a pre- 1285
dictable way, thereby informing the fish of their size, conductivity 1354
and relative movement. Thousands of electro-receptors constantly 1421
monitor the pattern of current flow around the fish. Predicted by 1489
Lissman's behavioural experiments, they were the subject of intense 1559
physiological and anatomical investigation throughout the 1960s. 1624
The receptors form conductive pores in the otherwise highly resistive 1695
skin of the fish so that current generated by the electric organ 1760
tends to leave the fish by those routes, returning along curved 1824
paths to re-enter the fish at its tail. The sensory cells at the 1891
base of the electro-receptors encode the current intensity directly 1960
into nerve impulses, which show the greatest modulation in the area 2028
of skin closed to the nearby object. This local modulation has been 2098
likened to projecting an electric image of the object on to the 2162
surface of the skin. 2183

Continued study revealed several different types of electro-receptor. 2255
So-called ampullary receptors monitor the surroundings for low- 2320
frequency electrical signals generated by the swimming muscles of 2386
non-electric fish and insect larvae, providing information about 2451
predators and prey. The sensitivity of such receptors is so great 2519
that navigation by measuring induced electric currents as the fish 2586
swims through the Earth's magnetic field has been shown to be 2648
possible. 2658

Ampullary receptors cannot, however, respond to the high-frequency 2727
content of electric fish signals. They are used only in a passive 2795
way and it seems that it is others, known as tuberous receptors, 2860
which are designed for the job of active electrolocation. If tuber- 2930
ous receptors code the fish's own electric field, it seems likely 2995
that they should at least be useful for detecting the EODs of other 3068
electric fish. 3084

WORDS: 617

## Exercise 110

**Form the exclamation mark by typing an apostrophe over a full stop.**

The BA's and BSc's conferred by the Colleges last year were ten times the number of MA's, MSc's and PhD's!

If wealth is lost nothing is lost; if health is lost something is lost; and if character is lost, all is lost!

A friend is a person with whom I may be sincere. Before him, I may think aloud. Happy is the house that shelters a friend!

# Correction Signs — 2

Study the meaning of the new correction signs and then produce a corrected copy of the exercise below.

Note: The marginal sign is written on the same line as the correction, in the margin nearest the correction.

| *Sign in Margin* | *Key to signs* |
|---|---|
| stet/ | Let it stand; i.e. type word *with dotted line underneath* as it was originally. |
| '/ | Insert apostrophe or single quotation mark. |
| ⌒/ | Close up space. |
| δ | Take out cancelled letter, and close up space. |

## Exercise 111

(a)

δ I am afraid ~~that~~ I shall be unable to accept your kind
invitation. Please accept my apologies and my ~~best~~ wishes stet/
for a very successful meeting.

(b)

At twenty a man is full of fight and hope. He wants
lc/ to reform the whole World. When he is over sixty he still
wants to reform the whole world, but ⁁ he cannot. he knows/

(c)

⌒/ The met hod of shopping by charge account means that
you can pay for all your month⁁s purchases with a single '/
cheque; you need no longer waste time waiting for change
δ or writ~~t~~ing cheques for ⁁ amounts. small/

## Exercise 322

Strokes

Ideally the size and design of office furniture, particularly of 65
desks, should be suitable for the work to be performed on it. 127
Unfortunately this is not always possible, and desks have to be 192
bought which can be fitted into the available office space. If a 259
clerk is working for most of the time on small 5 x 3 inch index 323
cards, a very small desk would be sufficient, but if another clerk 390
needs to spread out ledgers and working papers, a 6-feet-square 454
desk might be necessary and should be provided - regardless of 516
prestige considerations. There is, however, an advantage in having 585
all desks of a standard size. It adds to the appearance of the 650
office, allows interchange of units, and better terms are usually 716
obtained when buying. 738

With a chair of standard height, the height of a desk should not 805
be more than 28 inches. Some clerks with long limbs will doubtless 874
state that desks are never high enough for them to sit at comfort- 941
ably, and although the height of desks should be adjustable, it is 1008
usual to have chairs of adjustable height to fit the desk. It is 1075
preferable on grounds of hygiene and portability that desks should 1142
be light in construction, and they should be so made that the floor 1210
beneath can easily be cleaned. Some storage space is desirable, 1276
and the two drawers usually provided are adequate for normal pur- 1342
poses, but too much storage space should be avoided, as the inside 1409
of such extra drawer space is apt to get cluttered up with office 1475
bric-à-brac and personal belongings. 1512

As far as material is concerned, prior to about 30 years ago, all 1580
desks were made of wood, but nowadays metal furniture is also made; 1648
this has the disadvantages of being cold to work on, and may be harsh 1718
in appearance; in addition metal desks, when enamelled, are apt to 1785
chip in use. Modern processes have now introduced anodised metal 1852
furniture which cannot be chipped and which can also be supplied in 1920
pleasant pastel colours. Metal furniture is, of course, more fire- 1988
resistant than wooden furniture. 2021

Regarding the surface of a desk, bare wood is apt to get scratched 2090
and look rather dilapidated very quickly. Linoleum and rexine tops 2159
can be obtained which are warm and comfortable to work on. For 2224
some business routines, it is useful to have a plate-glass top to 2290
the desk, not only because of the hard writing surface it gives, but 2359
because of the great facility of sliding schedules of standing 2422
information under the glass for ready reference. 2471

When buying desks, cost should not be forgotten by the office 2535
manager, and the standard two-drawer desk meets the average require- 2604
ments at a reasonable cost. Simple wooden tables without drawers, 2672
and topped with linoleum, are a most useful adjunct for filing or 2738
for sorting correspondence, or occasional use in private or general 2806
offices. 2815

WORDS: 563

# Lesson 11

**Introducing**
**2 (")**
**9 (()**
**(-) ())**

Figure **2** is above *W* and is struck with the *S* finger; its shift is the **double quotation mark** (").

Figure **9** is above *O* and is struck with the *L* finger; its shift is the **opening bracket (()**.

The hyphen (-) is above *p* and is struck with the *;* finger; its shift is the **closing bracket ())**.

## Exercise 112

**Location drill**

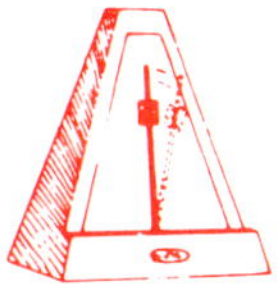

*Use rhythmic beats*

**The hyphen may pierce the paper; strike it lightly.**

```
sss sws s2s s2s s2s sss s"s s"s s"s sws s2s
lll lol l9l l9l l9l lll l(l l(l l(l lol l(l
;;; ;p; ;-; ;-; ;-; ;;; ;); ;); ;); ;p; ;);
```

## Exercise 113

**Traditional punctuation**

*Third line: The abbreviation full stop — that of «p.m.» — is omitted as it is replaced by the sentence full stop.*

*Fourth line: As the sentence ends in a question mark (a.m.?) the abbreviation full stop cannot be omitted.*

```
Twenty-one (21), Eighty-four (84), Ninety-two (92).
1, 2, (12), 4, 8, (48), 9, 0, (90), 2, 1, 8, (218).
Noon is written as 12.00 m.; midnight as 12.00 p.m.
Did you say the Committee was called for 9.20 a.m.?
```

*Jump confidently to distant keys*

## Exercise 114

**Accuracy**

**Use the hyphen to divide words at line ends.**

Jefferson said: "The will of the people is the only legit-
imate foundation of any government, and to protect its free
expression should be our first object."

Milton said: "He who kills a man kills a reasonable crea-
ture, God's image; but he who destroys a good book, kills reason itself, kills the image of God in the eye."

# Additional Speed Tests

**On a wide variety of vocabulary**

## Exercise 321

Strokes

In establishing office procedures specialisation is an important 65
factor, and one which has a distinct bearing on clerical work. 128
As with any other kind of work, it has the advantage of developing 196
specialists and experts in particular fields of work. To take a 262
mundane example, where one person is made responsible for all 324
outgoing mail that person soon becomes an expert on the various 388
rates of postage, and after a time can correctly stamp postal 450
packages without referring to rates of charges at all. Special- 516
isation helps when it is wished to centralise a service. The 579
best example of this is the establishment of a typists' pool, 642
where the typists concentrate on typing work only. It also pro- 708
duces a greater volume of work. 740

Specialisation helps to fix responsibility, for example where one 808
person is authorised to write orders of a certain kind. It helps 875
to establish routines, as there is only one particular clerk or 939
section which performs a certain specialised function. It helps 1005
in grading the jobs in an office, so that a person is a secretary, 1072
shorthand typist, or a copy-typist. 1108

Operations may be made simpler, more accurate, faster and more 1173
efficient, and the performance of work can be made more rhythmic 1238
by specialisation, which also makes it easier to train and engage 1304
people for certain specific jobs; thus a person is engaged as an 1369
accounts clerk, a cashier and so on. 1406

Fraud may be less likely, for example, where one clerk specialises 1475
in the preparation of the pay-roll, another in paying out wages 1539
and so on - there is less likely to be collusion. Uniformity of 1605
practice is assured; thus, in granting credit, a rigid code can 1669
be adhered to more easily. 1696

Disadvantages do exist with specialisation, and they should be 1761
quickly recognised. Workers may have only a very limited picture 1828
of the job, and unless a broad training programme is in being, 1891
it may not encourage the training of managers with all-round know- 1958
ledge. Because of this narrow vision, there may also be a lack 2023
of judgment and understanding of other departmental affairs. 2084

WORDS: 417

## Exercise 115

**Speed**

The blocked style — all lines beginning flush left — is the simplest arrangement of text.

(a)

I am going to meet Mr Anderson (though I am no admirer of him) on Monday next at his office. I expect to be there at 9 am as suggested, and look forward to a useful outcome.

(b)

I have just received your letter of 29 October and I am very pleased to learn that you will consider Mr Wilson for a position in your Bank.

## Exercise 116

**Accuracy**

For inner quotations within outer quotations use the apostrophe (')

(a)

"Have you read 'Nobody's Diary'?" the teacher asked his pupils. "No", was the pupils' reply; "could you please tell us who was the writer of it?"

A final full stop is placed inside the closing quotations — for the sake of appearance. If a phrase or word only is being quoted the final quotation mark is placed inside the punctuation.

(b)

The lecturer said: "For further reading, I would recommend you 'Modern Business Methods' by Professor B Morgan. You can find this book at the 'Central Bookshop'."

## Exercise 117

**Accuracy**

The hyphen needs no space before or after it; but when used as a dash a space must precede and follow it.

(a)

You will, I think, agree with the following words spoken by the late Lord Baden-Powell: "You never fail when you try to do your duty - you always fail when you neglect to do it."

(b)

It is quite interesting that farming takes up about three-tenths of the world's land. One-tenth is devoted to the cultivation of crops while two-tenths is used to feed livestock. Men occupy only a very small fraction of the land. The remainder is almost all forests, or mountains, deserts, and other waste land.

When spelt-out, fractions should be hyphenated (three-sevenths), unless the numerator or the denominator already has a hyphen (sixty-five hundredths).

**Exercise 320** **Type the following table, setting it out to the best advantage. Use the mixed method of ruling - in red colour if possible.**

MAJOR VITAMIN CHART

Prepared by the
National Vitamin Foundation, N.Y.

| | What it does | Major Dietary Sources |
|---|---|---|
| VITAMIN "A" | In general, Important for ~~the~~ normal growth in children. Necessary for good vision. Essential for healthy skin, eyes and hair and for the health of all the epithelial structures of the body. | Milk, butter, fortified margarine, ~~eggs~~, liver and kidney. Body also makes its own vitamin "A" from foods containing carotene, e.g. leafy green and yellow vegetables. |
| VITAMIN "$B_1$" | Necessary for proper function of heart and nervous system. Early signs of deficiency include loss of appetite, constipation, insomnia. Required to obtain energy from food. | Whole grain cereals, enriched cereals, enriched bread, fish, lean meat, liver, milk, dried yeast, pork, poultry. |
| VITAMIN "$B_2$" | Necessary for healthy skin. Helps prevent sensitivity of the eyes to light. Essential for building and maintaining body tissues. | Eggs, enriched bread, enriched cereals, dried yeast, liver, milk, lean meats, leafy green vegetables. |
| VITAMIN "D" | Helps utilization of calcium and phosphorus. Necessary for strong teeth and bones. Prevents rickets. | Egg yolk, cod liver oil, vitamin "D" fortified milk, tuna, salmon. |
| VITAMIN "$B_6$" | Important for healthy teeth and gums, the health of the blood vessels, ~~and~~ the red blood cells, and the nervous system. | Neat and whole grain cereals, wheat germ, vegetables, and dried yeast. |
| VITAMIN "$B_{12}$" | Helps prevent some anemia forms. Contributes to health of nervous system and proper child's growth. | Liver, kidney, salt water fish, oysters, milk, lean meat and foods of animal origin. |
| VITAMIN "C" | Essential for healthy strong teeth, gums, and bones. Builds body cells and blood vessels. | Citrus fruits, tomatoes, green vegetables, berries, peppers, cabbage, new potatoes. |
| VITAMIN "E" | Prevents abnormal peroxidation of tissue fats. Essential for integrity of red blood cells. | Whole grain cereals, lettuce, vegetable oils, wheat germ. |
| VITAMIN "K" | Necessary for normal blood clotting. | Leafy vegetables. |

# Correction Signs – 3

Study the third group of correction signs and prepare a fair copy of the exercise below.

Note: If there is more than one correction in the same line, the marginal signs must be written in the same order as the corrections, reading from left to right - on both sides of the paper.

| Sign in Margin | Key to signs |
|---|---|
| /-/ | Insert hyphen |
| /—/ | Insert dash |
| " / | Insert double quotation marks |
| (:)/ | Insert full colon |

## Exercise 118

**(a)**

Undoubtedly, education does not mean teaching people what they
stet/ do not know. Education, ~~indeed~~, is a painful, continual and dif /-/
ficult work to be done by kindness, by watching, by warning, by
ǂ/ precept, and by praised, but above all by example. /—/

**(b)**

ǂ J Rustkin (1810-1900), the well-known English author and social
reformer, speaking on the value of work said: "If you want know /-/
lc/ ledge, you must toil for it; If food, you must toil for it; and
if pleasure, you must toil for it: toil is the law. " /

**(c)**

A great wise man of the past was once asked "Is a good man one (:)
" / who is liked by all? He said, "No." "Is it, perhaps, one who
is disliked by all?" Again he said, "No; the good man is he who
all/ is liked by the good people and dis liked by all the bad." ⁀

# Exercise 319

Display effectively the following Balance Sheet using A4 paper, landscape. If necessary, fold the paper. Mixed ruling is not permissible.

THE MODEL ENGINEERING CO. LTD.

BALANCE SHEET AS AT 31ST DECEMBER 1980

| | £ | £ | £ |
|---|---|---|---|
| **Authorized Capital** - | | | |
| 40,000 7% Preference Shares of £1 each | 40,000 | | |
| 20,000 Ordinary Shares of £1 each | 20,000 | | |
| | 60,000 | | |
| **Issued Capital** - | | | |
| 30,000 Preference Shares fully paid | | | 30,000 |
| 15,000 Ordinary fully called | | 15,000 | |
| Less Calls in Arrear | | 100 | 19,400 |
| **Reserves** - | | | |
| Profit & Loss A/c | | 7000 | |
| Share Premium | | 2000 | 9,000 |
| **Current Liabilities** - | | | |
| Creditors | | 5,040 | |
| Bills Payable | | 2,600 | |
| Rent Due | | 200 | 8,200 |
| | | £ | 62,100 |

| | | COST | DEPR. | NET |
|---|---|---|---|---|
| **Fixed Assets** - | | | | |
| Buildings | | 30,000 | 6,000 | 26,000 |
| Machinery | | 24,000 | 4,000 | 18,000 |
| Furniture | | 4,000 | 1,000 | 47,000 |
| | | 58,000 | 11,000 | 3,000 |
| **Current Assets** - | | | | |
| Stock | | | 5,100 | |
| ~~Debtors~~ Debtors | | 7,000 | | |
| Less B.D. Provision | | 350 | 6,650 | |
| Bank | | | 2,900 | |
| Cash | | | 400 | |
| Insurance Prepaid | | | 50 | 15,100 |
| | | | £ | 62,100 |

**Lesson 12**

**Introducing**

**3 /**

**7 &**

Figure **3** is above *e* and is struck with the *d* finger; its shift is **the oblique line** / , known as **solidus.**

Figure **7** is above *u* and is struck with the *j* finger; its shift is the symbol **&**, known as **ampersand**.

## Exercise 119

**Location drill**

```
ddd ded d3d d3d d3d ddd d/d d/d d/d
jjj juj j7j j7j j7j jjj j&j j&j j&j
ddd d3d d3d d/d ddd jjj j7j j7j j&j
```

## Exercise 120

**Type brackets with one space before the opening and after the closing bracket; but with no space after the opening or before the closing bracket.**

```
We have just received your letter of 3rd May.
(1, 2, 3, 4).  (7, 8, 9, 10).  (17, 37, 373).
"G Long & Sons" is a well-known firm in York.
Tiberius was born in 42 BC and died in AD 37.
```

**BC (before Christ) follows the year; while AD (Anno Domini) precedes it.**

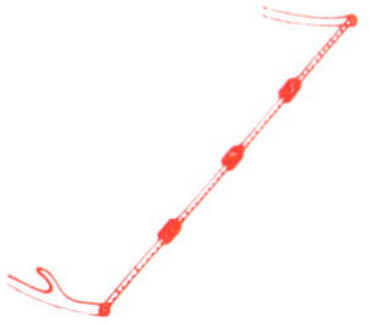

*Set paper grips in equal distances*

**Use the solidus (/):**

1. **To type references in correspondence;**
2. **As an alternative to the hyphen to represent 'to' in numbers;**
3. **To type sloping fractions.** *(In typing fractions leave no space between the numerator and the denominator, but separate fraction from its whole number with a space.)*

## Exercise 121

```
Thank you for your letter of 3rd August under reference KNR/sd.
Numbers 18/24 (or 18-24) have been omitted from our catalogues.
Three and one-third (3 1/3).  Seven and three-sevenths (7 3/7).
```

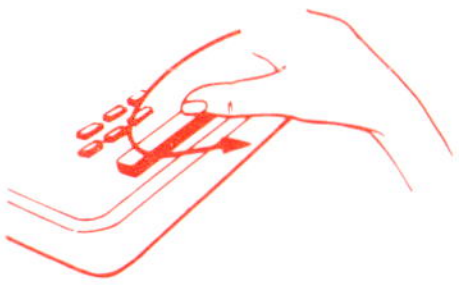

*Strike space bar sharply using right-hand thumb*

## Exercise 317

Type the following Balance Sheet with suitable display. Note that the totals in balance sheets should always be typed at the same level.

GENERAL MANUFACTURING CO LTD
BALANCE SHEET, 30TH JUNE 1982

| | £ | | £ |
|---|---|---|---|
| Capital | 150,000 | Freehold Premises | 103,000 |
| General Reserve (~~Revenue~~) | 95,000 | Machinery | 130,000 |
| Profit & Loss Account | 80,000 | Stock | 34,000 |
| Creditors | 15,000 | Debtors | 28,000 |
| | | Cash | 45,000 |
| | £340,000 | | £340,000 |

## Exercise 318

This is a modern method of displaying a Balance Sheet. Type it carefully, avoiding any appearance of crowding.

NORTH & SOUTH LTD
BALANCE SHEET AS AT 30TH JUNE, 1981

| | £ | £ | £ |
|---|---|---|---|
| CAPITAL EMPLOYED | | Authorised | Issued |
| SHARE CAPITAL | | | |
| 70,000 Ordinary shares of £1 each | | 70,000 | 70,000 |
| RESERVES | | | |
| Profit and Loss Account | | | 32,500 |
| | | | £102,500 |
| Represented by: (Typist: spaced letters) | Cost | Depr. | Net |
| FIXED ASSETS | | | |
| Freehold Land and Buildings | 60,000 | — | 60,000 |
| Motor Vehicles | 8,550 | 5,350 | 3,200 |
| | 68,550 | 5,350 | 63,200 |
| CURRENT ASSETS | | | |
| Stock | | 16,310 | |
| Debtors | | 27,440 | |
| Bank | | 19,430 | |
| | | 63,180 | |
| Less CURRENT LIABILITIES | | | |
| Creditors | 23,700 | | |
| Rates Outstanding | 180 | 23,880 | 39,300 |
| | | | £102,500 |

## Exercise 122

**Use the ampersand (&) in names of firms, street addresses, and certain abbreviations.**

Messrs Black & Brown's address is 99 & 101 Oak Avenue, Bristol.

E&OE, printed on invoices, means Errors and Omissions Excepted.

C & F is a very well-known abbreviation for "Cost and Freight".

## Exercise 123

**Ellipsis (omitted words in a sentence) is indicated by three spaced or unspaced full stops.**

Article 1 of the Declaration of Human Rights says: "All human beings are born free and equal ... and should act towards one another in a spirit of brotherhood."

OR

Article 1 of the Declaration of Human Rights says: "All human beings are born free and equal . . . and should act towards one another in a spirit of brotherhood."

## Exercise 124

**A punctuation mark following the omitted words is typed after the three dots.**

"This is not exactly in line with tradition . . . ; and it was not, as I recall, your style."

Article 2 of the Declaration of Human Rights says: "People of all races, colours, religions, languages, and countries should enjoy all the rights and freedoms . . . ."

## Exercise 125

**A punctuation mark preceding the ellipsis is typed before the dots, immediately after the last word.**

"How cold it was!... No one could work in that climate."

Haggadah (4th century AD) said: "I have learned much from my teachers,... and from my students more than from all."

## Exercise 126

**If using «am» or «pm» do not add «in the morning» or «in the evening». If «am» or «pm» is omitted, spell out the time; eg eight o'clock in the evening.**

After a hearty breakfast at 7.30 am and a satisfying vegetable lunch at 1.00 or 1.30 pm, a light meal in the evening is sufficient. Fruit (dried or fresh), a cereal such as toast, flakes, unleavened hot rolls or reheated wholewheat yeast rolls (baked the day before), make an excellent tea in the evening. By having fruit fresh, or stewed dried fruit, one's thirst for drink is satisfied.

**Exercise 316** **Type the following manuscript taking a carbon copy. Do not change the layout. First read it through carefully and make on it the necessary notes in pencil. Leave a top margin of 5 cm (6 lines).**

The Balance Sheet / Caps

which must be

The A ~~act~~ of 1929 contains important provisions relative to the matters disclosed in the Balance Sheets of Companies. Sections 122 to 131 of the Act give details in full [Briefly, these requirements may be summarised as follows: /N.P

1. Every Co. must keep proper books of Account.
2. Once at least in every calendar year the Directors must lay before the Co. in General Meeting:-
   (a) A Profit & Loss A/c;
   (b) A Balance Sheet, accompanied by a report on the state of the Company's affairs, stating the proposed disposal of profits. Authorised
3. The Balance Sheet must state the Capital (i.e. the Nominal Capital), the Issued Capital, the Liabilities and the Assets, ~~and stating how~~ distinguishing between Fixed Assets and Floating Assets, and stating ~~where~~ how the values of the Fixed Asset have been arrived at. separately
4. There must be shown in the Balance Sheet, so far as they have not been written off:
   (a) The Preliminary Expenses, i.e the costs of forming the Company;
   (b) The costs of issue of shares or debentures; or documents
   (c) If ascertainable from the books of the Co., the value of the Goodwill, Patent Rights and ~~Trade Marks~~ Trademarks
5. Any Liability which is secured (otherwise than by operation of law) on any asset of the Company must be stated to be so secured.

**Lesson 13**

**Introducing**

**5 £**

**6 (_)**

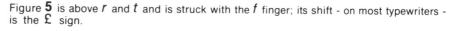

Figure **5** is above *r* and *t* and is struck with the *f* finger; its shift - on most typewriters - is the £ sign.

Figure **6** is above *y* and is struck with the *j* finger; its shift is the **underscore** (_).

## Exercise 127

**Location drill**

```
fff frf f4f f5f f5f f5f fff f4f fff f5f fff
jjj juj j7j j6j j6j j6j jjj j7j jjj j6j jjj
f5f f£f f£f f£f fff jjj j6j j_j j_j j_j jjj
```

*The use of a shield will protect neighbouring letters from accidental erasure*

To underscore a word:

1. Backspace to its first letter, depressing the backspace key with the right-hand little finger; if this is too weak, with your third or middle finger.
2. Type the 'underscore' key once for each letter in the word, striking it lightly to avoid piercing the paper.

## Exercise 128

```
£10, £29, £38, £47, £56, £39, £20, £93, £565.
The cheque for £56 will be mailed to you now!
Now is the time for all to aid their Country.
"Money often costs too much." - R. W. Emerson
```

*Release the paper occasionally to make sure that it is not crooked*

**Names of authors at the end of a quotation are often underscored.**

**The underscore does not extend to quotation or punctuation marks.**

**Exercise 315** **Re-type the following altered typescript keeping to the original display. Rule in ink, using full stops as guides.**

/Caps

Journal of John Lucas

| | | Dr | Cr |
|---|---|---|---|
| 1982 | | £ | £ |
| (1) | Fire Insurance unexpired . . . . . . | 25.00 | |
| | Fire Insurance . . . . . . . . . . | | 25.00 |
| | Transfer of prepaid insurance | | |
| (2) | Salaries . . . . . . . . . . | 125.00 | |
| | Salaries provision . . . . . . . . | | 1~~3~~25.00 |
| | Provision made for salaries due to partners A, B, and C. | | |
| (3) | Cash . . . . . . . . . . . . . . | 100.00 | |
| | (Contractee) R. Roberts . . . . . . . . | | 100.00 |
| | For receipt of £100 in full settlement of contract price | | |
| | R. Roberts (Contractee) . . . . . . . . . . | 50.00 | |
| | Contract (R. Robert's) . . . . . . . . . | 50.00 → | |
| | Transfer of amount ~~eual~~ equivalent to ½ (half) of value of contract | | |
| | Contract (R. Robert's) . . . . . . . . . | 39.~~5~~00 | |
| | Materials & Wages, etc. . . . . . . . . . | | 39.00 |
| | For materials and (for) labour on contract | | |
| | Contract . . . . . . . . . . . . | 11.00 | |
| | Profit & Loss A/C . . . . . . . . | | 11.00 |
| | For estimated profit on ~~full~~ (completed) portion of contract | | |
| (4) | Depreciation . . . . . . . . . . . . | 78.5~~5~~7 | |
| | Patents . . . . . . . . . . . . . | | 78.57 |
| | One-seven~~tieth~~th of £550 written off | | |

Foreign words or phrases that have not been anglicized are often underscored.

## Exercise 129

The French expression savoir vivre means 'refined manners'.

The Greek phrase ariston metron means 'moderation is best'.

The Latin ceteris paribus means 'other things being equal'.

Use the underscore to type a vertical fraction.

Type the whole number (if there is one); turn the platen half a space back and type the numerator; underscore it; backspace; turn platen down two half spaces; type the denominator. Note: Leave no space between the whole number and the fraction.

## Exercise 130

$25\frac{11}{12}$ x $30\frac{12}{13}$

$70\frac{9}{10}$ x $17\frac{8}{15}$

Leave a space before and after a mathematical sign.

To type one-digit numerators over the middle of two-digit denominators, back-space halfway. Or, backspace to first digit; then hold the space bar down.

**Numbers**

When typing numbers of one thousand or more, mark off the thousands with commas, as 1,500. This, however, does not apply to page, insurance policy and car licence numbers, street addresses or telephone numbers.

## Exercise 131

The highest recorded speeds attained with a ten-word penalty per error on a manual (non-electric) typewriter are the following: One minute: 170 words by Margaret Owen (USA) in the year 1918. One hour: 147 words (net rate per minute) by the American Albert Tangora in 1923. The official hour record on an electric machine is 9,316 words (40 errors) on an IBM machine, giving a net rate of 149 words a minute, by Margaret Hamma (USA) in 1941. In an official test in the year 1946 Mrs M Garnard attained a speed of 216 words a minute.

Omit the comma in four-digit year numbers; eg AD 1789; but use a comma with five-digit year numbers; eg 10,000 BC.

## Exercise 314

Type the following tabular matter in single line spacing, taking care to bring in the sentences from the foot, above the table. Ruling should be done in ink or on the typewriter but mixed ruling is not permissible. (Part of LCCI examination paper LC/53/A80 - Higher.)

TRANSOCEANIC CRUISES

Low Season Fares

| FARES (per adult) | | DATE-DURATION-SHIP-CRUISE NUMBER | | | |
|---|---|---|---|---|---|
| | | 10 June 15 days CANOPUS 180 | 11 July 16 days JUPITER 181 | 31 July 15 days CANOPUS 182 | 12 Sept 22 days JUPITER 183 |
| FIRST CLASS | | £ | £ | £ | £ |
| Cabins for ONE passenger | Outside single | 575 | 610 | 600 | 725 |
| | Inside single | 550 | 595 | 605 | 700 |
| | Court single | 600 | 645 | 650 | 770 |
| Cabins for TWO passengers | Outside two-bedded | 490 | 520 | 500 | 580 |
| | Inside two-bedded | 460 | 495 | 510 | 555 |
| | Outside two-berth | 400 | 425 | 435 | 620 |
| | Court two-bedded | 520 | 550 | 570 | 595 |
| | Court two-berth | 485 ~~[illegible]~~ | 520 | 535 | 580 |
| | Special staterooms | 675 | 755 ~~715~~ | 890 | 960 |
| Cabins for THREE passengers | Outside three-berth | 400 | 390 | 385 | 410 |
| | Inside three-berth | 390 | 380 | 370 | 400 |
| | Court three-berth | 435 | 415 | 410 | 450 |
| TOURIST | | | | | |
| Cabins for TWO passengers | Outside two-berth | 350 | 372 | 366 | 375 |
| | Inside two-berth | 320 | 325 | 330 | ~~345~~ 395 |
| Cabins for FOUR passengers | Outside three-berth | 290 | 300 | 315 | 330 |
| | Inside three-berth | 275 | 288 | 325 | 355 |
| Cabins for THREE passengers | Outside four-berth | 272 | 295 | 300 | 310 |
| | Inside four-berth | 260 | ~~[illegible]~~ 280 | 305 | 320 |

A port charge (for Southampton) of £3 per adult and £1.50 for children is payable for all passengers.

Inside two-berth 380 410 425 600

Each

[redacted] figure shown in this table is the minimum for each cabin or [redacted] for each Cruise. Full details are available upon request.

berth

# Accuracy Exercises

*In the exercises that follow repeat the same line until you have completed a correct typing. (If your typewriter differs in the position of some characters make the necessary allowances.)*

## Exercise 132

The discount on S Thompson's bill No 45 amounted to exactly £55.00.
Messrs Wilson & Anderson gave our Club cheques for £925 and £2,836.
The 1982 edition of the book has 3 parts, 9 chapters, and 99 pages.
Is R Johnson's report on bill No 14/2 on profits due June 12 or 13?

## Exercise 133

We have received a cheque from J Jones (dated 25/3) for £92.50.
D Brown's cheque for £740 (bill No 101) was cashed on 1st May.
Turn to pages 85–98 and answer questions 3, 5, 7, 10, 12 and 15.
The box is 10⅝ by 4½ feet long and weighs about 400 lb.

## Exercise 134

The question mark may be used to indicate uncertainty.

Hippocrates (460?-377 BC) has been called the "Father of Medicine".
Please send us by return: 5 sets M-2 @ £9.25 and 8 prs M-8 @ £8.95.
Order No 4 (for 9 desks @ £9.15 each) was shipped to us on 1st May.
In 1980, 52 clerks were working here; in 1981, 79; and in 1982, 99.

## Exercise 135

Approximately 120 of No 4382-BR machines were priced at £99.80.
Policy No 29-C for £8,500 has been renewed for another 5 years.
The following problem is correct: 30×2−20+10÷2−5 = 40.
Our order reads: Ship 2390 bags of 15 Kilos each @ 25p per Kilo.

## Exercise 313

**Type the following tabular matter, including the footnote, in single-line spacing. Avoid cramping. Ruling should be done in ink or on the typewriter. (Part of LCCI examination paper LC/53/Su78 - Higher.)**

NEW REGISTRATIONS OF ⟨NEW⟩ GOODS VEHICLES IN THE UNITED KINGDOM

(Total of New Registrations: 64,983 and 83,391 [redacted])

Renault (France) 1,384 -

| Manufacturer | Car-derived Vans and Pick-ups | Others, up to 3½ tons |
|---|---|---|
| BRITISH | | |
| Bedford | 11,719 | 13,310 |
| British Leyland | 29,394 | 19,428 |
| Chrysler | - | 7,131 |
| Ford | 16,233 | 31,990 |
| Others | 10 [redacted] | 64 |
| Total British | 57,356 | [redacted] ← 71,923 |
| IMPORTED | | |
| Daf (Holland) | 22 | - |
| Chrysler (France) | 4,255 | - |
| Citroen (France) | ← 123 | |
| Peugeot (France) | - | 163 |
| Mercedes-Benz (W. Germany) (Benz) | - | 898 |
| [redacted] (W. Germany) (Volkswagen) | - | 5,323 |
| Fiat (Italy) | - | 1,512 trs |
| Mazda (Japan) | - | 1,117 |
| Toyota (Japan) | - | 2,324 |
| Moskvich (USSR) | 485 | 122 |
| Others | 8 | |
| Total Imported | 7,627 | 11,468 |

Datsun (Japan) 1,350 - (light)

The most spectacular entry into the (light) commercial market has been by Datsun, the (Japanese) manufacturer better known in the United Kingdom for its successful leadership of the car importer league. Datsun, of course, like its great Japanese rival, Toyota, is a very large-scale manufacturer of commercial vehicles. The Japanese do not make any really heavy trucks like the Europeans.

# How to Emphasize Words

## Exercise 136

(a)

The most common way to emphasize a word is to underscore it.

People can generally find time for what they choose to do. If they cannot, it is not really the time but the <u>will</u> that is wanting.

(b)

A second method to emphasize a word is to use CAPITAL letters.

The greatest fact in life is this: "It is NEVER too late to start again." History is full of startling examples of this truth.

(c)

A third method to emphasize a word is to thicken it by overtyping it two or three times.

Never hold any one by the button or the hand in order to be heard out; for if people are unwilling to listen to you, you had better hold **your tongue** than them.

(d)

A fourth method to emphasize a word is to use s p a c e d letters with double spacing before and after it.

You may be waiting to do some  g r e a t  thing; however, do the small things that are unseen, and they will bring other and greater things for you to do.

(e)

A fifth method to emphasize a word is to use a different *typeface* – provided that you are using a machine that can change typeface heads.

Edgar Allan Poe (1809-1849), the well-known American poet, critic, and story writer, said: "With me poetry has not been a purpose, but a *passion*."

**Exercise 312** Type the following tabular matter, ruling only those lines shown in the draft. The margins must be justified, that is, the last figure of each line should form a straight right-hand margin. (Part of LCCI examination paper LC/53/S/Sp79 - Higher.)

INTER-CONTINENTAL HOTEL RESERVATIONS

A computerised reservations system and a vast international communications network ensure [redacted] ^ confirmation of your reservations around the world. (instant)

"As near at hand as your telephone"

AFRICA

| | | | |
|---|---|---|---|
| Abidjan | 34-94-81 | Libreville | 32023 |
| Lusaka | 51000 | Nairobi | 355550 |

EAST ASIA/PACIFIC

| | | | |
|---|---|---|---|
| Bangkok | 48370 | Bombay | 297756 |
| Colombo | 20836 | Hong Kong | 5-229879 [redacted] |
| Jakarta | 59860 | Manila | 89-40-11 |
| Sydney | 215-0888 | Melbourne | 288025 [redacted] |
| Tokyo | 637219 | Wellington | 49-524 [redacted] |

MIDDLE EAST/CENTRAL ASIA

| | | | |
|---|---|---|---|
| Amman | 41361 | Beirut | 252900 |
| Jerusalem | 282551 | Karachi | 515021 |
| [redacted] Rawalpindi | 66011 | Tel Aviv | 611059 |

LATIN AMERICA/CARIBBEAN

| | | | |
|---|---|---|---|
| [redacted] (Barranquilla) | 40001 | Buenos Aires | 45-0111 |
| Panama City | 27090 | Quito | 230300 |
| Rio de Janeiro | 224-512 | San Salvador | 23-62-77 |

EUROPE

| | | | |
|---|---|---|---|
| Amsterdam | 237510 | Berlin | (312) 332 - 517 |
| Bonn | 57600 | Copenhagen | (303) 222 - 6695 |
| Geneva | 346091 | Hamburg | (808) 955 - 9356 |
| [redacted] Lisbon | 321697 | ~~Hanover~~ | ~~28359~~ |
| Paris | 2254300 | London | (514) 861 - 0521 |
| ~~Rotterdam~~ | ~~182246~~ | Rome | (206) 624 - 0400 |
| Stockholm | 201007 | [redacted] Vienna | (604) 682 - 6656 |

UNITED STATES AND CANADA

| | | | |
|---|---|---|---|
| Boston | (617) 482-6681 | Chicago | 881 0691 |
| Dallas | (214) 821-3030 | Denver | 110 200 |
| Detroit | (313) 354-1400 | Honolulu | 441081 |
| [redacted] Houston | (713) 225-4900 | Montreal | 01-734-7445 |
| New York | (212) 973-3800 | Seattle | 476892 |
| Toronto | (416) 368-2941 | Vancouver | 536611 |

For any foreign city not listed, dial Operator and ask for Explorer 030713

# Correction Signs – 4

| Sign in Margin | Key to Signs |
|---|---|
| N.P./ or Para/ | Begin new paragraph immediately after bracket sign [ |
| Run on/ | Run on; no new paragraph is required. In text this is indicated by ⤺ |
| # | Insert space. |
| Caps/ | Use closed (unspaced) capitals when there are two lines under the word(s). |
| trs/ | Transpose letters or words. If necessary, number the words 1, 2, 3, etc., to make their order clear. The sign used in text is ∽ |

## Exercise 137

**Make a fair copy of the corrected typescript below using double-line spacing. Leave an additional line space between heading and text and between paragraphs.**

*The heading, whether at the left-hand margin (blocked style) or in the centre of the typing line (traditional method) must be typed in capital letters and — if preferred — underscored.*

Noise in Britain

Britain is one of the noisiest countries in the world and every year there is yet further invation of silence and privacy. motor traffic, factories, aircraft overhead, transistor radios, are among the main noise-makers. At home, the whirl of vacuum cleaners, washing machines and toys compete with radio, television and recordplayers. Far worse comes from outside, with the snarl of motorcycles, revving of cars, growl of lawnmowers, and the crazy symphony of the City streets.

Living standards and spiral costs as we surround ourselves with more and more machine-made noises until our eardrums are full and clamouring for silence. There appears to be little that return us to a golden age of silence in this era of the modern machine and din. Noise has become nearly everyones problem, from those living close to motorways to those directly in the path of the latest sonic boom.

Noise is rapidly becoming one of the most disturbing faetures of all. The World Health Organization has al ready warned us that "Noise is not as evident aform of assault as a blow on the head, but it is nevertheless likely to cause some kind of damage, imperceptible, but none the less dangerous.

**Exercise 311** Type a copy of the following table in single-line spacing. Ruling should be done in ink or on the typewriter. (Part of LCCI examination paper LC/53/S/Sp79 - Higher.)

FURAMA IMPORT-EXPORT CORPORATION

Five-Year Import Figures - All Divisions

| Year | Cameras and Binoculars | | Washing Machines and Dishwashers | |
|---|---|---|---|---|
| 1975 | 27 | 1080 | - | - |
| 1976 | 38 | 1466 | - | - |
| 1977 | 42 | 1500 | 19 | 7600 |
| 1978 | 43 | 1525 | 26 | 9228 |
| 1979 | 55 | [redacted] 2344 | 29 | 9855 |
| | **Business Machines** | | **Radio and Television Sets** | |
| 1975 | 73 | [redacted] 3650 | 33 | 360 |
| 1976 | 81 | 3780 | 39 | 400 |
| 1977 | 122 | 6950 | 45 | 425 |
| 1978 | 128 | 7000 | 48 | 450 |
| 1979 | 140 | 8200 | 69 | 911 |
| | **Musical Instruments** | | **Record Players** | |
| 1975 | 9 | 270 | 14 | 640 |
| 1976 | 15 | 346 | 20 | 775 |
| 1977 | 21 | 500 | 22 | 800 |
| 1978 | 20 | 510 | 25 | 860 |
| 1979 | 26 | 663 | 33 | 996 |

1 The figures in each column represent, firstly the number of thousands of units imported, and secondly their value in thousands of Malaysian dollars.
2 Our importation of Washing Machines and Dishwashers did not commence until 1977.
3 Last year the Corporation's total import [redacted] exceeded 350 000 items ← as compared with 156 000 in 1975.
4 'Business Machines' includes Typewriters, Photo-copying Machines, Adding Machines, and Shredders.

Shredders

# Accuracy Exercises in Hanging Form

Exercises 138, 139 and 141 are examples of **hanging paragraphs**. This style is used mainly for sub-paragraphs. Its characteristic is that the first line *overhangs* to the left all the other lines by *two* or *three* spaces.

To type a hanging paragraph: either set the tab key three spaces to the right of the normal margin, depressing it whenever required; or, remove the margin three spaces to the right. When this is the case, backspace for the sub-heading and the first line of each paragraph by depressing the Margin-Release Key.

The sub-headings «Deposit Account» and «Current Account» are examples of shoulder headings.

**Shoulder headings** are used for sub-headings in a text that bears a main heading (in this example the main heading is «How to Open an Account»).

A shoulder heading commences at the left-hand margin and must not be followed by a full stop. It may be typed in lower case with initial capitals and underscored, or in closed capitals without underscoring.

Shoulder headings are separated from their text with one line of space whereas the main heading is separated from its text with two lines of space.

## Exercise 138

**Compare with other forms of typing paragraphs and sub-paragraphs described on page 87.**

HOW TO OPEN AN ACCOUNT

It is very simple to open an account with a bank. You go to the bank you have chosen and in an interview with the Manager he will explain to you the different types of account. He will ask you for some personal information including a specimen of your signature which must be the one you intend using when signing documents for the bank.

Deposit Account

If you have money which is not needed immediately, you may open a deposit account. The bank will pay interest on this money, but will require up to ten days' notice before withdrawal. It does not make any charges for this account.

Current Account

This is the most suitable for everyday business or private use, as deposits and withdrawals may be made at any time and advantage taken of the many services which the bank has to offer. For this the bank may make charges based on the number of transactions passed through the account, and it allows little or no interest on this type of account.

When you open a current account you will receive a book of paying-in slips, to be used when putting money into the bank, and a cheque book. You should make arrangements to receive your bank statement when required.

**Exercise 310** Type a copy of the following table, taking care to place it centrally on the page. Pencil ruling is not permissible. (Part of LCCI examination paper LC/54/Sp79 - Intermediate.)

Matter appearing above and or below a table is expected to be typed over the full width of the tabular work. To plan this, proceed as follows:

Tab out first line of the preamble, using the space bar, over the width of the table as already determined. If the width of the matter above the table fits within one or two spaces, that is acceptable; if a long word (which cannot be suitably broken) goes beyond the table's width make a slight adjustment in the width of the main column.

If the preamble has been 'squared off' with the tabular matter, there should be no difficulty with a footnote.

## TANKER CHARTERING ACTIVITY

lc/ Reported chartering and new orders have been at a reasonable level. In the Caribbean area - on which most of the recent fixing centred - Rates fluctuated somewhat. The dirty tanker market index at the last showing was Worldscale 99 compared with Worldscale 95.

| | Company | Voyage | Tonnage | Worldscale |
|---|---|---|---|---|
| CLEAN TANKERS | | | | |
| LIBRA | Anco | Cherbourg - Montreal | 35,000 | 235 |
| ANCHORA | Ascot | Barcelona - New York | 19,000 | 150 |
| ESTORIL | Soco | Curacao - Rotterdam | 38,000 | 24 |
| DIRTY TANKERS | | | | |
| BARTEL | Anco | Caribbean - U.K. | 42,000 | 145 |
| ROKOS | Novoil | Persian Gulf - Boston | 35,000 | 170 |
| GREENWAY | Sanco | Caribbean - Piraeus | 50,000 | 145 |
| MOSSPOINT | Anco | Caribbean - New York | 46,000 | 142 |
| BRITANNIC | Tampol | Persian Gulf - U.K. | 40,000 | 24 |
| CAROLINE | Novoil | Curacao - Piraeus | 31,000 | 145 |
| AMOS | Anco | Indonesia - Rotterdam | 52,000 | 142 |
| LA PLUME | Tampol | Persian Gulf - Boston | 48,000 | 140 |
| RINGO | Sanco | Caribbean - U.K. | [redacted] | 66 |
| SUNSET | Anco | Indonesia - U.K. | 60,000 | 117 |
| PRIMULA | Soco | Persian Gulf - Brest | 105,000 | 37 |
| PENNYWISE | Soco | Caribbean - St. John's | 225,000 | 24 |
| [redacted] | Anco | Persian Gulf - Halifax | 98,000 | 45 |
| ZEPHYR | Sanco | Indonesia - U.K. | 67,000 | 66 |

BELLMAN

57,000

NOTE: Sanco took another 275,000 tonnes for another three years' trading at rates averaging out at Worldscale 31.

## Exercise 139

*Copy the following exercise. Note the hanging form of the sub-paragraphs.*

**Between main heading and text turn up three.**
**Between paragraphs turn up two.**
**Between numbered items turn up one-and-a-half.**
**After the item numbers leave two thumb spaces.**

HOW TO EXPRESS NUMBERS

Numbers are sometimes expressed in figures and sometimes in words.

Expressed in figures

1 In scientific matter; e.g. The atomic number of Oxygen is 8.
2 When denoting weight, quantity, and measurement; e.g. 3 kg, 30 miles, 240 Volts.
3 In sums of money, dates, invoices, statistical tables and reports.
4 In house numbers, postcodes, telephone numbers, policy and certificate numbers, after "No." (for number), with the per cent (%) symbol, before a.m. and p.m. and in the 24-hour clock (0640 hours).
5 From number 10 upwards. (In commercial correspondence figures are preferred from No. 2 upwards.)
6 For specific amounts under 100 (not used in a general sense).

Expressed in words

1 When beginning a sentence; e.g. Sixty soldiers marched past the church.
2 For numbers one to nine inclusive in general work.
3 In the names of streets under one hundred; e.g. My address is 10 Eighty-seventh Avenue.
4 For numbers under 100 when expressing indefinite numbers; e.g. We drove eighty or ninety miles.
5 In legal work.
6 For approximation; e.g. The box weighed about eight kilos.
7 When used in an indefinite way; e.g. There are about two hundred pupils in the top class.
8 For ages, used in ordinal form; e.g. In her twenty-first year she had already an M.A. degree.

ATTENTION

1 In certain documents (cheques and legal work) both figures and words are used to ensure accuracy or to prevent fraudulent alteration; e.g. A cheque for £60 (sixty pounds) was mailed.

2 Words and figures should never be mixed. For example, type either 10,000 or ten thousand, but not 10 thousand. Millions are an exception to this: you can type either £6,000,000 or £6m or £6m. or £6 million.

3 A fraction standing alone is spelt out; e.g. Three-tenths of the income is spent on food. But a whole number and a fraction should be expressed in figures; e.g. The dimensions of the box were $5\frac{1}{2}$" x 7" x $8\frac{1}{4}$".

4 Several round numbers are expressed in words; e.g. More than thirty thousand students enrolled in the University. However, round numbers occurring close together are expressed in figures; e.g. There were 10,000 students in the first year, 8,000 in the second and 6,500 in the third.

**Exercise 309** Place the following table centrally on the page. Errors should be corrected as undetectably as possible, preferably with a rubber eraser. (Part of LCCI examination paper LC/54/S/Sp79 - Intermediate.)

UNITED KINGDOM MARKET FOR
ELECTRONIC OFFICE EQUIPMENT
(£m)

| MACHINES | Actual figures | | | Estimated figures | |
|---|---|---|---|---|---|
| | 1976 | 1977 | 1978 | 1979 | 1980 |
| Calculators | 43 | 48 | 53 | 58 | 63 |
| Electric typewriters | 24 | 25 | 26 | 28 | 31 |
| Automatic typewriters | 3 | 4 | 4 | 9 | 10 |
| Electronic cash registers | 6 | 7 | 8 | 6 | 8 |
| Electronic accounting systems | 31 | 34 | 37 | 45 | 50 |
| Dictation equipment | 4 | 5 | 5 | 6 | 7 |
| Direct electrostatic copiers | 9 | 12 | 14 | 15 | 16 |
| Plain paper copiers | 40 | 46 | 70 | 84 | 89 |
| Small copiers | ·25 | ·30 | ·50 | ·40 | ·30 |

## Exercise 140

*Type the following paragraph first in the blocked form and then in the indented.*

**The numbers used to enumerate items in text stand out better when they are set out in brackets than when followed by full stops.**

Cheques

Cheques have the following advantages over cash: (1) They are more convenient to carry about. (2) A cheque can be made out at any time and place. (3) A cheque can be filled in for any amount, exact to the nearest penny. (4) Cheques are more convenient to send through the post than cash. (5) Cheques are only of any value after they are signed. (6) The used cheque form itself serves as evidence of payment after it has been cleared.

## Exercise 141

*Type a copy of the following manuscript setting out the sub-paragraphs in hanging form.*

**Treble space between main heading and text; double space between paragraphs.**

How to type continued numbers.

Continued numbers — used mostly in years or pages — are the fist and last numbers of a sequence; e.g. 2-9. These are separated by a hyphen and expressed as follows:

If the first number is less than twenty, use both digits of the second number; e.g. 11-18; but 45-6.

If the first number is 100 or multiple, again use all the digits of the second number; e.g. 100-104, 800-825.

If the first number is more than 100 but less than 110 (in multiples of 100) in the second number use only the changed part; e.g. 107-8, 1002-3.

If the first number is more than 109 (in multiples of 100), in the second number use the last two digits; e.g. 623-28, 1646-48. But if more than the last two digits change, use all the digits of the second number; e.g. 1789-1821.

## Exercise 308

**Type a copy of the following subscription list, which is to be placed centrally on the page. Pencil ruling is not permissible. Centre the heading. (Part of LCCI examination paper LC/54/M2/Sp79 - Intermediate.)**

NOTES: 1. The £ sign is centred over the figures in the column - if there is no decimal point.

2. Where the figures in the column are no more than two, place the £ sign over the units column.

(Spaced caps) → THE RIVERSIDE CLUB

(Caps) → GOLF AND COUNTRY CLUB MEMBERSHIP

| Membership | Entry Fee | Annual Subscription April 79 to March 80 | Total | Entry fee and Sub Total for 10 months June 79 to March 80 | Reduced Total for Membership if Paid before 1 April 1979 |
|---|---|---|---|---|---|
| | £ | £ | £ | £ | £ |
| Individual | 45 | 70 | 115 | 105 | 95 |
| Husband and Wife | 60 | 115 | 175 | 155 | 145 |
| Children under 2 | - | - | - | - | - |
| 2 - 6 | - | 5 | 5 | 4 | - |
| 7 - 12 | - | 10 | 10 | 8 | - |
| 13 - 18 | - | 15 | 15 | 13 | - |
| Country (outside 40 mile radius) | 35 | 35 | 70 | 65 | 62 |
| Overseas | - | 50 | 50 | - | - |

FOOTNOTE: All fees and subscriptions listed above are subject to VAT (8% at time of publication). Planned payment arrangements available on application to the Club.

# Correction Signs (5th and last)

| Sign in Margin | Key to Signs |
|---|---|
| ⊙/ | Insert full stop. |
| Spaced Caps/ | Use spaced C A P I T A L S when there are three lines under the word(s). Between words typed with spaced capitals allow three spaces. |
| [ ] | Move matter to right or left, as shown in the text. |
| "Balloon" (no sign) | Where many words have to be inserted in a certain point in the text, a line leads to a "balloon" drawn at a convenient place. |

*Margin on both sides 15(20) spaces. Double-line spacing. Leave an additional line of space between heading and text as well as between paragraphs.*

## Exercise 142

**Check the typescript before removing it from the machine. Ensure that spelling is correct, particularly that of unfamiliar words.**

spaced caps/ GOOD SPELLING

Because good spelling is considered ~~very~~ important by employ ers, they place it high on the list of qualifications when they are hiring a secretary; some girls find it easy to spell correctly, but whenever they came up against a troublesome word, they do the same as secretaries not so gifted and immediately look up the word in the office dictionary. /most/ /-/ ⊙/ uc/ of/ o/ /stet

[The carelessness of mis/spelled words becomes an affront when ~~proper~~ a proper name is spelled incorrect. The person reci/eving a letter feels that if he was important enough for a firm to write to him ~~feels that if he was important enough for a firm to write to him~~ soliciting his business and promising de luxe service, and so on and on, his name should have written correctly. [It takes ~~just~~ a few seconds to look in the Office files, the telephone b ook, or the city directory, in order to verify ~~at once~~ the ~~right~~ spelling of a name. /f /ly /trs " " been/ /NP /stet lc/ /correct

to be a small matter,

run on Although this effort to ensure accuracy in letter writing may seem ~~unimportant~~, firms have found through experience that it helps surprisly in building up goodwill towards their customers. ing/

**Exercise 307** Type the following table, centralizing it on the page. All the figure columns are to be of equal width. (Part of LCCI examination paper LC/54/M2/Sp77 - Intermediate.)

Do not waste time on a false start. Note the instructions and, having read through the assignment and decided on the display, type the exercise carefully. If you make a mistake correct it.

(Spaced caps) → STATISTICS OF VISITORS FOR 1975

(Caps + centre) → 1 – Total number of Visitors: 1,183,014

→ 2 – Distribution of Visitors by Nationality

| Country of → Nationality → | Air | Sea | Road | Rail | Total | % of Total |
|---|---|---|---|---|---|---|
| Asia | 121,595 | 40,064 | 362,343 | 123,141 | 647,143 | 54.7 |
| Continental Europe | 33,672 | 1,849 | 21,187 | 5,769 | 62,477 | 5.3 |
| India | 87,023 | 2,024 | 49,329 | 5,470 | 143,846 | 12.1 |
| Japan | 33,960 | 408 | 26,166 | 587 | 61,121 | 5.2 |
| Australia/New Zealand | 11,283 | 5,577 | 24,607 | 3,540 | 45,007 | 3.8 |
| Canada | 5,240 | 551 | 3,807 | 614 | 10,212 | 0.9 |
| UK and Ireland | 45,643 | 1,323 | 40,462 | 3,748 | 91,176 | 7.7 |
| USA | 32,344 | 1,935 | 28,970 | 3,763 | 67,012 | 5.7 |
| Others | 29,257 | 2,162 | 20,926 | 2,675 | 55,020 | 4.6 |
| Total | 400,017 | 55,893 | 577,797 | 149,307 | 1,183,014 | 100% |
| % of Total | 33.8 | 4.8 | 48.8 | 12.6 | 100 | |

There are also visitors from Singapore coming by road via Johore, Bahra Causeway.

## Exercise 143

**Type the following passage in double-line spacing. Before attempting it, read it through quickly to ensure that everything is clear and makes sense, and mark distinctly all corrections and balloons. (LCCI assignment from examination paper LC/54/S/Sp77 - Intermediate.)**

Between the heading and the text — when typed in the blocked style — leave an extra line over and above the set spacing. This applies also to the spacing between the paragraphs of the text.

Caps Trade Prospects Better

uc lc Some of the small countries (in the Far East) have begun to recover from the world recession, ~~This~~ which hit their terms of trade so badly. Last year's average real economic growth rate was about four per cent. [redacted] For this year the best current estimate is six and a half [redacted] to seven per

NP cent. [Inflation ~~having~~ has however been brought down, so that the outlook is definitely good. Indonesia has done remarkably well. ~~where~~ sliding money values used to be the byword in that country. Last year the rise in prices was ~~reduced by half~~ halved to nineteen per cent. In the other countries (Malaysia, Philippines,

trs Singapore, Taiwan, South Korea and Thailand) the average rate of inflation last year was between five and six per cent.

Another factor which has affected trade adversely is the recession in western markets, ~~and~~ as well as the falling world prices for most of this region's primary commodities. Just recently an improvement has been discernible in the ~~deterioration of~~ terms of trade.

Caps Forecast for trade (definitely for better times)

The forecast is ~~good.~~ ~~Inspite of~~ (Despite) the lack of official government relations, trade with Japan goes on, and new foreign investment continues. The Gross Domestic Product (GDP) grew by only two and a half per cent last year, but the forecast for ~~1977~~ (this year) is six [redacted] to seven per cent. Expenditure for the coming fiscal year is budgeted as forty-three per cent higher than in the current year.

(Prices for consumer goods rose by only five per cent last year.)

## Exercise 306

**Type this table so that it is centred both vertically and horizontally on the page. (Part of LCCI examination paper LC/54/S/Sp77 - Intermediate.)**

Make correct use of tabulator stops; guesswork is usually disastrous.

Caps and centre

SOME UNITED KINGDOM BANKS' BUSINESS WITH OFF-SHORE CENTRES* - (£m)

| | 1972 | 1973 | 1974 | 1975 | % Increase 1974-75 |
|---|---|---|---|---|---|
| UK LIABILITIES | 524 | 893 | 1,127 | 2,291 | + 102.4 |
| Bahamas | | | | | |
| Hong Kong | 158 | 560 | 957 | 1,380 | + 44.2 |
| Cayman Islands | 27 | 174 | 245 | 691 | + 182.0 |
| Singapore | 91 | 347 | 480 | 652 | + 35.8 |
| New Hebrides | – | 2 | 8 | 2 | – |
| | | | | | |
| UK CLAIMS | | | | | |
| Bahamas | 1,888 | 2,994 | 3,025 | 5,363 | + 77.3 |
| Hong Kong | 113 | 435 | 965 | 1,529 | + 58.3 |
| Cayman Islands | 24 | 244 | 406 | 1,333 | + 228.3 |
| Singapore | 392 | 664 | 1,237 | 1,742 | + 40.3 |
| New Hebrides | – | 29 | 27 | 19 | – |

Source - Bank of England Quarterly Bulletin

* External liabilities and claims of UK banks in foreign currencies

Footnotes are expected to occupy the full width of the tabular work.

# Additional Keyboard Characters

The following characters appear mostly on American typewriters:

The $ (Dollar sign), which is the shift key of numeral 4;
The ¢ (Cent sign), which is the shift of numeral 6; and
The # (No or lb sign), which is the shift of numeral 3.

*N.B. The # sign before a figure stands for 'number'; after a figure, it stands for 'pound' or 'pounds'.*

## Exercise 144

The month's expenses included rent $300 and food $500.
The Firm's offices are at #150 Lincoln Street, Apt #8.
Order #560 for 20# of powder will be despatched today.
Emily bought 10# of flour @ 75¢ and 6# of sugar @ 90¢.

If you are using an American typewriter, look for any additional differences in the top row of the keyboard and practise on them. A typical arrangement of the top row characters on American machines is the following:

### Manual Typewriter

### Electric Typewriter

The backspace key, the space bar, the carriage return key, the hyphen-underscore, and sometimes the x and the full stop keys have a 'repeat' action, i.e. they continue their action as long as they are depressed.

**Exercise 305** **Type the following table, leaving a double-line space between each of the six entries. Ruling should be in ink or on the typewriter, but mixed ruling is not permissible. (Part of LCCI examination paper LC/54/Su78 - Elementary.)**

When an item in the first column continues to a second line, that second line should be indented to the third space. This applies to both the blocked and the indented style.

MASON BROTHERS

New Salary Scales – June 1978

| Position | Qualifications | Salary Range |
|---|---|---|
| | | £ |
| Junior Clerk I | CSE in English and two others | 1600-2000 |
| Junior Clerk II | CSE in English, Mathematics and two others | 1850-2250 |
| Typist | LCC Typewriting ~~(Elementary)~~ (Intermediate) | 1750-2300 |
| Senior Typist | LCC Typewriting (Higher) | 2000-2550 |
| Secretary/ Shorthand Typist | LCC Shorthand (80) Typewriting (Intermediate) | 1900-2400 |
| Secretary II | LCC Secretarial Studies Certificate | 2000-2600 |

# Part 3

## Contents

## Exercise 304

**Type a copy of the following table centralizing it on the page (LCCI).**

NOTE: Every figure of 1,000 or more must have a comma (or a space); these commas or spaces should be vertically aligned. Aligned also should be the 'plus' and the 'minus' signs.

B A S I C   S T A T I S T I C S

EXPORTS AND IMPORTS 1973

| E X P O R T S | | | |
|---|---|---|---|
| | $m | Percentage Change on 1972 | |
| | | Volume | Value |
| Rubber ................ | 2,242 | + 16 | + 73 |
| Tin ................... | 888 | - 6 | - 4 |
| Saw Logs .............. | 929 | + 7 | + 57 |
| Sawn Timber ........... | 592 | + 40 | + 115 |
| Palm oil .............. | 464 | + 17 | + 28 |
| Petroleum ............. | 238 | - 12 | + 7 |
| Other ................. | 1,523 | - | + 27 |
| Total ................. | 6,876 | - | + 42 |

| I M P O R T S | | | |
|---|---|---|---|
| | $m | Per cent | Per cent Change 1972-73 |
| Machinery and transport equipment .......... | 1,720 | 31 | + 15 |
| Manufactures .......... | 1,300 | 24 | + 23 |
| Food, drink and tobacco | 1,210 | 21 | + 25 |
| Chemicals ............. | 500 | 9 | + 31 |
| Mineral Fuels ......... | 400 | 7 | + 8 |
| Raw materials ......... | 340 | 6 | + 9 |
| Other ................. | 110 | 2 | + 41 |
| Total ................. | 5,580 | 100 | + 20 |

# Combination Signs and Special Characters

## I. Combination Signs

The signs in groups A and B below may or may not appear on your keyboard. In either case, try to form them yourself by combining two other characters. First study carefully both groups, and then **combine** each sign at least twice.

### GROUP 'A'

| | |
|---|---|
| Pound(s) Sterling: | Type (-) over (L), as Ł |
| Dollar(s): | Type (/) over (S), as $ |
| Cent(s): | Type (/) over (c), as ¢ |
| Exclamation: | Type (') over (.), as ! |
| Cedilla: | Type (,) slightly below (c), as ç |
| Asterisk: | Type (-) over (x), as * |
| Caret: | Type (/) over (_), as /̲ |
| Plus: | Type (-) over (/), as + |
| Division: | Type (-) over (:), as ÷ |
| Equals: | Type (-) slightly over another (-), as = |

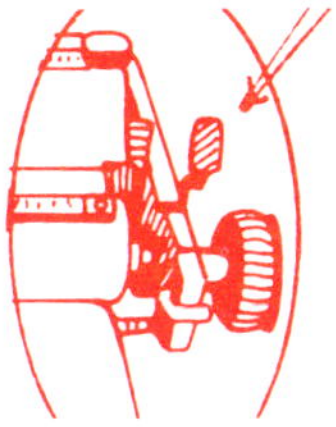

**To raise or lower the platen by less than half space, use the line finder — not the variable line spacer. Thus, the platen will return to its normal position.**

### GROUP 'B'

| | |
|---|---|
| Square brackets: | Type the solidus, and underscore at both ends, as [ ] |
| Dagger[†]: | Type (-) over (I), as † |
| Double dagger[‡]: | Type (I) slightly above another (I), as ‡ |
| Section[§]: | Type (s) over another (s) but slightly below it, as § or § |
| Per cent: | Type (o) raised by half space; continue with the solidus and another (o) on the normal line, as 15°/o |
| Per mille: | Type (o) raised by half space; continue with the solidus and two more (o's) on the normal line, as 15°/oo |

* The asterisk, being a footnote sign, is raised by nearly half a space.

† The dagger, also being a footnote sign - next to the asterisk - is also raised.

‡ The double dagger, a third footnote sign - next to the dagger - must also be raised.

§ The section sign, a fourth footnote sign - next to the double dagger - is also raised.

## Exercise 303

**Type a copy of the following table placing it centrally on the page (LCCI).**

The items in first column should be aligned with their related items in the columns.

If the first column item occupies more than one line and the column entry one, align on the last line of the first column.

**Ensure that the longest line does not extend beyond the leader dots.**

CONSOLIDATED PROFIT AND LOSS ACCOUNTS

Years to 31 December

| | 1979 £'000 | 1978 £'000 | 1977 £'000 | 1976 £'000 | 1975 £'000 |
|---|---|---|---|---|---|
| Turnover | | | | | |
| Sales of Rubber .. .. .. | 4,355 | 4,308 | 3,260 | 2,210 | 3,172 |
| Sales of Palm Oil .. .. .. | 4,479 | 4,250 | 3,746 | 4,277 | 4,343 |
| | 8,834 | 8,558 | 7,006 | 6,487 | 7,515 |
| Cost of sales and administration | 6,134 | 6,102 | 4,519 | 4,923 | 5,065 |
| Profit before interest and taxation .. .. .. .. | 2,700 | 2,456 | 2,487 | 1,564 | 2,450 |
| Interest receivable .. .. .. | 3 | 2 | 4 | 2 | 3 |
| Profit before taxation .. .. | 2,703 | 2,458 | 2,491 | 1,566 | 2,453 |
| Taxation .. .. .. .. .. | 1,273 | 1,194 | 1,179 | 812 | 1,170 |
| Profit after taxation .. .. | 1,430 | 1,264 | 1,312 | 754 | 1,283 |
| Extraordinary credits .. .. | 44 | - | - | - | 114 |
| Surplus for the year .. .. | 1,474 | 1,264 | 1,312 | 754 | 1,397 |

## Exercise 145

*Type once, making the signs by combination.*

A rate of $2.50 to £1 means that the price of 50¢ is 20p.

(a) 5 + 4 = 9. (b) 13 + 6 = 19. (c) 20 ÷ 2 = 10. Fine!

The / sign marks where a letter or word has been omitted.

Liz sat for the Alliance Française Examination in August.

# II. Special Characters

The following characters - already known to you - can also be used for a different purpose. Thus:

The [x] is used for *multiplication*, as 4 x 2 = 8.

The [-] is used for *minus*, as 4 - 2 = 2; also for *to* in numbers, as 18-25 (no spaces).

The [o] slightly raised, is used for *degrees* of a circle or temperature, as $32^{o}$.

The [(] or [)] is used for the *brace*, as

```
(        )
(   or   )
(        )
```

The ['] is used for *feet* and *minutes*, as 15'.

The ["] is used for *inches* and *seconds*, as 12"; also for *diaeresis*, as Noël, Zoë.

The [.] is used for the *decimal* point, as 3.14.

A numeral, slightly raised, is used for an *index*, as $5^2$. Also, within brackets, for a footnote sign.

**The mathematical signs (+), (−), (×), (:) and (=) must be preceded and followed by a space. However, no space is left if these connect simple expressions enclosed in brackets, as (x=ab), or form part of a superior or inferior expression.**

## Exercise 146

(a) 28 + 3 = 31. (b) 11 + 11 = 22. (c) 526 - 509 = 17.

(d) 649 - 42 = 607. (e) 5 x 6 = 30. (f) 100 ÷ 10 = 10.

(g) (5x12) - (2x13) = 34. (h) $5^3$ = 125. (i) $(2x+3)^{3x-2}$

# Typing Money in Column Forms

*Before copying each money column study carefully the accompanying instructions*

```
  p
 18
  3
 11
 —
 32p
 ══
```

All units should line up.
p (for pence) is separated from its column with an additional half line space, and lines up with the column units.
Leave half a line space above and below the top line of the 'total sum'; likewise, leave half a line space between 'total sum' and the first of the double lines.
p (for pence) follows the 'total sum' without a full stop.

A halfpenny is represented in fraction form.
When items exceed one hundred pence (over £1), the total must include the £ sign, without the addition of p for pence.
The lines above and below the total sum should not extend to cover the £ sign.

```
     p
   84½
   28
   ───
£1.12½
   ═══
```

```
          £
    256,720
 12,632,356
      4,830
 ──────────
£12,893,906
 ══════════
```

This column consists of pounds only (the commas mark the millions and the thousands).
The £ sign is centred over the longest item, which is usually the *total*. (In the blocked style the £ sign appears over the first digit.)

When a column, including the total, is not more than two figures wide, the monetary sign is positioned over the units column. (This applies to all signs, as £, $, m, etc.)

```
  $
 20
 12
 ──
$32
 ══
```

```
      £
 110.03
   2.00
  45.10½
    .30
 ──────
£157.43½
 ══════
```

This column consists of pounds and pence (the full stops mark the decimal point).
The £ sign is typed over the decimal point; you may, however, type it over the units of the pounds.
*After the decimal point, use two digits for more clarity, e.g., 0.30 (30p), 0.03 (3p).*

When using single or 1½ spacing in a money column, allow a half space above and below the lines of the total sum (see **a** and **b**).

When using double spacing in the column, allow one space above and below the lines (see **c**).

```
    £            £            £

  2,345        2,345        2,345
  3,456
  4,567        3,456        3,456
 ──────
£10,368        4,567
 ══════                     4,567
              ──────
             £10,368       ──────
              ══════
                          £10,368

                           ══════

    a            b            c
```

```
   630 000
     2 045
 2 725 678
 ─────────
 3 357 723
```

To mark millions and thousands, some offices use a space instead of a comma.

*Fractions are on different keys on different makes of typewriters. Locate them on your own machine – if they exist at all – and practise on them before you copy the exercise below. If they are not included in your keyboard make them by combination. (If there are several fractions to be typed and the machine does not have keys for all of them, use the combination method throughout.)*

## Exercise 147

Miller borrowed £300 at an interest of 9½% p.a.

The cabinet dimensions are: 40⅜" x 24¼" x 17⅝".

The sum of 45½, 56¼, 17¾, 28⅛ and 139⅝ is 287¼.

## Exercise 148

**To type degrees raise 'o' slightly.**

Butter melts at ordinary table temperature. Tar on roads melts only on exceptionally hot days. Most solids melt at much higher temperatures than 32°F (0° Centigrade). For example, glass is known to melt at a temperature of approximately 2000°F, iron at about 2700°F, platinum at about 3100°F and tungsten at 6300°F.

## Exercise 149

**(a)** 1/5 + 3/5 = 4/5 **(b)** 8/9 - 2/9 = 6/9

**(c)** 1/2 x 3/4 = 3/8 **(d)** 3/8 ÷ 1/2 = 3/4

## Exercise 150

**The apostrophe stands for 'feet'; the quotation marks for 'inches'.**

The most massive living thing on earth is a California big tree standing 272' 4" tall. It has a base circumference of 101' 7". Its mean base diameter is 32' 3" (with a maximum of 34'). This tree was estimated to contain the equivalent of 600,120 board feet of timber, sufficient to make 40 five-bedroomed bungalows.

## Exercise 302

**Type a copy of the following table placing it centrally on the page. Pencil ruling is not permissible (LCCI).**

Use the half spacer for the leader dots in the first column.

Uncorrected errors lose many marks. After completing an assignment, and before removing your work from the typewriter, check the typescript carefully against the examination paper.

**Words in any one line must not extend beyond the leader dots.**

PROPERTIES ON THE GLOBAL MARKET

| Location | Type of Accommodation | Number of Floors | Sale, Lease or To Let |
|---|---|---|---|
| ADELAIDE<br>Australia .. .. .. | Professional Centre | 2 | Sale |
| AMSTERDAM<br>Holland .. .. .. | Warehouse/Wholesale Centre | 3 | To Let |
| GLASGOW<br>Scotland .. .. .. | City Centre Offices | 3 | To Let |
| HOUSTON<br>United States of America | Office Tower | 40 | To Let |
| KUALA LUMPUR<br>Malaysia .. .. .. | Industrial Complex | Up to 3 | Sale |
| LONDON<br>England .. .. .. | Office Accommodation | 8 | To Let |
| MADRID<br>Spain .. .. .. .. | Office Accommodation | 10 | Sale |
| MELBOURNE<br>Australia .. .. .. | Adjoining Towers | 30 | Lease |
| PARIS<br>France .. .. .. .. | Office Tower | 20 | To Let |

## Exercise 151

(a) $\frac{7}{2} \div \frac{3}{2} = \frac{7}{2} \times \frac{2}{3} = \frac{7}{3} = 2\frac{1}{3}$

(b) $\frac{1}{2} + \frac{13}{16} + \frac{14}{21} + \frac{46}{24} + 3\frac{23}{24}$

**Whole numbers, mathematical signs and fractions lines should all be aligned.**

## Exercise 152

*Ignore the £ sign on your keyboard; make it yourself by combination. Do not put a full stop after* £ and p (pence).

Before cash is paid into the bank it must be counted and put into packets which are provided by the bank. The accepted method of making up is as follows: £20, £10, £5, or £1 notes into bundles of 100 notes; 50p pieces into bags of £10; 10p and 5p pieces into bags of £5; decimal bronze into bags of 100p, 50p or 25p; the old sixpenny pieces ($2\frac{1}{2}$p) must be packed separately.

**A halfpenny is represented in fraction; e.g. $25\frac{1}{2}$**

## Exercise 153

*To type superior or inferior characters use the line finder to move platen slightly forwards or backwards.*

Repeat these mathematical equations: $5^2 = 25$; $25^2$ or $5^4 = 625$.

The formula for water is $H_2O$; the one for nitric acid is $HNO_3$.

The area of the square is: $A = a^2$ ('a' representing the side).

**Study once again the functions of all the controls on your typewriter and be sure that you use each one automatically: Tabulator, ribbon, line finder, variable line spacer, line-space selector, etc.**

## Exercise 301 **Type the following tabular matter. No ruling is required except that shown in the table (LCCI).**

NOTES: 1. When the open space between the first column and the columnar matter to which it refers is such that the eye does not move easily from one to the other, leader dots should connect the two.

2. When a 'Total' or 'Average' appears in the first column, the word should be indented. If both 'Total' and 'Grand total' are given, the latter is indented further.

THE 'EASTERN' PROJECT (SOUTH CHINA SEA)

Comparative Statistics for Four Years

| | 1972 | 1973 | 1974 | 1975 |
|---|---|---|---|---|
| Opening cash surplus .................. | 1.4 | 1.6 | 1.7 | 1.9 |
| CASH OUTFLOWS | | | | |
| Capital expenditure ................... | 7.2 | 7.3 | 7.7 | 8.1 |
| Other costs ........................... | 0.2 | 0.3 | 0.4 | 0.4 |
| Interest paid ......................... | 2.1 | 2.1 | 2.2 | 2.3 |
| Gross payments on SCS ................. | - | - | - | - |
| Repayment of Loan Stocks .............. | 5.6 | 5.8 | 5.9 | 6.3 |
| Total cash outflow ................ | 15.1 | 15.5 | 16.2 | 17.1 |
| CASH INFLOWS | | | | |
| Net proceeds of present issues ........ | 15.9 | 15.8 | 15.2 | 15.3 |
| Interest received ..................... | 0.7 | 0.6 | 0.8 | 0.9 |
| Sale of spare capacity ................ | 0.6 | 0.8 | 0.8 | 0.9 |
| Net revenue from Sales ................ | 2.2 | 2.7 | 4.6 | 7.3 |
| Total cash inflows ................ | 19.4 | 19.9 | 21.4 | 24.4 |
| Net charges ........................... | 4.3 | 4.4 | 5.2 | 7.3 |
| Closing cash surplus .................. | 5.7 | 6.0 | 7.9 | 9.2 |

NOTES 1. The cash surplus at the start of the period includes the proceeds of the final call of 10 cents per share received on or before 31st March in the given year.

2. Interest received is calculated at the rate of 8 per cent per annum on the basis of an average of opening and closing balances.

Use the square brackets [ ] :

(1) when correcting part of quoted matter;

(2) when clarifying part of quoted matter; and

(3) when requiring additional parentheses (an insertion in an already complete sentence) in matter which is already enclosed in brackets.

## Exercise 154

(a)

"The recipient of the Nobel Peace Award for 1965 [1964] was the American Martin Luther King, Jr. . . ."

(b)

"It seems to me that I see in my mind a noble and powerful Nation [England under Cromwell] rousing herself . . ."

(c)

The various arguments advanced (these include certain anonymous writers [Public Economy, London 1978]) may be formulated thus: . . .

## Exercise 155

**To call attention to an error in a quotation (faulty logic, error in fact, incorrect word, wrong spelling, etc.) place the word 'sic' underscored and in square brackets after the error.**

He wrote: "It is a good idea for the typist to make a list of words she finds difficult, and when she gets spare time to practice [sic] typing them."

## Exercise 156

**The accents: acute (´), grave (`) and circumflex (^), unless existing on the keyboard, will have to be made with pen (in same colour).**

Do not use foreign words or phrases if you can use English ones. It is certainly better to sacrifice a shade of meaning than to employ such terms as: congé (leave), à la Française (after the French mode), à votre santé (to your health), façon de parler (manner of speaking), coup de grâce (finishing stroke), enfant gâté (spoiled child), etc.

## Mixed Column Headings

### Horizontal and Vertical

When column headings are much wider than the spaces taken by the columns themselves, you may type them vertically, as shown in the example at right.

*If the sheet of paper, turned sideways, is longer than the platen, fold it in two before typing the vertical headings.*

MILEAGE BETWEEN PRINCIPAL POINTS IN CANADA

(via rail or water)

| Distance | St. John's | Halifax | Charlottetown | Saint John | Fredericton | Quebec City | Montreal | Ottawa | Toronto |
|---|---|---|---|---|---|---|---|---|---|
| St. John's | 0 | 930 | 1,041 | 1,081 | 1,094 | 1,466 | 1,563 | 1,675 | 1,897 |
| Halifax | 930 | 0 | 239 | 279 | 292 | 664 | 761 | 873 | 1,095 |
| Charlottetown | 1,041 | 239 | 0 | 215 | 230 | 600 | 684 | 795 | 1,018 |
| Saint John | 1,081 | 279 | 215 | 0 | 67 | 425 | 482 | 594 | 816 |
| Fredericton | 1,094 | 292 | 230 | 67 | 0 | 403 | 454 | 565 | 788 |
| Quebec City | 1,466 | 664 | 600 | 425 | 403 | 0 | 164 | 276 | 498 |
| Montreal | 1,563 | 761 | 684 | 482 | 454 | 164 | 0 | 112 | 334 |
| Ottawa | 1,675 | 873 | 795 | 594 | 565 | 276 | 112 | 0 | 247 |
| Toronto | 1,897 | 1,095 | 1,018 | 816 | 788 | 498 | 334 | 247 | 0 |

### How to type the above table

1. Centre the main heading;
2. Calculate the depth of space required by the vertical headings, as follows:
   *Count the number of letters/spaces in the longest vertical heading (Charlottetown = 13 letters). Add one space before and after the heading = 15 spaces. The length of 15 spaces in elite pitch is 1¼ inches, or 7½ lines (six lines to the inch);*
3. Centre the horizontal heading (Distance) to the longest vertical heading (Charlottetown);
4. Add the spaces required above and below the horizontal lines (within which the headings will be typed);
5. Complete all horizontal lines of tabulation;
6. Insert paper sideways and type the vertical headings, starting them at the same point of the scale, and centring them over their columns.

## Exercise 300

**Repeat the above example making the calculation yourself; rule in ink or on the typewriter.**

## Diagonal Column Headings

Compared to the vertical column headings, the diagonal ones are more convenient to read but more elaborate to type.

Calculations are rather similar to those made for the vertical headings; however, before deciding to use this method you should make sure that the platen of your typewriter is longer than the diagonal measurement of the sheet you are using.

SOME GROUNDS FOR DIVORCE IN THE U.S.A.

| State | Adultery | Cruelty | Desertion | Alcoholism | Impotence | Insanity | Bigamy | Separation |
|---|---|---|---|---|---|---|---|---|
| Alabama | yes | yes | yes | yes | yes | yes | - | yes |
| Alaska | yes | yes | yes | yes | yes | yes | - | - |
| Arkansas | yes | yes | yes | yes | yes | yes | yes | yes |
| Connecticut | yes | yes | yes | yes | - | yes | - | - |

## Exercise 157

The question or the exclamation mark may precede or follow the closing quotations according to their correct grammatical position.

1(a) Do you know that it was John Milton who wrote: "Paradise Lost"?

The (?) follows the (") because it refers to 'Do you know'.

1(b) The Justice of the Peace asked the witness: "What is your age?"

The (?) precedes the (") because it refers to 'What is your age'.

2(a) He does not know the name of the author of: "Romeo and Juliet"!

The (!) follows the (") because it refers to 'does not know'.

2(b) Running naked out of his bathroom Archimedes shouted: "Eureka!"

The (!) precedes the (") because it refers to 'Eureka'.

## Exercise 158

Another use of the quotation sign is to stand for the *ditto marks* (meaning *the same, as before*).

| | | | |
|---|---|---|---|
| To convert | kilos to pounds | multiply by | 2.205 |
| " | pounds to kilos | " | 0.454 |
| " | metres to yards | " | 1.090 |
| " | yards to metres | " | 0.910 |

The *ditto marks* should not be confused with the *leader dots* (for which see page 183)

# Typing Sums of Money

A. SUMS OF £1 and over:

1. If they include pence, they are shown as decimals; e.g. £2.45
2. If they do not include pence, they can be shown:

   a Either without the decimal point, e.g. £50
   b Or with the decimal point, e.g. £50.00

B. AMOUNTS UNDER £1 can be typed:

1. Either without the £ symbol but with the p or pence following the figure; e.g. 35p or 35 pence
2. Or with the £ symbol and a decimal, e.g. £0.35

*No full stop should follow the £ or p sign – except at the end of a sentence.*

*Never use both the £ and the p signs in a single money expression.*

## Exercise 159

*Type the following sums of money in figures.*

(a) Eighty-five pence

(b) Twelve and a half pence

(c) Forty-six pounds and thirty pence

(d) One hundred and sixty-five pounds

## Exercise 298

**Display the following table to the best advantage.**

Useful Weights and Measures /Caps

| To change | to | Multiply by |
|---|---|---|
| yards | metres | 0.9144 |
| Metres | yards | 1.0936 |
| Inches | centimetres | 2.5400 |
| Centimetres | inches | 0.3937 |
| Feet | metres | 0.3048 |
| Metres | feet | 3.2808 |
| Pounds avdp. | Kilograms | 0.4536 |
| Kilograms | pounds avdp. | 2.2046 |
| Miles | Kilometres | 1.6093 |
| Kilometres | miles | 0.6214 |

## Exercise 299

**An example of 'three-level' column heading. First-level heading is divided into two second-level headings, each of which is sub-divided into two third-level headings. NB Do not place horizontal rules immediately beneath a heading, lest they should be mistaken for an underscore.**

To allow for vertical rules leave at least one space at either end of the widest line of each heading.

ENERGY, PETROLEUM, AND COAL, BY COUNTRY

| Country | Energy consumed (coal equivalent) | | | |
|---|---|---|---|---|
| | Total (mil. metric tons) | | Per capita (kilograms) | |
| | 1976 | 1970 | 1976 | 1970 |
| Algeria . . . . . . . . . . . | 12.6 | 6.6 | 729 | 460 |
| Argentina . . . . . . . . . | 46.4 | 39.2 | 1,804 | 1,691 |
| Australia . . . . . . . . . | 90.8 | 67.2 | 6,657 | 5,375 |
| Austria . . . . . . . . . . . | 30.2 | 25.3 | 4,013 | 3,424 |

# Remedial Drills

**For letters of the alphabet that you may usually type incorrectly**

**Choose the line you need and type it rhythmically two or three times**

| | | |
|---|---|---|
| A | alarm ahead again away apart avail aware awake adapt affair advance | 3 |
| B | ebb bob baby bomb bulb bribe ebb robber briber barber baboon barbed | 20 |
| C | clock check cycle civic click chance choice circle contract concern | 12 |
| D | dated indeed candid demand defend decided divided deducted depended | 10 |
| E | even ever never event every cease lever clever cheque degree extent | 1 |
| F | fifth fifty fluffy fifteen fifth fifty fluffy fifteen fifty fifteen | 16 |
| G | gauge garage grudge ginger gauge garage grudge ginger garage grudge | 18 |
| H | high height highly highway high height highway high highest highway | 9 |
| I | civil limit rigid crisis inside insist invite finish cities incline | 6 |
| J | job joy join just jury jump jail joy job join jury joke judge jelly | 25 |
| K | kick knock khaki kick knock khaki kick knock khaki kick knock khaki | 22 |
| L | local legal libel label likely little lively lawful loyalty clearly | 11 |
| M | madam mimic member moment memory murmur mammals mumps member memoir | 15 |
| N | nun nine noon none ninth ninety nun nine noon none nun ninth ninety | 5 |
| O | motor motion colony control colour option conform comfort condition | 4 |
| P | paper pupil prompt proper perhaps prepaid prosper property prepared | 19 |
| Q | quit quite quiet quick quart quarter quick qualify quality quantity | 24 |
| R | rare rear error refer juror rare career rather report regret return | 7 |
| S | sense series census splash success session suppose sustain suppress | 8 |
| T | that tent test text trust state typist tested thirty intent content | 2 |
| U | future unduly unjust untrue museum usually curious unlucky cultured | 14 |
| V | vivid valve revive evolve revolve vivid valve revive evolve revolve | 21 |
| W | willow withdraw woodwork westward windward withdrew willow woodwork | 13 |
| X | next exit taxi exist extra index exact exert expect excuse explored | 23 |
| Y | yet yes your year yard yours yet young years yield yearly yesterday | 17 |
| Z | zoo zone zinc zero zeal zest zebra zenith zoo zone zinc zero zenith | 26 |

**Numbers at ends of lines show the order of frequency with which letters are used in the language; eg No 1 shows that «e» is the most frequently used letter, whereas No 26 shows that «z» is the least frequently used letter.**

## Exercise 295

**A tabulation, without ruling, except for the column headings which are underscored.**

OCEANS AND SEAS

| Name | Area (in sq. miles) | Average depth (in feet) |
|---|---|---|
| Pacific Ocean .................... | 64,000,000 | 13,215 |
| Atlantic Ocean ................... | 31,815,000 | 12,880 |
| Indian Ocean .................... | 25,300,000 | 13,002 |
| Arctic Ocean .................... | 5,440,200 | 3,953 |
| Mediterranean Sea ............... | 1,145,100 | 4,688 |
| Caribbean Sea .................... | 1,049,500 | 8,685 |

## Exercise 296

**An example of table with main heading and one-level column headings.**

PRODUCER PRICE INDEXES BY MAJOR COMMODITY GROUPS
(1967 = 100)

| Commodity | 1980 | 1978 | 1975 |
|---|---|---|---|
| Farm products | 233.4 | 212.5 | 186.7 |
| Processed foods | 233.8 | 202.6 | 182.6 |
| Textile products and apparel | 182.4 | 159.8 | 137.9 |
| Hides, skins, and leather products | 241.0 | 200.1 | 148.5 |
| Fuels and related products and power | 574.8 | 322.5 | 245.1 |
| Chemicals and allied products | 261.7 | 198.8 | 181.3 |
| Rubber and plastic products | 217.1 | 174.8 | 150.2 |

## Exercise 297

**An example of two-level column headings. First-level heading is separated by a line and centred above the subsumed headings below. The heading to the first column (Year) is centred within its box. Each heading is centred above the column it identifies.**

PUBLIC DEBT OF THE UNITED STATES

| Year | Gross debt | |
|---|---|---|
| | Amount (in millions of dollars) | Per capita (dollars) |
| 1920 (Jan.1) .......... | 24,299 | 228.23 |
| 1930 .................. | 16,185 | 131.51 |
| 1940 .................. | 42,968 | 325.23 |
| 1950 .................. | 256,087 | 1,688.30 |
| 1960 .................. | 284,093 | 1,572.31 |

Commas (for thousands) and full stops (for decimals) must be vertically aligned.

# Division of Words

## At Line End

After the bell rings you can still type six to nine letters depending on your machine. If, however, you want to keep a relatively even right-hand margin, you must divide long words. To do so, observe the following rules:

### When The Bell Rings:

1. If you have just completed a word and the next one is short (up to four letters), start and finish it on the same line.

2. If you have just completed a word and the next one is long but divisible, start it and divide it at a suitable point.

3. If you have just completed a word and the next one cannot be divided, turn up immediately. However, if that word (or number) would extend only one or two characters into the margin, start and finish it using the margin release key.

### How to Divide Words

1. Divide between syllables, e.g. *par-cel, post-age.*

2. Divide after the prefix and before the suffix, e.g. *con-tract, need-less.*

3. Divide between double consonants which are in the middle of a word, e.g. *mil-lion, lug-gage.*

4. When a final consonant is doubled in order to add a suffix, divide between the doubled letters, e.g. *refer-ring, submit-ting.*

5. If a root word ends in double consonant, divide after the root word, e.g. *drill-ing, add-ing.*

6. When three consecutive consonants exist in the middle of a word, divide before or after those that are pronounced together, e.g. *stum-bling, bank-rupt.*

7. Hyphenated words are divided into their original components, e.g. *head-teacher, text-book.*

NOTE that the division of English words is governed by sound - not by spelling. This means than when dividing after an accented syllable, the consonant stays with the vowel when it is short: *dimin-ish, prob-ably, sched-ule* but goes with the following syllable, if it is long: *stu-dent, peo-ple, divi-sive.* When in doubt - do not divide.

### You Cannot Divide

1. Words of one syllable, e.g. *thought, drained.*
2. The last word of a paragraph or page.
3. The first two or last two letters of a word, e.g. *PEnalty, musicAL.*
4. Words of five or fewer letters, e.g. *also, going.*
5. Numbers and sets of figures, e.g. *£900.50 or (3 x 4) - (2 + 3).*
6. Acronyms, e.g. *NATO, COMECON.*
7. Proper nouns (unless necessary), e.g. *Germany, Elizabeth.*
8. Persons' names with or without titles or degrees should be typed on the same line. Do not type *Mrs W.E.* on one line and *Gladstone* on the next.

### Never End A Line With:

The divisional mark: *(a) or (1),*
a £ sign,
an opening quotation mark,
an opening bracket.

### Never Begin A Line With:

A closing quotation mark,
a closing bracket,
a punctuation mark
- except only a dash.

Examples of preferred division of words in typewritten work:

**(a)**

```
inter-est
prop-erly
chil-dren
earli-est
mini-ster
```

**(b)**

```
abun-dance
depen-dent
elimi-nate
terri-tory
fac-tories
```

**(c)**

```
appli-cable
dis-connect
illus-trate
impor-tance
origin-ally
```

**(d)**

```
respon-dent
regard-less
change-able
philo-sophy
fanati-cism
```

## Exercise 293

**Type the following in two columns using the indented style. Divide the list into two equal parts, separated from each other by at least one inch and a vertical double line. Justify the *gift* columns. No leader dots are required.**

Display Table like this →

WEDDING ANNIVER....

| Anniversary | Gift | Anniversary | Gift |
|---|---|---|---|
| 1st | Paper | | |
| 2nd | Cotton | | |
| etc... | | | |

Wedding Anniversary Gift List

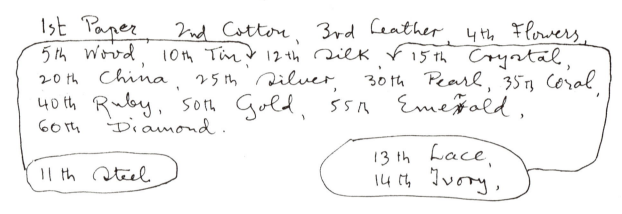

1st Paper, 2nd Cotton, 3rd Leather, 4th Flowers, 5th Wood, 10th Tin, 12th Silk, 15th Crystal, 20th China, 25th Silver, 30th Pearl, 35th Coral, 40th Ruby, 50th Gold, 55th Emerald, 60th Diamond.

11th Steel

13th Lace, 14th Ivory,

## Exercise 294

**An example of tabulation, in blocked style, without border or column lines. Between column headings allow three spaces; but after the first column allow wider spacing for better appearance.**

CONSUMER PRICE INDEXES
(1967 = 100)

| Year | Commodities | Services | Housing | All items |
|---|---|---|---|---|
| 1940 | 40.6 | 43.6 | 52.4 | 42.0 |
| 1945 | 56.3 | 48.2 | 59.1 | 53.9 |
| 1950 | 78.8 | 58.7 | 72.8 | 72.1 |
| 1955 | 85.1 | 70.9 | 82.3 | 80.2 |
| 1960 | 91.5 | 83.5 | 90.2 | 88.7 |
| 1965 | 95.7 | 92.2 | 94.9 | 94.5 |

# Typewriter Pitch

Type 'pitch' means the number of characters that print in each horizontal inch of space. The most common pitches are the pica (10 characters to the inch) and the elite (12 characters to the inch). Some electric typewriters are dual-pitch, i.e. they can be adjusted to both the pica and the elite size.

**On 'pica' machines (ordinary carriage size), the range of the carriage scale is from 0 to 91.**

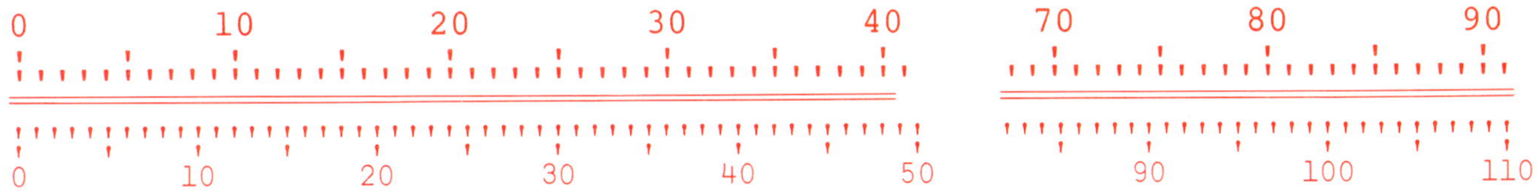


**On 'elite' machines (ordinary carriage size), the range of the carriage scale is from 0 to 110.**

The paragraph below is typed twice: with elite size letters and with pica size, so that you can compare the two pitches. Copy it out, setting your margins and tabulator as follows:

For pica size - margins 15 and 75, tab 20;
for elite size - margins 20 and 85, tab 26.

## Exercise 160 (a) Elite size

*Make your own line endings keeping the right margin as even as possible. Try to keep your word division to a minimum and, in any case, do not divide on more than two consecutive lines.*

The capital of a business can be divided into that part which
is FIXED and that which is CIRCULATING. The fixed capital consists
of those assets which have been acquired for retention in the business, to be used for an indefinite period to produce output until
they are worn out or become obsolete. Circulating capital includes
all those assets which have been acquired for the sole purpose of
selling them again, e.g. raw materials, work-in-progress and stocks
of finished goods.

## Exercise 160 (b) Pica size

*Use the dividing hyphen only at the end of the line; not at the beginning of the following line.*

The capital of a business can be divided into that part which
is FIXED and that which is CIRCULATING. The fixed capital consists
of those assets which have been acquired for retention in the business, to be used for an indefinite period to produce output until
they are worn out or become obsolete. Circulating capital includes
all those assets which have been acquired for the sole purpose of
selling them again, e.g. raw materials, work-in-progress and stocks
of finished goods.

## Exercise 290

**Type the following table in the indented style. The sub-heading should be centred beneath the main heading.**

LEADING NATIONS IN COAL PRODUCTION
(mil. metric tons, 1973)

| | | | |
|---|---|---|---|
| United States | 530.1 | West Germany | 103.0 |
| U.S.S.R. | 461.2 | India | 77.1 |
| China | 428.0 | South Africa | 62.4 |
| Poland | 156.6 | Australia | 54.6 |
| United Kingdom | 132.2 | North Korea | 30.0 |

Long and narrow tables can be divided into two (or more) equal parts, placed side by side.

Such parts are separated with a vertical double line.

## Exercise 291

**Type the following list dividing it into three equal parts. Separate parts from one another by 8-10 spaces and a vertical double line. Arrange the countries alphabetically.**

NB The commas, used in the columns as thousand markers, should be vertically aligned.

THE MAIN ORANGE PRODUCING COUNTRIES
(In thousand tons, 1975)

U.S.A. 8,740 - Brazil 3,500 - Mexico 2,013 - Spain 1,830 - Italy 1,700 - Israel 1,180 - India 900 - Argentina 774 - Morocco 765 - China 729 - Egypt 725 - S. Africa 600 - Greece 590 - Turkey 578 - Algeria 385 - ~~Pakistan 330~~

## Exercise 292

**Copy the following table justifying the right-hand margins. (To 'justify' the right-hand margin is to make it *even*, i.e. to bring the last letter of each line to form a straight line.) Leader dots connect the two columns, and give a better appearance to the table.**

E.E.C. COUNTRIES AND THEIR CAPITALS ⟶ (Centre)

| Country | Capital | Country | Capital |
|---|---|---|---|
| France .................. | Paris | Luxembourg ......... | Luxembourg |
| W. Germany ............... | Bonn | United Kingdom ......... | London |
| Italy - - - - - - - - - | Rome | Norway - - - - - - - - - | Oslo |
| Belgium - - - - - - - | Brussels | Ireland - - - - - - - | Dublin |
| The Netherlands - - - | The Hague | Greece - - - - - - - - | Athens |

## Part 4

# Contents

## Exercise 289 **Repeat the previous exercise in the indented style. Rule with the typewriter.**

*Centre main heading; also each column of figures under its column heading.*

*Where the column heading is wider than the widest column line, treat it as the widest line in determining positioning. The widest line must then be centred under the heading, and the tab stops set accordingly.*

*Where the column heading is narrower than the widest column line, centre heading over the widest line; e.g. in column one below, centre «Country» over «The Netherlands».*

**Before typing the tabulation make accurate calculations on the diagram below.**

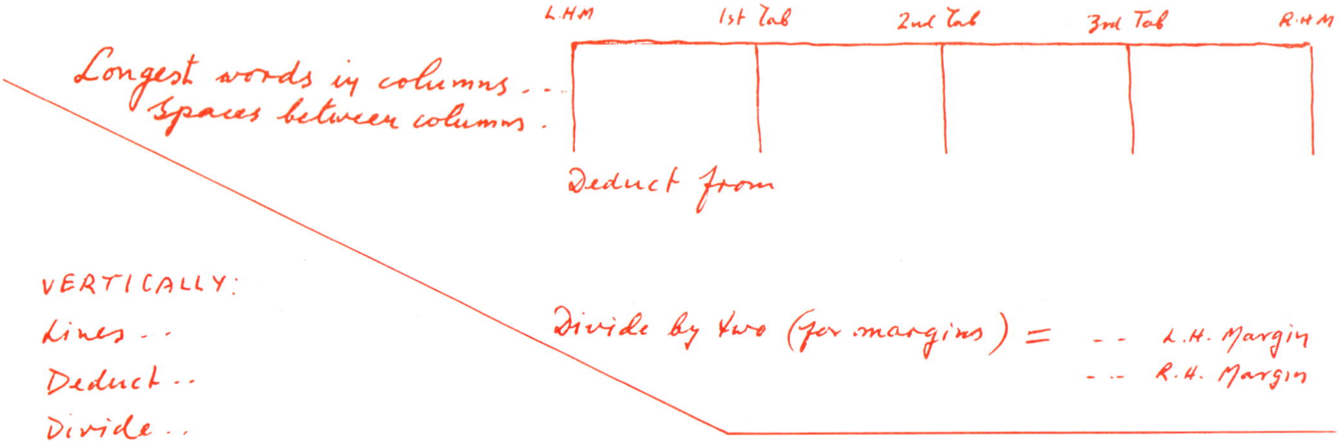


THE TEN COUNTRIES
WITH THE HIGHEST LIFE EXPECTANCY

| Country | Male Population | Female Population | Average |
|---|---|---|---|
| Sweden | 71.8 | 76.5 | 74.2 |
| The Netherlands | 71.0 | 76.4 | 73.7 |
| Iceland | 70.8 | 76.2 | 73.5 |
| Norway | 71.0 | 76.0 | 73.5 |
| Denmark | 70.6 | 75.4 | 73.0 |
| Ryukyu Islands | 68.9 | 75.6 | 72.3 |
| Canada | 68.7 | 75.2 | 72.0 |
| France | 68.0 | 75.5 | 71.7 |
| Japan | 69.0 | 74.3 | 71.7 |
| United Kingdom | 68.5 | 74.7 | 71.6 |

# Speed Tests — Assessing Your Typing Speed

## Assessing the Typing Speed

### To calculate your typing speed proceed as follows:

1. Count the strokes typed. (Speed tests usually bear a column showing the cumulative number of strokes at the end of each line.)
   Note that changing line counts as one stroke while capitals and changing paragraph count as two strokes.
2. Divide the number of strokes by five to find the number of *standard words.* (A *standard word* consists of five strokes.)
3. Divide the number of standard words by the number of the minutes of typing to obtain the typing speed *in words a minute* (wam).
4. Count the number of errors and find the *rate of error* and the *accuracy rate* as follows:

$$\textbf{Rate of error (\%)} = \frac{\text{number or errors}}{\text{number of standard words}} \times 100$$

$$\textbf{Accuracy rate (\%)} = 100 - \text{rate of error (\%)}$$

Note: The mininum accuracy accepted for a pass is 98 per cent.

A second method, still used by some examining boards, is the following:

1. Count the number of strokes.
2. Count the number of errors and subtract 50 strokes for every error from the total number of strokes, to find the *net* number of strokes.
3. Divide by five to obtain the *net* number of standard words.
4. Divide again by the number of the minutes of typing.

Both methods may be illustrated by the following example:

In a speed test of 1500 strokes typed in 10 minutes six errors were made. What is the typing speed?

First method

| | | |
|---|---|---|
| 1. Number of strokes typed | 1500 | |
| 2. Divide by five | 300 | (number of standard words) |
| 3. Divide the number of standard words by 10 (minutes of typing) | 30 | |
| 4. Six errors in 300 words corresponds to (6 x 100) ÷ 300 = 2 | 2% | (Accuracy 98%) |

Therefore, the typing speed is 30 wam with an accuracy of 98 per cent.

Second method

| | |
|---|---|
| 1. Number of strokes typed | 1500 |
| 2. Six errors correspond to 6 x 50 = 300 strokes to be subtracted from 1500 | 1200 |
| 3. Divide by five to obtain the number of net standard words | 240 |
| 4. Divide the number of net standard words by 10 (minutes of typing) | 24 |

Therefore, the typing speed is - by this method - 24 wam.

## Typing Errors

**1. Each letter or character: (a) missing, (b) additional, (c) unrecognisable, (d) wrong, (e) piled, (f) clearly above or below the line.**
**2. Each word wrongly divided at the end of line.**
**3. Each whole word omitted or in excess. In rewritten matter, every error is penalized whether in first or second writing; and one additional error is charged for rewriting.**
**4. Each space omitted or in excess.**
**5. Each transposition of: (a) letters, (b) characters, (c) words. (Errors in transposed words are additionally penalized.)**
**6. Each incorrect line spacing.**
**7. Any letter, except those beginning an indented paragraph, printed to the left or right of the left-hand margin.**
**8. Each letter or character which overlaps any portion of the body of another letter or character or extends into the space between words.**
**9. Typing the correct letter over a faulty one, and x-ing out errors.**
**10. Omission or repetition of a line.**

**N.B. Only one error is penalized in any one word.**

## Exercise 161

**Re-type correctly and say in which category of the above list each error falls.**

The great advantage of hire purchase to a byyer is that it allows him to enjoy the immidiate use of the goods whilst giving him time to pay for them. If it were not for the possivility of paying by the instalments, the sale of many kinds of consumer durable goods would bee greatly reduced and the benefits derived fromtheir use would be lost. Some people also beleive that the get better after-sale service from a firm wich has supplied goods on hire purchase than they xxxxdxbx would do otherwise.

## Exercise 288

**Copy out the following tabulation in the blocked style. Centre it both horizontally and vertically on A5 paper, landscape. Use the mixed method of ruling.**

*INSTRUCTIONS:* 
1. *As main heading is long, it is set in two lines, single spaced.*
2. *Start main heading one space to the left of first column so that it will be in line with the vertical ruling.*
3. *Start column headings at the tab points set for the columns.*
4. *Allow 3 spaces above and below the column headings.*
5. *Use the half spacer to get all column headings lined up exactly.*

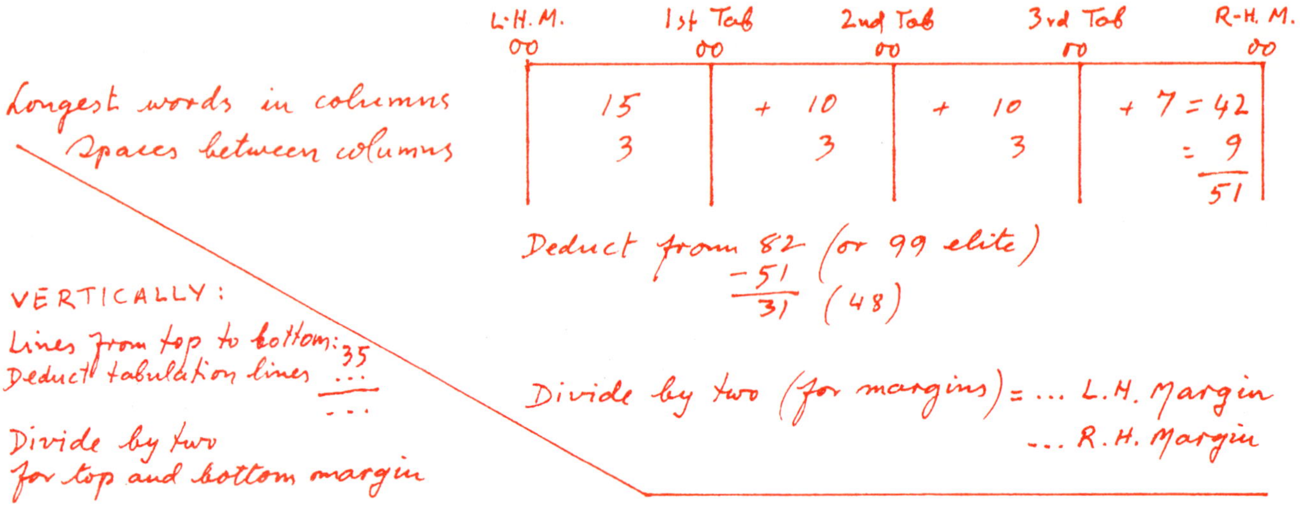


**With fully blocked tabulation it is better to align column headings with either the top or the bottom line - provided there is consistency.**

THE TEN COUNTRIES
WITH THE HIGHEST LIFE EXPECTANCY

| Country | Male Population | Female Population | Average |
|---|---|---|---|
| Sweden | 71.8 | 76.5 | 74.2 |
| The Netherlands | 71.0 | 76.4 | 73.7 |
| Iceland | 70.8 | 76.2 | 73.5 |
| Norway | 71.0 | 76.0 | 73.5 |
| Denmark | 70.6 | 75.4 | 73.0 |
| Ryukyu Islands | 68.9 | 75.6 | 72.3 |
| Canada | 68.7 | 75.2 | 72.0 |
| France | 68.0 | 75.5 | 71.7 |
| Japan | 69.0 | 74.3 | 71.7 |
| United Kingdom | 68.5 | 74.7 | 71.6 |

# Accuracy and Speed Tests

**Sit comfortably, with the lower and middle back area supported by the chair back. Upper body and head leant slightly forward. Shoulders down, chest forward, elbows loose by the sides, arms parallel to keyboard slope, fingers curved, feet vertical to floor, and eyes fixed on book.**

## Exercise 162

**Align machine with edge of desk; adjust paper guide and paper bail; set line selector for single space.**

Strokes to line end

It is impossible to get the reader of a sales letter to act 60
favourably until you have built up a desire for your product in 124
his mind. But you cannot build any desire till you have aroused 190
his interest. And you cannot arouse interest until you have 252
secured his attention. That is why a sales letter must first 315
capture the reader's attention. Once that is secured it must be 382
held till his interest is awakened. Then, while he is still 444
interested, your letter must make him desire the product. After 510
that, you must tell him specifically what to do. 560

WORDS: 112

## Exercise 163

The successful secretary cultivates a uniformly poised and 59
cordial manner that will enable her to meet callers and, if neces- 126
sary, turn them away with diplomacy and friendliness. She realizes 195
that the impression which she makes determines, to a great extent, 262
their opinion of the organization. It is imperative that this be 328
favourable. She discovers the caller's mission, mentally classi- 395
fies him, and decides whether she will interrupt her employer for 461
an immediate interview, arrange one for the future, or whether she 528
can give the information herself. 562

WORDS: 112

## Exercise 164

A wolf, seeing a lamb drinking from a river, wanted to find 60
a pretext for eating him. He stood high up the stream, and in a 126
loud voice accused the lamb of muddying the water so that he 187
couldn't drink. The lamb said that he drank only with the tip of 255
his tongue and that in any case he was standing lower down the 318
river and couldn't possibly disturb the water high up. When this 386
excuse failed the lamb, the wolf said: "Well, six months ago you 453
insulted my father." "I was not even born then", replied the 519
lamb. "You are good at finding answers," said the wolf, "but I'm 587
going to eat you all the same." 620

WORDS: 124

## CALCULATIONS FOR ELITE MACHINES:

A. Longest words in each column: 9 + 8 + 9 + 9 = 35
Spaces between columns: 3 + 3 + 3 = 9

44 Subtract from 99 (number of spaces across paper) = 55
Divide by two for margins: 55 ÷ 2 = 28 (Lt-hd margin)
+ 27 (Rt-hd margin)

B. Setting margins and tab stops:

**28** + 9 + 3 = **40** + 8 + 3 = **51** + 9 + 3 = **63** + 9 = **72** (+ 27 = **99**)

| 28 | 40 | 51 | 63 | 72 | 99 |
|---|---|---|---|---|---|
| ↑ | ↑ | ↑ | ↑ | ↑ | ↑ |
| Left-hand margin | 1st tab | 2nd tab | 3rd tab | Right-hand margin | Total spaces |

## BACK-SPACE METHOD

Another method of centring tables horizontally is by back-spacing, as follows: find the horizontal centre on the paper; count the number of characters in the longest word(s) in each column; add to them the blank spaces between the columns; divide by two. The answer gives the number of spaces to be back-spaced from the centre.

EXAMPLE (Paper A4, pica letters)

Horizontal centre: 41
Longest words in each column: 10 + 7 + 7 + 8 = 32
Blank spaces between columns: 4 + 4 + 4 = 12

Total 44 Divide by two: 22

*Therefore, back-space 22 times from the centre and set the left-hand margin. Now, count 10* + 4 for the first tab, 7 + 4 for the second and 7 + 4 for the third.

## VERTICAL CENTRING

**If the previous table is to be centred vertically (using again A5 paper, landscape), you will calculate as follows:**

Lines from top to bottom of paper: 35
Subtract lines occupied by table 10
(typed in one-and-a-half line spacing) —
25

Divide 25 by 2 = 12.5. Allow 12 at the top and 13 at the bottom.

## RULING THE TABULATION

**To rule the above tabulation proceed as follows:**

1. Turn platen 2 spaces above the first line of columns.
2. From left-hand margin backspace twice and insert a guide sign (light full stop or sign in pencil).
3. Move to the first tab stop, backspace twice, and insert a guide sign.
4. Follow the same procedure with second and third tab stops.
5. Go to the last column, tap twice from longest word and insert another guide sign.
6. Turn platen 1.5 spaces below the last line of columns and repeat procedure of numbers 2-5.
7. Now, remove paper from machine and join the dots with a ball-point of matching colour.

**NOTE:** The heading may be vertically aligned with the first column or with the vertical ruling.

## Exercise 165

**Type smoothly, with steady continuity; this IS the foundation for accuracy.**

Strokes

The proper handling of everyday complaints does not receive 59
the attention it deserves. In too many cases, businessmen ignore 125
complaint letters or answer them in an unfriendly manner. A grudg- 193
ing answer is as bad as no answer at all. At the other extreme is 260
the policy that the customer is always right. The trouble with 324
this attitude is that some customers take advantage of the situa- 389
tion and send false complaints. The vast majority of complaints 454
are on the level and should be treated as such. To handle them 518
properly might be temporarily expensive, but there is no alterna- 583
tive if you expect to retain the goodwill of your customers. 643

WORDS: 129

## Exercise 166

**Keep paragraph indentations uniform throughout; five spaces for pica letters and six for elite.**

The office practice - or secretarial practice - course is a 59
general course for all business students without distinguishing 122
between secretarial and non-secretarial students. It covers the 187
information, procedures, and machines with which all office workers 253
need to have a familiarity before accepting an office position. 316
It ties together and integrates on a vocational level the know- 380
ledge and skills gained in other business courses and introduces 445
certain new related subject matter which will make a more compe- 508
tent and more highly informed office worker. 552

WORDS: 110

## Exercise 167

Every business makes efforts to build up a reputation for 58
good service, quality of product, fair prices and anything else 122
which will attract customers and make them stay as such. This 185
reputation is known as "goodwill". Goodwill is very valuable 252
because no businessman can exist without it. For this reason, 316
if a businessman sells his business he will ask for a sum for 378
the goodwill. Goodwill may be said to be the value given a 441
business over and above the value of the net assets. As a judge 507
defined it, goodwill is "the likelihood that the old customers 572
will return to the old place". 604

WORDS: 121

## Exercise 168

**At the end of each passage put a circle around each mistake and write number of errors in the margin.**

An ass which saw a wolf running toward him while he was 56
grazing in a meadow, pretended to be lame. When the wolf came 120
near and asked what made him lame, he said that he had trodden 183
on a thorn in jumping over a fence and advised the wolf to pull 247
it out before eating him, so that it would not prick his mouth. 311
The wolf fell into that clever trap and, at once, lifted up the 376
ass's foot. As he was intently examining the hoof, the ass gave 443
him a kick in the mouth, and knocked out his teeth. "I have got 509
what I deserved," said the wolf in this sorry plight. "My good 577
parents taught me the trade of a butcher and I had no business 640
whatever to meddle with doctoring." 677

WORDS: 135

## Exercise 287

**You are required to centre horizontally the table at right:**

**Paper A5, landscape, one-and-half-line spacing, pica letters.**

SOME CLASSICAL NAMES

| | | | |
|---|---|---|---|
| Achilles | Calypso | Galatia | Penelope |
| Amazons | Claudius | Julius | Phaedra |
| Apollo | Croesus | Narcissus | Philippus |
| Atlantis | Daphne | Niobe | Stentor |
| Autolycus | Electra | Oedipus | Virgil |

### HOW TO CALCULATE (using pencil and paper):

1. Count the longest line in each column: Autolycus = 9 + Claudius = 8 + Narcissus = 9 + Philippus = 9: total 35.

2. Decide the distance between each column, say 3 spaces: (3 + 3 + 3 = 9).

3. Add together the above totals (35 + 9 = 44), and subtract from 82, which is the number of spaces across the paper: (82 − 44 = 38).

4. Divide this number by two to find the width of each margin: (38 ÷ 2 = 19). Therefore, the left-hand margin will be set at 19.

***Your notes will be something like this:***

| | | | | | |
|---|---|---|---|---|---|
| Longest word in each column | 9 + | 8 + | 9 + | 9 = | 35 |
| Plus spaces between columns | 3 + | 3 + | 3 + | = | 9 |
| | | | | | 44 |

Subtract from 82 = 38

Divide by two (for margins) = 19 left-hand margin

+ 19 right-hand margin

### NOW SET MARGINS AND TAB STOPS

Insert paper into machine with edge at zero, and:

1. Set left-hand margin at 19; count the longest word of first column (which is 9 spaces) and add the 3 spaces between first and second columns (19 + 9 + 3 = 31). Set a tab stop there to begin the second column.

2. From first tab stop (at 31) count the longest word of second column (8 spaces) and add the 3 spaces between second and third columns (31 + 8 + 3 = 42). Set a second tab stop there to begin the third column.

3. From second tab stop (at 42) count the longest word of third column (9 spaces) and add the 3 spaces between the columns (42 + 9 + 3 = 54). Set third tab stop there to begin the fourth column.

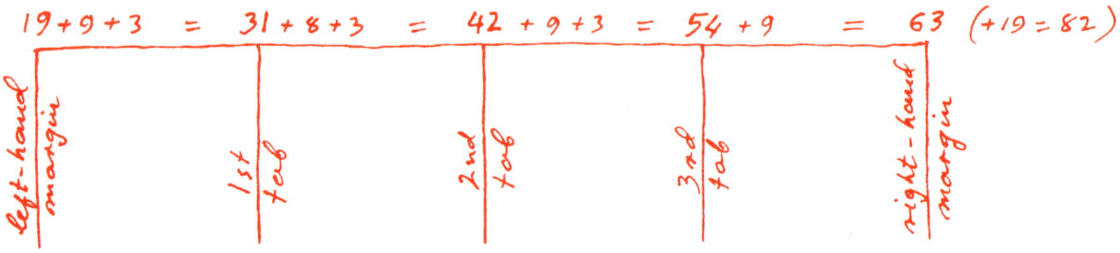

## Exercise 169

Strokes

A girl who has obtained a position in a business house and 59
who has ambition should be very careful, by her manner and by the 125
way in which she performs her work, to earn the respect of her 188
employers. Giggling and chattering, loud laughing, and talking 253
on staircases and in passages in business hours are very bad form. 320

Any show of ill-temper or impatience is to be deprecated; 381
if there is anything to which a girl can reasonably object, she 445
should state her objections quietly and in a pleasant manner. If 511
punctual, methodical, competent, and pleasant, she will win her 574
way; but if she wishes to make a career, she must also show her- 639
self able to take responsibility and to be capable of initiative. 705

WORDS: 141

## Exercise 170

**Pay particular attention to accuracy.**

The secretary, when in the office, should dress neither too 60
casually nor too formally. She should dress simply and taste- 124
fully in conservative colours. She will not hesitate to consult 189
experts on the most becoming hair-style for her and on the care 253
of her hands and skin. Make-up and nail polish should be used 317
conservatively. 333

Matters of personal cleanliness and hygiene have always 396
been stressed by employers. The intelligent secretary guards 459
with extreme care against giving the slightest hint of offence. 522
She takes a shower regularly, uses deodorants moderately, sends 587
her clothing to the cleaners frequently and wears perfumes with 651
discretion. 663

WORDS: 133

## Exercise 171

**Try to read quickly and accurately well ahead of what you are typing.**

General Business, or Elementary Business Training, as it is 64
called in some schools, is an excellent foundation course for all 130
future training in the commercial field. It is designed to ful- 196
fil the ordinary needs of individuals in conducting their per- 259
sonal business. Students are taught the proper use of the tele- 325
phone as well as the service it offers. They also learn to write 392
efficient messages for the various kinds of telegrams and to 453
compose attractive business letters. Here, too, they become 515
aware of the practical uses of filing for everyone, regardless 578
of profession or career. The proper methods of writing and 639
endorsing cheques, budgeting, and borrowing money, and of per- 702
forming other transactions of a financial nature that the modern 767
world requires are included. The General Business course is like 836
a travel folder, for it highlights the qualifications necessary 900
for and the opportunities offered in various types of work. 960

WORDS: 192

# Leader Dots

**Leader dots are used in tabular statements to carry the eye from one point to another on the same line. The most common methods of typing them are:**

**(a) Two dots followed by three spaces, as**

..   ..   ..   ..   ..   ..

**(b) Three dots followed by two spaces, as**

...  ...  ...  ...  ...  ...

**(c) One dot followed by four spaces, as**

.    .    .    .    .    .

**(d) A continuous row of dots, as**

..........................

**Allow at least one blank space between the leader dots and the columns they join.**

**When leader dots are typed in groups they should fall in line under each other, and all end at the same point.**

## Exercise 285

**Type the table at right, using any one of the above styles of leader dots**

THE FIVE LONGEST RIVERS
(Length in miles)

| | | |
|---|---|---|
| Nile | ... ... ... ... ... ... | 4,160 |
| Amazon | ... ... ... ... ... ... | 4,080 |
| Mississippi | ... ... ... ... ... | 3,740 |
| Yangtze | ... ... ... ... ... ... | 3,720 |
| Yenisey | ... ... ... ... ... ... | 3,650 |

## Exercise 286

**Repeat the above table typing the leader dots in a different method.**

**NOTE:** Do not confuse 'leader dots' with 'ditto marks'. The latter are placed under a word or phrase to indicate repetition (see page 68).

# Tabular Display

Tabular display is the orderly columnar arrangement of words and figures in tables. To serve their purpose satisfactorily, tables must be so arranged that they can be easily read and interpreted and at the same time give the page an artistic effect.

Tabular display is an arduous task. It needs concentration and careful planning. The width of margins, the distance between columns, the depth of line spacing etc should all be calculated accurately before starting the table.

### COLUMN WORK

To display matter arranged in columns proceed as follows:

1. Allow equal side margins (unless otherwise demanded).
2. Leave equal distance (usually 3 or 4 spaces) between columns.
3. Use single, one-and-a-half or even double spacing between lines, depending on the space available and the nature of the work.

xxxxxxxxxxxx xxxxx xxxxxxxxxxxx

| xxxxxxxxxxxxxxx | xxxx | xxxx | xxxx | xxxx | xxxx |
|---|---|---|---|---|---|
| xxxxxxxxxxxxxxxxxxxxxxx | xx | xx | xx | xx | xx |
| xxxxxxxxxxxxxxxxxxxxxxx | xx | xx | xx | xx | xx |
| xxxxxxxxxxxxxxxxxxxxxxx | xx | xx | xx | xx | xx |
| xxxxxxxxxxxxxxxxxxxxxxx | xx | xx | xx | xx | xx |
| xxxxxxxxxxxxxxxxxxxxxxx | xx | xx | xx | xx | xx |

Blocked style

xxxxxxxxxxxx xxxxxx xxxxxxxxxxxx

| xxxxxxxxxxxxxxx | xxxx | xxxx | xxxx | xxxx | xxxx |
|---|---|---|---|---|---|
| xxxxxxxxxxxxxxxxxxxxxxx | xx | xx | xx | xx | xx |
| xxxxxxxxxxxxxxxxxxxxxxx | xx | xx | xx | xx | xx |
| xxxxxxxxxxxxxxxxxxxxxxx | xx | xx | xx | xx | xx |
| xxxxxxxxxxxxxxxxxxxxxxx | xx | xx | xx | xx | xx |
| xxxxxxxxxxxxxxxxxxxxxxx | xx | xx | xx | xx | xx |

Traditional style

## Exercise 172

**To get the best possible results keep your typewriter clean and in good condition.**

Strokes

King John was described as the worst king who ever ruled in 61
England. He had brilliant abilities, which he occasionally brought 131
into play in brief spasms of energy, but he was the slave of his 196
own passions and inordinate vices. He was a tyrant and a murderer, 265
faithless, reckless, vindictive and cruel; but oddly enough, England 333
was the gainer. For he made himself so generally detested that all 401
the best elements in the country united in opposing his oppression 467
and forcing him to seal, in 1215, the Great Charter (Magna Carta), 539
which proclaimed the fundamental principle that no man, high or low, 607
king or noble, gentle or simple, may override or break the law of 672
the land with impunity, and that none has power to change the law 737
without the general assent. 765

WORDS: 153

## Exercise 173

In industry and intelligence the ant is not surpassed even 59
by the bee and the wasp. Certain groups perform certain duties. 125
Labour-saving devices are adopted; the workers will drop food or 191
building stuff to other groups below and thus save carrying. The 258
ants build roads by the removal of obstacles, and even arch them 323
over with earth to form covered ways; sometimes they excavate 385
tunnels of considerable length. Ants have their own way of com- 451
municating with one another; when one of their number is injured, 516
the news is passed along and a rush is made to the rescue. If an 583
injured ant is partly buried the debris is removed, or a fallen 647
ant is lifted out of pitfalls. Food is carried by a company of 712
ants when it is too heavy for one. A remarkable fact is that some 780
species of ants go on regular forays to seize the larvae and pupae 847
of certain other species, which they carry to their own nests, to 913
rear and use as slaves. 936

WORDS: 187

## Exercise 174

**To limit the number of errors work at a controlled speed.**

The typewriter is to the pen as the modern motorcar is to 58
the horse. Years ago, when a girl applied for a position in an 122
office, she was asked if she wrote "a good hand", meaning whether 190
she had neat and legible handwriting. Now, an employer asks an 255
applicant how many words a minute she can type. A high level of 321
typewriting ability is required of secretaries, shorthand-typists, 388
typists and general office workers. In fact, there is no office 454
job of a "white-collar" nature where typewriting is not expected. 522
The book-keeper types statements and reports; the filing clerk 586
types labels, and the receptionist types letters and statements, 651
too. Students learning to type early in their school careers 714
can use this skill to great advantage in saving time and improving 781
grades. Typed term papers, because of their legibility, neatness 848
and accuracy, are required in many college courses. Since the 912
average typewriting speed is more than twice that of the average 977
longhand speed, the saving in time to the student is obvious. 1040

WORDS: 208

**Exercise 284** **Type a copy of the following advertisement and reply-slip. Display it centrally on the page. (Part of LCCI examination paper LC/54/S/Sp 78 - Intermediate.)**

(Caps) → Straits Office Supplies Limited

Our latest copier for quick and inexpensive operation with excellent reproduction is now available.

It is compact - takes up half a desk in space, yet has all the features of larger, more expensive machines. There is a support for large books and a manual over-ride which allows for odd-sized paper to be inserted without reloading the automatic paper system. Double-sided copies and offset masters can be produced. NP [SOS 500 can be purchased outright or it can be leased.

Please send me details .....
I would like a demonstration .....

NAME ..........................................

ADDRESS ..........................................

..........................................

..........................................

TELEPHONE ..........................................

Straits Office Supplies Limited
GPO Box 1789
676 Shenton Way
Singapore #9

## Exercise 175

Strokes

When great numbers of people work together, they will find 59
that, unless they show the utmost courtesy toward one another, 122
their days can be unbearable. In a big organization, with floor 187
after floor of office space, in order that not an inch may be 249
wasted, desks are lined up close together. For that reason, it 314
is inconsiderate of the newcomer, who may be a little worried 376
about some new tasks, to hum or whistle at his work and disturb 440
those nearby. The girl who is short of patience should not start 507
sighing and snapping her fingers when she makes a mistake over 570
new work, for it may cause a half dozen people around her to make 636
mistakes, too. Everyone is expected to work as quietly as pos- 701
sible, without adding unnecessarily to the noise from telephone, 766
machines, and the unavoidable motions of a large number of people. 833

WORDS: 167

## Exercise 176

**Speed without accuracy is of no value; accuracy without speed is of no value.**

Do you know that all the business, military, and political 59
leaders are salesmen? No matter what you do you must know how 124
to sell your product, your services, and yourself if you are to 188
be successful. Therefore, the course in Salesmanship should be 254
considered seriously by everyone. Selling becomes an art only 318
after the "mechanics of selling" have been learned. There are 384
definite steps in the selling process that must be followed before 451
an article or idea is sold. The course in selling gives the 513
basic information needed by all young men and women who would 575
like to work full or part time in selling jobs. There are many 640
students in high school who must work to defray the expense of 703
their education. Most of these students work in neighbourhood 767
or downtown stores as sales-people. Salesmanship also teaches 831
one how to look after merchandise, and how to take care of other 896
details necessary for success in this type of work. 948

WORDS: 190

## Exercise 177

**Correct machine manipulation will give you better results.**

Athena was not only the goddess of wisdom among the Olympians 63
but also she was the weaver of the gods. It was, therefore, quite 131
natural that she considered the stuffs she wove unapproachable 194
for fineness and beauty and she was very angry indeed when she 257
heard that a simple peasant girl who was called Arachne declared 323
her own work to be superior. The goddess went forthwith to the 388
maiden's hut and challenged her to a contest. Arachne accepted. 455
Both set up their looms and stretched the warp upon them. Then 521
they went to work. Heaps of skeins of beautiful threads coloured 588
like the rainbow lay beside each and threads of gold and silver 652
too. Athena did her best and the result was a marvel, but 712
Arachne's work was in no way inferior. In a fury of anger, the 779
goddess slit the web from top to bottom and beat the girl around 844
the head with her shuttle. Arachne, disgraced and mortified and 910
furiously angry, hanged herself. Then a little repentance entered 978
Athena's heart. She lifted the body from the noose and sprinkled 1047
it with magic liquid. Arachne was changed into a spider and her 1113
skill in weaving was left to her. 1146

WORDS: 229

**Exercise 283** Type a copy of this entry form, taking care not to type the dots too hard. All the words in the left-hand margin are to be typed in capital letters with the exception of the word 'Free' which is to be typed in spaced capitals. (Part of LCCI examination paper LC/54/S/Sp79 - Intermediate.)

lc

Please complete this form in full and hand it to the Receptionist when you arrive at the exhibition.

Capital letters please

NAME .............................

JOB TITLE .............................

ORGANISATION .............................

BUSINESS ADDRESS .............................

.............................

.............................

BRING THIS SECTION WITH YOU FOR F R E E ENTRY INTO EXHIBITION

| Type of Organisation | Mainly interested in |
|---|---|
| .... Export/Import | .... Typewriters |
| .... Security | .... Copiers |
| .... Group Plantations | .... Telephones |
| .... Clerical Training | .... Telex |
| .... Education | .... Reprography |
| .... Transport | .... Computers |
| .... Advertising | .... Calculators |
| .... Information | .... Post Room |
| .... Exhibitions | .... Projectors |
| .... Entertainment | .... Audio machines |

| Other organisations Specify | Other interests Specify |
|---|---|
| ........................ | ........................ |
| ........................ | ........................ |
| ........................ | ........................ |
| ........................ | ........................ |

## Exercise 178

**Return carriage rapidly and correctly; this will save you valuable time.**

Strokes

The management of every progressive firm lays much stress on 61
the appearance of its correspondence. There is general agreement 128
that if a letter is worth writing it is worth writing well, and 192
that, like the products it sells, a letter should be attractively 258
presented to the one who will receive it. 299

The first thing that anyone notices is the way that a letter 362
is placed on the paper. It shouldn't take long for a girl who 427
has received a thorough training in shorthand and typing to be 490
able to judge from her shorthand notes the approximate length of 555
a letter. Then as she rolls the paper into the machine, she can 621
plan how far down to begin and what marginal stops to set, in 683
order to have the best possible arrangement. 727

However hurried a girl may be, she is expected to take the 788
time to camouflage her typing errors. It is a little difficult 853
sometimes to turn out good work on low quality office stationery, 919
but with patience you can do a passable erasing job. Instead of 985
using a typewriter eraser, use the softer kind, like that on the 1050
end of a pencil; rub lightly and stop after every few strokes to 1115
see whether you have erased enough. Erasing cannot be allowed in 1182
school or you would never learn how to type, but in a business 1245
office you are supposed to have left your practice days behind 1308
you and to use no more stationery than is necessary. 1361

WORDS: 247

## Exercise 179

**Do not overtype; correct errors properly.**

The House of Commons meets in Westminster from Mondays to 62
Fridays throughout the year, except when Parliament is in recess. 130
The hours of sitting for normal business are: Mondays to Thurs- 198
days from 2.30 p.m. to 10 p.m., and Fridays 11 a.m. to 4.30 p.m. 264
Certain business is exempt from normal closing time and other 327
business may be exempted if the House chooses, so that the Commons 392
often sits later than 10 p.m. on the first four days of the week, 457
and all-night sittings are not unknown. 502

On ordinary occasions, members of the House of Commons, who 566
also have much committee, party and constituency business to 627
attend to, are not expected to be in constant attendance in the 691
debating chamber. When any special business is about to be 752
taken - for instance, if a vote on some legislative or other 813
matter is pending - special steps are taken to secure their pres- 878
ence. At other times, the chamber may be relatively full or 941
relatively empty, depending on the speakers and the subject for 1005
debate. Some members leave the House altogether for a few hours, 1073
but the majority remain within its precincts so as to be able to 1138
reach the lobbies within a few minutes of being called. 1194

In the past, members wishing to be away from the House for 1256
a period of days during the session, were obliged to apply for 1319
'leave of absence'. This is not now considered necessary, but 1385
may be granted formally to an official delegation from the House. 1452

WORDS: 249

**Exercise 282** Type a copy of the following application form, displaying it centrally on the page. Take care not to type the dots too hard. (Part of LCCI examination paper LC/54/M2/Sp79 - Intermediate.)

The Riverside Club ← (Spaced caps + centre)

Membership Application Form ← (Caps + centre)

Family Name .................... Other Name (s) ................

Address ........................ ..............................

........................

........................

Occupation ...................... Tel No ......................

List of Sporting Interests ....................................

..............................................................

..............................................................

Other Club Memberships currently held ..........................

..............................................................

Type of Membership sought (Tick relevant)

| | | Country Club | Golf and Country Club |
|---|---|---|---|
| Self | .... | .... | .... |
| Spouse | .... | .... | .... |
| Children | .... | | |

| | Name of Child | Date of Birth | |
|---|---|---|---|
| 1 | .................... | ................ | .... |
| 2 | .................... | ................ | .... |
| 3 | .................... | ................ | .... |
| 4 | .................... | ................ | .... |

I accept that the decision of the Club in respect of this application is final.

Applicant's Signature .................... Date ................

## Exercise 180

Strokes

A business telephone is not to be used for chatting and date 61
making. This has a bad effect on customers who overhear such calls, 131
and who will think that the firm can't be very busy - or very 195
businesslike. Besides, it has a bad effect on the boss. Just because he 271
is out, it's not a good idea to use the line for long talks with your 342
friends. All the time you are using the phone, he may be trying to call 416
you. 421

Whenever it is necessary that you use the telephone for a 486
personal call, offer to pay for it. In the case of an out-of-town call, as 563
soon as you have hung up call the operator and ask her what the 627
charge for the call is. In making your reimbursement, add the tax. The 702
firm may not require you to pay for a local call, especially if the 770
employees do not abuse this privilege; but unless you know this 834
definitely, make the offer to the switchboard operator or to someone in 906
charge of the office. 928

WORDS: 186

**Type each speed test three times. Your first typing should aim at complete control and accuracy; the second one should aim at an increased speed; and the third one at maximum accuracy and speed.**

## Exercise 181

The value of training of staff is often overlooked, and it is not 66
until an office manager hires a junior straight from school that he 134
realises the need for it. There is hardly a single clerical job which does 211
not require some training. Even answering the telephone properly or 281
sorting alphabetically needs some instruction. 328

Education and training have been described as the "balance 395
wheel" in harmonious staff relationships, and although this is only 464
partly true, its importance is more than in just giving workers the "know 532
how" of their job. Full and proper training gives workers the fresh 604
interest in their work; it increases their capacity for doing better 679
things; it gives them pride in their work, increases morale, and gives 750
them better chances of promotion. 784

From an economic point of view, training is essential if new 852
workers are to be fully productive in the minimum of time. Techniques 924
of office work as well as of industry are for ever changing, and it is 995
necessary that training should be given in order to keep abreast of 1063
modern developments. It is also essential from a national viewpoint that 1138
training should keep up with the latest in technology. 1193

Training should not be viewed in isolation, but as an integral part 1268
of the whole personnel programme. It should be linked up with the 1336
recruitment of staff, with their promotion, and with their staff reports. 1410
Workers feel it is a good employer who pays to have them trained; it 1480
gives them a feeling of security. 1514

WORDS: 303

## Exercise 281

**Type the following announcement in duplicate, ruling with the typewriter. Separate main text from order form slip by a line of dashes. Before tearing off slips fill them in as follows:** *Top copy* **Ronald Jameson, 25 Merc Lane, Queniborough, Leicester LE7 8DC.** *Second copy* **Miss Elizabeth Irving, 1016 Adley Road, Ottawa, Ontario, K1J 8B9, Canada.**

---

# COMLON

*Journal of the Commercial Education Scheme*

COMLON is the new quarterly magazine of The London Chamber of Commerce and Industry, Commercial Education Scheme. It aims to provide commentaries on examination questions, subject matter, educational topics and matters of interest in the fields of Business and Secretarial Studies. We hope it will appeal both to students and college staff.

Subscription rates for 4 copies per annum are:

Inland - £2.70 (UK)
Overseas - £3.50 (Seamail)
Overseas - £4.85 (Airmail)

Order your subscription today by completing and posting the form below.

- - - - - - - - - - - - - - - - - - - - - - - - - - - - - - - - - - - - - - - -

SUBSCRIPTION ORDER FORM

To: MS5., LONDON CHAMBER OF COMMERCE AND INDUSTRY
Commercial Education Scheme, Marlowe House, Station Road, Sidcup, Kent DA15 7BJ

Please send me the next four quarterly issues of COMLON
to the address below. I enclose remittance to the value of £....

Name ..............................................................
(Block letters please)

Address ...........................................................

Remittances payable to 'The London Chamber of Commerce and Industry (CES)'.

## Exercise 182

Strokes

Letters of application are the most personal of business letters 65
and as such they are often the most difficult to write. They should 135
follow business letter forms, but they should also have the appeal and 206
sparkle (whatever it is that gives personality to a letter) which personal 272
letters contain. Yet they must not be familiar; familiarity in a business 348
letter shows lack of respect for persons on whom we wish to make a 417
favourable impression. A letter of application should give full details; 490
but it should not be too long, for a long letter might be discarded by 557
a busy official who has scores of other letters to read. And the letter 627
must be neat. No employer will hire a person whom he knows to be 696
slovenly. No employer will be favourably impressed by a letter which 766
contains common errors in spelling and grammar. 827

WORDS: 165

**Type continuously for 10 minutes. If you finish before the expiration of time start the passage from the beginning. At the end of the test count the number of strokes typed, circle your errors and calculate your speed, as described on page 73.**

## Exercise 183

Not only is it good manners for a caller to be on time for an 62
appointment, but it ensures him a good reception. The latecomer who 132
strolls in at a quarter to three for a 2.30 appointment is likely to learn 207
that Mr. Smith is busy now with another caller and won't be free for 279
the rest of the day. Even when Mr. Smith's secretary pretends to 349
believe the caller's lame excuse for his lateness and gives him another 422
appointment, the caller will still be faced with the prospect of making 494
his apologies to Mr. Smith when he finally does see him. 553
To be sure of keeping an appointment on time, it has been 618
found best in big cities to allow from 10 to 15 minutes in addition to 689
the amount of time that a trip would ordinarily take. Delays by traffic, 764
bad weather, and slow lift service consume a surprising amount of 830
time. In less congested localities and where the distances between 899
buildings are not great, it is well to allow for about five minutes' 969
leeway. 977
When something occurs that will prevent you from keeping an 1044
appointment altogether, you are expected to telephone at once and 1115
give your reason - either to the person with whom you have the 1185
appointment or to his secretary. You will have a far better chance of 1254
securing another appointment than you will if you call up after the 1323
hour when you were expected. 1342
When you know that you will be delayed at all - even for only a 1413
few minutes - telephone to the person's secretary and explain the 1480
delay. When you arrive, make your explanation to the person with 1547
whom you had the appointment, just in case his secretary may not 1612
have bothered to explain so short a delay; her boss will probably have 1683
noticed your lateness, even though he may not have mentioned it. 1748

WORDS: 350

## Exercise 279

**Type the exercise at right in duplicate. Use A6 paper (half that of A5). Then, type on the top copy your own data, and on the second copy those of a friend.**

NAME ..............................

ADDRESS ..........................

..........................

..........................

COUNTRY ..........................

## Exercise 280

**Type the following form letter in duplicate. Subsequently, address top copy to Mr B Richards, 5 Queen Court, Leeds LS2 9JT (inviting him to be present on 2nd July); and second copy to Miss Jane Riley, 90 Church Street, Leeds AS3 RU7 (to be present on 3rd July).**

WHW/VB/496 26th June, 19--

*Insert here the name and address of each recipient*

*For students with access to a word processor (see p 257) this exercise could be fed into it, recalled, printed out and, finally, the variables inserted.*

Dear *(Insert surname)*

I enclose a copy of the notes on the Presentation Ceremony which will be held on July at 5.00 p.m. May I emphasize that candidates should be in their seats not later than 4.45 p.m.

Yours sincerely,

## Exercise 184

Strokes

Manufacturers, wholesalers and jobbers list the prices of their 69
articles in catalogues. These catalogues are printed only once or twice 143
a year because they are very expensive. The prices listed in such 211
catalogues are generally very much higher than the market price. To 281
bring the catalogue or the list price down to the market price, the 349
seller offers the buyer a discount on the list price. This discount is 422
called 'trade discount'. Thus, if an item is listed at £50 and the trade 500
discount is 20%, the actual price to the buyer is £40. Since the trade 575
discount is used only for the purpose of finding out the 'invoice price' 650
of the goods neither the buyer nor the seller makes a record of the list 723
price or of the trade discount in any journal. 770

WORDS: 154

**The "inverted commas" are placed only at the beginning of each quoted paragraph and at the end of the last one.**

## Exercise 185

Gettysburg Address is the famous speech delivered by President 70
Abraham Lincoln at the dedication of the battlefield of Gettysburg as a 145
soldiers' cemetery, on November 19, 1863. This Address is universally 220
recognized not only as a classic model of the noblest kind of oratory, 291
but also as one of the most moving expressions of the democratic 356
spirit ever uttered. The text of the address is the following: 422
"Fourscore and seven years ago, our fathers brought forth on 491
this continent a new nation, conceived in liberty and dedicated to the 562
proposition that all men are created equal. 606
"Now we are engaged in a great civil war, testing whether that 677
nation, or any nation so conceived and so dedicated, can long endure. 747
We are met on a great battlefield of that war. We have come to 813
dedicate a portion of that field as a final resting place for those who 885
here gave their lives that that nation might live. It is altogether fitting 963
and proper that we should do this. 998
"But, in a larger sense, we cannot dedicate, we cannot 1060
consecrate, we cannot hallow this ground. The brave men, living and 1130
dead, who struggled here, have consecrated it far above our poor 1195
power to add or detract. The world will little note nor long remember 1267
what we say here but it can never forget what they did here. It is for 1341
us, the living, rather, to be dedicated here, to the unfinished work 1409
which they who fought here have thus far so nobly advanced. It is 1477
rather for us to be here dedicated to the great task remaining before 1547
us; that from these honoured dead we take increased devotion to that 1616
cause for which they gave the last full measure of devotion; that we 1685
here highly resolve that these dead shall not have died in vain; that 1755
this nation, under God, shall have a new birth of freedom, and that 1824
government of the people, by the people, for the people, shall not 1891
perish from the earth." 1916

WORDS: 383

# Form Letters and Forms

## FORM LETTERS

**Form letters are standardized letters used by enterprises to give routine information to a number of correspondents on such subjects as acknowledgement of orders or complaints, collection of debts, etc.**

## FILLING IN FORM LETTERS

When inserting details on a form letter you should take care to make the letter appear as if it were individually typed; specifically:

1. Type details in the correct position in order to ensure proper alignment.

2. Use the same typeface for the details and a similar colour of ribbon as those used in the form letter. *(If this is difficult to achieve use a contrasting colour to distinguish details from form letter.)*

## FILLING IN FORMS

When transferring information on a printed form:

1. Release the line finder so that you can bring the base of the typed characters *slightly* above the dotted line:

..slightly above..

not too high
...............

..nor.on.the.dots..

..nor.cutting.dots.through..

2. See that inserted matter is parallel with dotted line:

..parallel with line..

..not crossing it through..

3. If the form is typewritten: Find the correct position for the first line and follow the line spacing of the original; if the form is printed, use the line finder for finding the correct typing position for each line.

I should like .3. ticket(s) for the Sun
and enclose my remittance for £9.75

Name .BETTY S DONALDSON (MRS).....

Address .48 Ingleby Way...........

WALLINGTON.......................

SURREY SM6 9LR.......

Filling in a typewritten form

Foreign Report

A private intelligence report on world affairs

Published by The Economist

Please enter a subscription for 1 year (48 issues)

| | | |
|---|---|---|
| UK | £50.00 | [X] |
| Europe | £65.00 (US $150.00) | [ ] |
| Rest of world | £80.00 (US $180.00) | [ ] |

Your copies will be sent to you by first class post in the UK and by first class airmail outside the UK.

I undertake to respect Foreign Report's confidential character and have noted that in no circumstances may its contents be reproduced in whole or in part.

Signed A P Livingstone

Name Arthur P Livingstone

Address Principal, Newton College
Sunningdale Drive
STAFFORD ST17 OHT

**Payment** NFR40

I enclose cheque/money order for £50.00

Filling in a printed form

## TYPING FORMS

1. Show blank spaces with dotted lines; not with underscore, for these may cut through the sheet, especially the stencil.

2. Type dotted lines in single unspaced full stops, and use double line spacing.

3. To decide how much space to allow for the completion of a form, anticipate the answers of a typical respondent.

4. Allow one space to separate a dotted line from the word that precedes or follows.

## Exercise 186

Strokes

An auction is a public sale in which articles ranging from cows to 66
precious stones are sold to the person who offers to pay the most. The 139
would-be buyer — or bidder — must make a sign to show that he is 204
prepared to pay more than someone else and if he succeeds in out-bidding 277
other people, the auctioneer bangs a hammer three times to show that the 352
article has been sold. Each item or each group of items to be sold is called 431
a 'lot' and is given a special number. Needless to say, a good auctioneer 509
must have a strong voice and sharp eyes, and by his skill he can often 579
obtain a much higher price for articles than the owners expected. 644

WORDS: 129

**Towards the end of a speed test your nervous energy and mental concentration will sag. To build your stamina practise on 15 minutes continuous typing two or three times a week.**

## Exercise 187

With proper training an office worker will become faster and 66
more accurate, his methods will be standardised by his training and he 137
will usually require less supervision than otherwise. Although training 211
schemes may be expensive, they reduce costs ultimately, and this fulfils 284
a moral obligation of management to develop subordinates and gives 351
them chances of promotion. 377

From the worker's point of view, he is then prepared for 442
promotion, particularly where he has been trained to act as substitute 513
for others when they are absent. The clerk feels that he has a better 585
basis for his opinions, and he is more willing to co-operate with 651
management when desired. Incidentally, in the course of training, quite 725
a great deal can be learned about the trainees which may be of use in 795
their subsequent placing. 821

There are no real disadvantages to training, but there are 887
difficulties, and these must be recognised and avoided or minimised. In 961
the first place, training requires expenditure of both time and money; it 1035
cannot be done for nothing. Also, it must be recognised that during a 1107
training period work may become dislocated and the output may be 1172
reduced. A second and very important point is that an expert is not 1242
necessarily a good teacher, whereas a good teacher may not be a star 1311
performer himself. It is difficult to get the right type of person with all 1389
the qualities necessary for teaching, in which case it is better to 1457
arrange training outside the concern. 1495

Again, a training scheme must be linked with the promotion 1561
policy; it is unwise to train a member of staff for promotion where the 1633
vacancies are not likely to occur in sufficient numbers. Staff quickly 1706
become dissatisfied if this happens, and if staff leave after training, the 1782
management has lost all the time, money, and effort in having them 1849
trained. Training may inculcate standard working habits and perpetuate 1922
mediocre methods; opportunity should be given for trainees to improve 1992
on these methods. Lastly, if junior staff is trained, it must be realised 2068
that the brightest of them will aspire to senior posts, and the problems 2141
of the young supervising the old have to be considered. 2197

WORDS: 440

# Ruling – Horizontal and Vertical Lines

Horizontal rules are usually made with the typewriter. Vertical rules can be made by hand provided the colour of the pen matches that of the ribbon. This is called mixed ruling.

If the carriage of the typewriter takes the paper sideways, all lines may be made with the typewriter.

**Horizontal lines have been drawn with the typewriter**

**Vertical lines have been drawn by hand**

## Ruling with the typewriter

Type first the horizontal lines; then, turn paper sideways and type the vertical lines.

NOTE: The two underscores which form an angle must coincide - not overlap.

**underscores coinciding**

**underscores overlapping**

## Ruling on platen with a pen

Insert the point of a pen into one of the holes of the card holder (or on the typebar guide above the ribbon).

For horizontal lines, move the carriage sideways; for vertical lines, release the line finder and turn platen forwards or backwards.

NOTE: Do not press pen too hard; it may tear the paper.

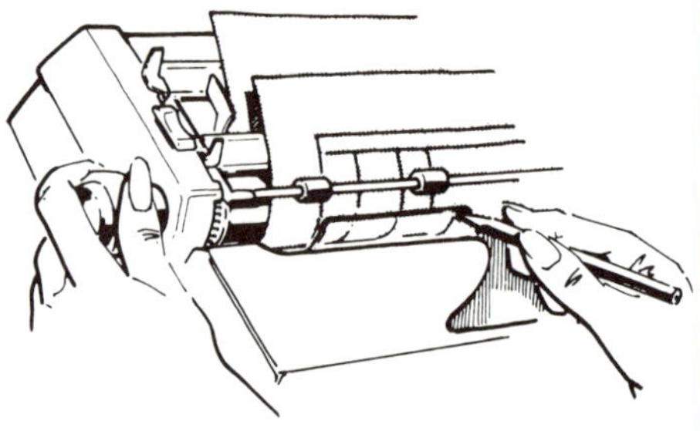

## Ruling with a pen and ruler

Before removing typescript from machine insert light pencil dots (or full stops lightly impressed) as guides to mark the desired line ends. Remove paper from typewriter and, using a ruler, draw the lines from dot to dot.

NOTE: When ruling top and carbon copies together clip the four corners of the work so that the carbons will not move during ruling.

**Guide marks should not be visible; switch ribbon to neutral position before striking them.**

## Exercise 277

**Repeat the following card ruling with ball point pen.**

Lilian Wilson, M.A.
Economist

## Exercise 278

**Copy the following account ruling with the typewriter**

Dr Cash Account Cr

| | | | |
|---|---|---|---|
| Sales | 3100 | Wages | 520 |
| Debtors | 627 | Rent | 415 |

# International Paper Sizes

The following ten paper sizes - known as International Paper Sizes (IPS) - are widely used today. They are based on a rectangle 841 x 1189 mm, called A0, which retains the proportions of the original each time it is halved.

Half the size of A0 is A1 (594 x 841 mm)
Half the size of A1 is A2 (420 x 594 mm)
Half the size of A2 is A3 (297 x 420 mm)
Half the size of A3 is A4 (210 x 297 mm)
Half the size of A4 is A5 (148 x 210 mm)
Half the size of A5 is A6 (105 x 148 mm)
Half the size of A6 is A7 ( 74 x 105 mm)

*Sizes A8, A9 and A10 are not of any particular interest.*

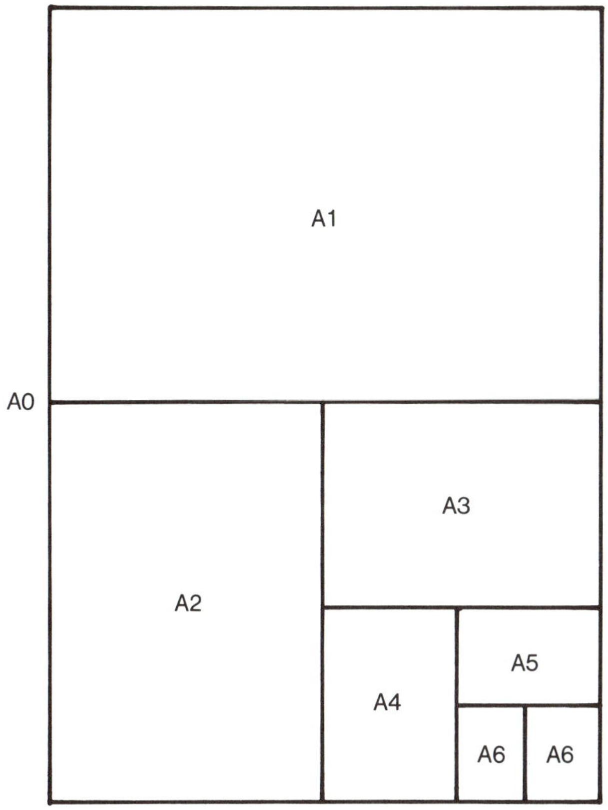


**Relative size of paper A0, A1, A2, A3, A4, A5 and A6**

## USES OF THE VARIOUS SIZES

A4 is used for business letters, long memorandums, agendas, minutes of meetings, tabulated statements, literary work, reports, specifications, long invoices, etc.

A5 is used for ordinary-size memorandums, debit and credit notes, and short invoices, letters, notices, etc.

Two-thirds A4 is used for documents which are too small for A4 and too large for A5.

A6 is used for postcards, index cards and receipts.

A7 is used for compliment slips, business cards, index cards, and labels.

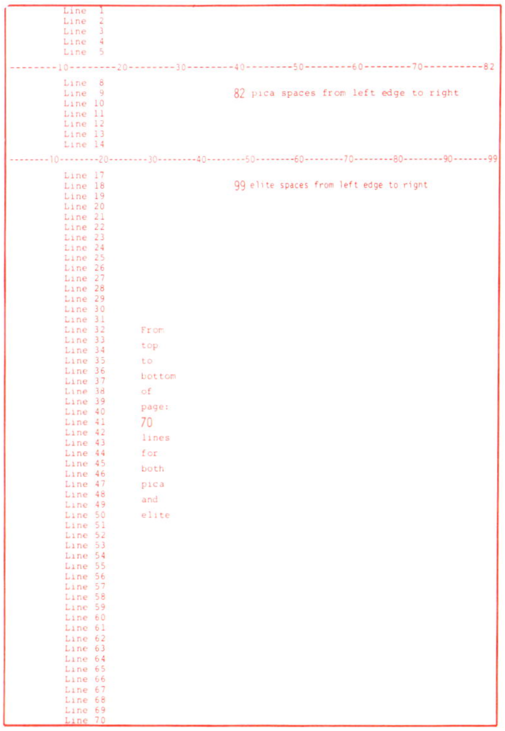


**Reduced A4 size**

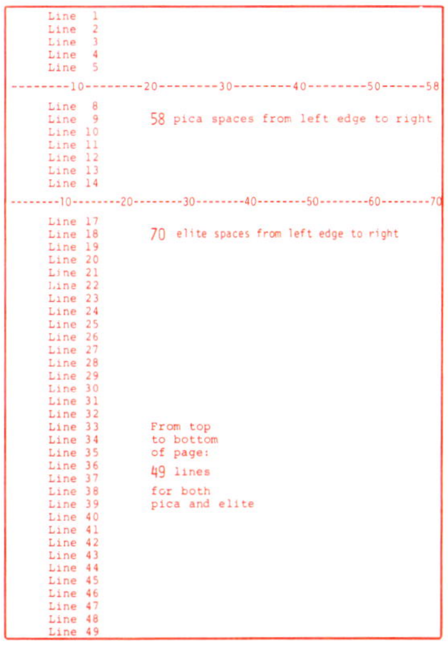


**Reduced A5 size (portrait)**

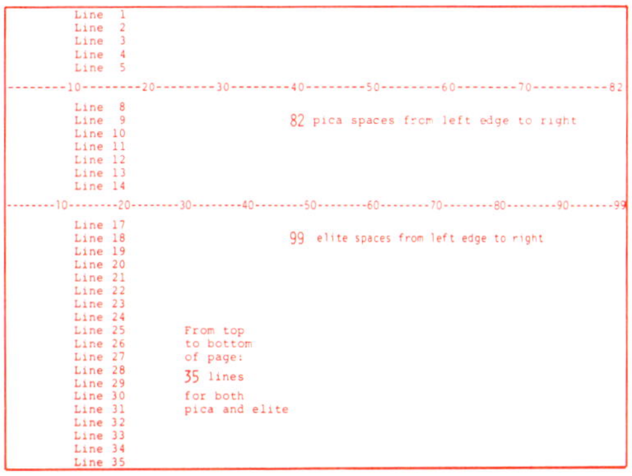


**Reduced A5 size (landscape)**

# Exercise 276

**Civil Service letters are typed on paper A4 or A5, in blocked or semi-blocked style and in open punctuation.**

**Foreign and Commonwealth Office**
London SW1A 2AH

**Telephone 01-**

J R Venning Esq
British High Commission
NICOSIA

**Your reference**
INF 312/1
**Our reference**
PBE 312/441/1
**Date**
11 April 1980

Dear Venning,

INFORMATION EXPENDITURE 1980-81

1. Your approved Information Budget for / the year 1980-81 is attached. I hope you will find the notes useful.

2. We appreciate your efforts to hold down expenditure, and will be quite prepared to restore the reductions you have made should it be necessary during the course of the year. In that event, however, would you be good enough to give us prior warning as requested in paragraph 3 of our estimates letter.

Yours ever

RA Brown

R A Brown
Information Policy
Department

# Display of Typing Work

**Display is the even spreading of typing work over the paper so as to present a pleasing effect.**

Artistic display involves symmetry both in horizontal and vertical positioning of the text. Therefore, it is important that you should be well acquainted with the number of horizontal spaces and vertical lines in each size of paper, as shown on previous page.

## How to Centre Horizontally

**A. Between equal margins**

Assuming you want to type the heading INTERNATIONAL TYPEWRITING. Insert sheet between 0 and 82(99) which is the width of A4 paper (figures in brackets apply to elite machines); move carriage to the centre 41(49); keep your eyes on the words to be centred and backspace once for every two letters, including blank spaces. You will thus arrive at space 29(37); and this is the starting point.

**Alternatively:** Count the letters+space of the heading - in this case 25. Deduct it from 82(99) - the width of A4 paper - and divide answer by two (ignoring fractions). This will give you 28.5 for pica (say 29) and 36.5 for elit (say 37). Commence typing at this point.

*Centre of paper*

*29(37)* *41(49)*

INTERNATIONAL TYPEWRITING

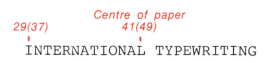

**B. Between unequal margins**

The same heading will now be typed in the centre of unequal margins, say 15(25) and 75(85). To find the new centre, add the margin-stop settings: 15 + 75 = 90 (25 + 85 = 110), and divide by two: 45(54). Move to this point and backspace once for each pair of letters+space.

**Alternatively:** Add the margin-stop settings: 15 + 75 = 90 (25 + 85 = 110). From this total deduct 25, which is the number of letters+space of heading and you have 65(85). Half of 65 (for pica) is 32.5 (say 33); half of 85 (for elite) is 42.5 (say 43); therefore, the new starting point is 33(43).

*Centre of line*

*33(43)* *45(54)*

INTERNATIONAL TYPEWRITING

To centre more than one line use the same procedure. It will help if you remove margin stops to the extreme ends and set a tab in the centre of paper to use for each line.

**Alternatively:** You can centre each additional line according to its length in relation to the previous line. For example: If the second line is six characters wider than the first, divide six by two - which gives 3 spaces - and backspace three times from where you started the previous line.

## How to Centre Vertically

To centre vertically is to allow equal top and bottom margins. Procedure: 1. Count all lines (including blank line spaces) to be centred. 2. Subtract them from total number of line spaces in sheet, i.e. 70 in A4 and 49 in A5 (or 35 if A5 is used sideways). 3. Divide answer by two (if result is odd, allocate remaining space to the bottom margin).

NOTE: Between a heading and its text always allow an extra line.

# Civil Service Letters

## SPECIAL POINTS TO NOTE

*(See the sample letter on page 175 — Exercise 276)*

**1. Printed parallel lines.** Below the printed letterhead there are two printed parallel lines, about 3 cm apart, extending from margin to margin. Within these lines there should be typed the *inside name and address* on the left-hand margin, and the *references* and *date* at the right-hand side (beginning two-thirds across the typing line).

**2. Margins.** These are indicated by the printed horizontal lines referred to above. Their width is 6-7 pica (8-9 elite) at left, and 4-5 pica (5-6 elite) at right.

**3. Subject heading.** As with the business letter but always in capitals.

**4. Salutation.** This starts two spaces beneath the bottom horizontal line. For formal letters 'Sir' or 'Madam' are preferred, while for informal correspondence 'Dear Sir', 'Dear Madam', 'Dear Jones' etc.

NB In interdepartmental correspondence the Salutation and the Complimentary Close are inserted in ink.

**5. Paragraphs.** Subject paragraphs begin at the margin and are introduced with arabic numbers followed by a full stop and three spaces. Sub-paragraphs are usually indented five spaces to the right; they are introduced with letters of the alphabet and are also followed by a full stop and three spaces. Example:

```
1.   -----------------------------------
----------------------------------------
----------------------------------------
----------------------------------------

     a.   ------------------------------
     -----------------------------------
     -----------------------------------

     b.   ------------------------------
     -----------------------------------
     -----------------------------------
```

NB In interdepartmental Civil Service letters all paragraphs should be numbered.

**6. Signature.** If the signatory is a woman her marital status (Mrs/Miss/Ms) should be typed **before** her name.

**7. Enclosures.** As with business letter but as a rule they should indicate the enclosed documents. Alternatively, a 'solidus' is typed in the left-hand margin against each line where mention is made of an enclosure. (See 2nd line of letter on following page.)

**8. Security classifications.** Such classifications as SECRET, CONFIDENTIAL, etc. are usually pre-printed or added with a rubber stamp. If not, they should be typed in capitals in the centre of the top and bottom margins of each page.

**9. Continuation sheets.** A long letter is continued on the back; the width of margins should be reversed (narrow at left, wide at right) and the typing lines superimposed. If a third page is needed, it will be necessary to number both the second and the third; on the new sheet, however, you will type the addressee's name, the reference and the date. Example of a third page (top part):

```
J R Venning Esq
PBE 312/441/1
11 April 1980

3

xxxxxxxxxxxxxxxxxxxxxxxxxxxxxxxxxxxxxxxxxx
xxxxxxxxxxxxxxxxxxxxxxxxxxxxxxxxxxxxxxxxxx
xxxxxxxxxxxxxxxxxxxxxxxxxxxxxxxxxxxxxxxxxx
xxxxxxxxxxxxxxxxxxxxxxxxxxxxxxxxxxxxxxxxxx
```

**10. Catchword.** Below the last line of the previous page it is usual to type a **CATCHWORD**, i.e. the first word to appear on the next page.

Example:

```
to return herewith the form for your

                          /information
```

NOTES:
1. In the body of Civil Service letters all numbers are typed in figures, except number 'one'; also when a number begins a sentence.

2. Civil Service letters are usually enclosed in 'window' envelopes except when they bear a security classification.

## Exercise 188

*Type a 3-inch line (30 pica or 36 elite strokes); locate its middle point, and centre the heading opposite on it.*

Typing Display

## Exercise 189

*Type in double-line spacing the information opposite, centring each line horizontally.*

The name of your school
The street address
The town and the country
Your name in full

## Exercise 190

*On A5 paper, landscape (i.e. with longer side up), centre horizontally the following letterhead. Start on the eighth line from top.*

THE LONDON CHAMBER OF COMMERCE AND INDUSTRY

COMMERCIAL EDUCATION SCHEME

Marlowe House, Station Road, Sidcup, Kent DA15 7BJ

## Exercise 191

*Centre horizontally and vertically on A5 paper, portrait, (i.e. with shorter side up). List the lines in alphabetical order.*

**The extended or indented letters of a line should be equal - in relation to the previous line.**

**To avoid odd letters allow two spaces between any two words in a line.**

SOME ECONOMIC ORGANIZATIONS

Central American Common Market
European Free Trade Association
Alliance for Progress
West African Regional Group
Asian and Pacific Council
Benelux Economic Union
European Economic Community
East African Common Market

## Exercise 192

*Type in double-line spacing this corrected invitation on A5 landscape, and centre both horizontally and vertically.*

Dr. and Mrs. K. ~~Bell~~ Sutherland
request the pleasure of ~~the~~ your company ~~of~~
Mr. and Mrs. B Johnson
at a ~~drinks~~ cocktail party
on ~~Thursday~~ Friday, 9th July 198~~1~~2 ~~between~~ from 7.30 ~~and~~ to 9.30 p.m.

# Exercise 275

SPECIMEN

PERSONAL LETTER

(Friendly nature)

in

indented style

194 Westminster Road,
Burn Bridge,
Harrogate,
Yorkshire.

17th April, 198-

Dear Elsie,

We arrived home safely on Monday reaching Harrogate at five thirty in the evening. A very comfortable journey as there were only about a third of the normal passenger quota travelling on the plane.

All our friends tell us how fortunate we were not to have experienced the coldest Easter weather for forty years! Certainly there are very few signs of Spring around as yet; the daffodils which were just in bud as we left home for our holiday are only now beginning to bloom.

The children are back at school and Peter is hard at work at the Institute though term does not commence till next Thursday.

Peter joins me in sending our thanks for the wonderful holiday we have just spent with you in Cyprus. It gave us special pleasure to be accepted as part of the family. As you must surely know, we thoroughly enjoyed every minute of the visit and have come home refreshed and with a host of happy memories.

We hope the whole family is in good health and wish you all the best.

With love,
Caroline

**POINTS TO NOTE:**

1. Use plain paper (no business letterhead).
2. Type sender's address 4 to 6 lines from top of paper using 1.5 spacing. Begin first line about two-thirds across typing line indenting each subsequent line 3 to 5 spaces.
3. 'Salutation' and 'complimentary close' are not typed; they are completed in ink by signatory.
4. In continuation sheets type only page number; name of addressee and date are omitted.
5. Margins range between 5 and 10 pica (6 and 12 elite) spaces.

## Exercise 193

*Type the following text noting carefully its contents*

METHODS OF TYPING
PARAGRAPHS AND SUB-PARAGRAPHS

This is an example of an "indented" paragraph. The first line is indented five spaces (six elite) to the right while all subsequent lines commence at the left-hand margin.

2. This one is an example of a "numbered indented" paragraph. It is similar to the previous one except for the number which is typed at the margin followed by a full stop and three spaces (four elite).

3. This is another example of a numbered indented paragraph - in fact, a sub-paragraph. The number is typed at the margin while the text is indented five spaces with an additional indentation of five spaces for the first line.

(4) This is again a "numbered indented" sub-paragraph similar to the previous one. The only difference is that the number at margin is enclosed in brackets, instead of followed by a full stop. You will now allow two spaces after the final bracket before the main body of the paragraph.

(i) An example of a "blocked" paragraph or sub-paragraph. The opening bracket is typed at the margin while all lines of the text - including the first one - start five spaces to the right of the margin or two spaces after the closing bracket.

(ii) This is the same style of "blocked" sub-paragraph as the above. However, the opening bracket has been backspaced into the margin in order to keep the closing bracket in line with that of (i) above.

(a) This is an example of a "hanging" sub-paragraph (see also p 56). The first line is typed in exactly the same way as for a blocked paragraph. All the subsequent lines are typed in blocked form but are indented two or three spaces from the first line.

<u>Note</u>

The numbering of sub-paragraphs may commence at the margin (as in the examples above) or alternatively it may commence five spaces to the right of the margin. It will help, therefore, if you set two or three tabular stops at five space intervals from the margin.

When typing sub-paragraphs remember to move the right-hand margin at least five spaces backwards in order to give your work a balanced appearance.

# Personal Letters

Personal letters may be of a business or a friendly nature. Depending on their length they can be typed on A4 or A5 paper size, in blocked, semi-blocked or indented style.

## Exercise 274

SPECIMEN

PERSONAL LETTER

(Business nature)

in

semi-blocked

style

135 Dorryn Court
Trewsbury Road
Sydenham
LONDON
SB1 4LB

28 September 198-

Prof. Anthony Rudkin
University of Liverpool
LIVERPOOL
L16 4WN

My dear Professor

I regret very much that an unexpected but necessary change in my plans will make it impossible for me to attend the meeting of the Lancashire Teachers' Association at Manchester.

I sincerely hope that my inability to be present will not put you to any serious inconvenience, and that you will readily succeed in finding someone to take my place on the program.

Please be assured that I would not disappoint you in this way if circumstances did not make it imperative for me to be elsewhere.

Yours sincerely

### POINTS TO NOTE:

1. Type on plain paper - although headed paper may be used.
2. Start sender's address 4 to 6 lines from top of paper, using either single or 1.5 spacing.
3. Set tab stop at about two-thirds across typing line and use it for positioning *sender's address, date* and *complimentary close.*
4. Continuation sheets follow the procedure used in ordinary business letters.
5. The envelope is headed 'Personal' so that it will be opened by the addressee himself.

## Exercise 194

*Type the following text noting carefully its contents*

HEADINGS AND SUB-HEADINGS

Headings can be typed in various styles: Centred or blocked, in closed or spaced capitals, in lower case with initial capitals, with or without underscoring.

MAIN HEADINGS

A main heading is typed at least six line spaces from the top of the paper. However, it often starts a few lines lower down - known as "dropped head".

If closed capitals are used for a main heading you may leave one or two spaces between its words; but if spaced capitals are used you should leave three spaces between each word. Underscoring a main heading is a matter of personal taste.

If the text is typed in single-line spacing separate it from the heading with two line spaces; but if the text is in double-line spacing separate it from the heading with three line spaces.

The vertical spacing between the lines of a main heading varies according to the nature of work. In the example below there are 1½ spaces between first and second lines, and two vertical spaces between second and third lines.

SUB-HEADINGS

Where the main heading is typed in spaced capitals the sub-heading should be typed in closed capitals; but where the main heading is typed in closed capitals the sub-heading should be in lower case with initial capitals.

L E D R A   P A L A C E   H O T E L

NICOSIA - CYPRUS

Lunch Menu

T H E   H I L T O N   H O T E L

NICOSIA - CYPRUS

Lunch Menu

SHOULDER HEADINGS

These are used mainly for sub-headings in a text that bears a main heading. Shoulder headings commence at the left-hand margin and are never followed by a full stop. They are separated from the text with one line of space.

Shoulder Headings

This is an example of a shoulder heading typed in lower case with initial capitals and underscored. It can also be typed in closed capitals without underscoring, as shown in the paragraph above. The text under a shoulder heading may be blocked or indented.

**Exercise 273** Display the following memorandum, using today's date. (Part of LCCI examination paper LC/53/Sp78 - Higher.)

MEMORANDUM

To Mr E. Chippindale (Aircraft Section) Ref. FLPT/Sp/78/3

From (General Manager) Mr H. Rawlings

AIRCRAFT PREMIUMS

I am preparing the draft of a new pamphlet covering all our activities and it is hoped that this will be ready for publication at the end of the year.

[run on/] Naturally, the part devoted to aircraft business in the old leaflet will be [substantially] retained, but a short section on jets should now be fitted in. Will you please read through the following, amend if and where necessary, and return to me.

When the [wide-bodied] jets were first introduced, being a new type of aircraft with highly insured values, they were specially rated until they had proved themselves as safe aircraft. Experience with these aircraft in the early years was very satisfactory, with the result that [premium] rates started to fall sharply, and these aircraft are now insured at normal rates.

[NP/] In the same way, a special rating has been applied on the hull insurance of Concorde. If all goes well this should be cleared up shortly. British Airways has arranged insurance for its Concordes on [an] value agreed [trs/] basis for £21m. Only a proportion of the risk[, however,] is covered under the main fleet policy.

Paragraph Headings. This is an example of a paragraph heading. It is typed in lower case, and it is underscored. A full stop is optional; if used, it should be followed by two or three spaces.

PARAGRAPH HEADINGS A paragraph heading may be typed in closed capitals and, preferably, underscored. Paragraph headings usually commence at the left-hand margin; they may, however, be indented five spaces to the right (six elite).

MARGINAL HEADINGS This is an example of a marginal heading - also called "side heading". The preferred style is in closed capitals without underscoring, although lower case with initial capitals may be employed.

Marginal headings commence at the left-hand margin and are separated from the text by two or three horizontal spaces. The subject matter may be blocked or indented.

When typing this style of paragraph set the left-hand margin stop where the lines of the text will begin and move the carriage back for the typing of marginal headings by depressing the margin release key.

## Exercise 195

*Display the following on A5 paper, portrait, in the indented style. Margins 1.5 cm wide for pica or 2 cm for elite pitch. Use double-line spacing. Start heading 8 lines from top of paper.*

Partnership Accounts [Spaced Caps]

Retirement of a Partner [Closed Caps]

Profit Share

It often happens that a partner retires during the course of a normal accounting period. He will be entitled in the ordinary way to his share of profits, including interest on capital, if any, to the date of retirement. This will be ascertained by:

1. Drawing up accounts to the actual date of retirement, or
2. Drawing up accounts for the full normal accounting period and splitting them into the (a) pre- and (b) post-retirement period.

[single-spaced]

The former method is the more satisfactory, but circumstances may prevent this being carried out. In regard to the second method the procedure is the following: . . .

## Exercise 272

**Type a copy of the following memorandum. Insert today's date and the reference MHM/Sp/79/M1/1. Leave a 3 cm top margin. (Part of LCCI examination paper LC/54/M1/Sp79 - Intermediate.)**

MEMORANDUM

To All District Representatives Date

From The Sales Manager Ref

DISCUSSION - EXHIBITION IN BIRMINGHAM ENGLAND IN JULY

There will be a meeting at this office to discuss
lc the forthcoming exhibition at 1400 hours on
25 May 1979.

(Spaced Caps) → AGENDA

1 Rota ~~to be agreed~~ for manning our stand for the week.

2 Final decision ~~with regard to~~ about the slide sequence to be shown on the stand.

NP [We shall need to run through the commentary to be used for the slide sequence and decide whether to ~~have~~ (add) music.

If you have any other items you wish to be added to the agenda, please let my secretary have details of
NP them by 21 May. [Enclosed is the list of area ~~representatives~~ of our Company in the United Kingdom. This list should prove useful when we commence our tour after the Exhibition.
(representatives)

Enclosure

## Exercise 196

*Type the following exercise paying particular attention to the headings and the paragraphs. Set tab stops in units of six (five for pica). Note that sub-paragraphs end a few spaces before the right-hand margin.*

II. AIMS OF THE CONVENTION

Article 2

1. The Contracting States intend to contribute through their joint action both to the promotion of the active co-operation of all the countries in the European region in the cause of peace and international understanding and to the . . . .

2. The Contracting States solemnly declare their firm resolve within the framework of their legislation and constitutional structures to co-operate closely with a view to:

(a) enabling the educational and research resources available to them to be used as effectively as possible in the interests of all the Contracting States, and, for this purpose:

(i) to make their higher educational institutions as widely accessible as possible to students or researchers from any of the Contracting States;

Six-space indentation

Six-space indentation

(ii) to recognize the studies, certificates, diplomas, and degrees of such persons; . . .

(b) constantly improving curricula in the Contracting States and methods of planning and promoting higher education, on the basis of not only the requirements for economic, social and cultural development, the policies of each country and . . . ;

(c) promoting regional and world-wide co-operation in the matter of the recognition of studies and academic qualifications.

3. The Contracting States agree to take all feasible steps at the national, bilateral and multilateral levels, in particular by means of bilateral, sub-regional, regional or other agreements, arrangements with the competent national or international organizations and other bodies, with a view to the progressive attainment of the goals defined in the present article.

III. UNDERTAKINGS FOR IMMEDIATE APPLICATION

Article 3

1. The Contracting States agree to give recognition, as defined in Article 1, paragraph 1 to secondary school leaving certificate and other diplomas issued in the other Contracting States that grant access to higher education with a . . . .

2. Admission to a given higher educational institution may, however, be dependent on the availability of places and also the conditions concerning linguistic knowledge required in order profitably to undertake the studies in question.

## Exercise 271

**Type a copy of the following memorandum in double-line spacing inserting today's date and the reference MHM/LCSm/80. Leave a top margin of 6 cm. (Part of LCCI examination paper LC/54/S/Sp80 - Intermediate.)**

MEMORANDUM

To The Accountant Date

From The Managing Director Ref

VISIT OF MR J R THOMAS FROM LONDON

Mr Thomas of Medico Services Limited is coming out here next month for three weeks, arriving on
uc 4 ~~July~~ June. ~~when~~ he will be touring around seeing prospective sites for the construction of the new
uc medical centre for which the government has given him sanction to tender. Please would you [redacted] that you are free during ~~those dates~~ that period and also ~~I should be grateful if~~ would you ~~could~~ make out a list of prospective sites for Mr Thomas to visit.

I should also like him to have a copy of the rules regarding foreign ~~firms~~ companies registering [redacted] in [redacted] Singapore. I shall be writing to him tomorrow and should like to enclose ~~these~~ this with my letter, so may I (please) have the rules on my desk first thing in the morning.

ensure

**Allow four line spaces from top of paper and type your name and the date in the right-hand corner; e.g.**

Elizabeth Williamson, 15 April 1982.

# More Manuscripts and Typescripts

This and the following 12 pages will give you further practice on graded manuscripts and typescripts. Out of these, pages 96-103 are London Chamber of Commerce and Industry's assignments.

As manuscripts often include abbreviations it will help if you learn at least the most common ones so that you can type them out in full whenever you come across them. Some of these abbreviations will follow in three sets in the form of tabulator drills. (Note that a few generally accepted abbreviations, such as 'i.e.', 'viz.' etc. keep always their abbreviated form.)

## Exercise 197

**Set margin at 8(10) and tab stops at 33(39) and 55(66). Centre the heading.**

SIMPLE ABBREVIATIONS - I

| | | | | | |
|---|---|---|---|---|---|
| A/c | Account | Ad | Advertisement | Agt | Agent; against |
| Amt | Amount | Assn | Association | Asst | Assistant |
| Bal. | Balance | B/d | Brought down | B/E | Bill of Exchange |
| B/f | Brought forward | B/L | Bill of Lading | B.S. | Balance Sheet |
| Cr. | Credit | C/d | Carried down | C/f | Carried forward |

## Exercise 198

**Type the following sentences rendering in full all abbreviated words. Left-hand margin 15(20).**

1. The amt b/d on the cr. side of the Expense a/c is shown in the B.S. as an asset.

2. The seller does not release the B/L until the B/E is accepted by the buyer.

3. An agt informs us that there has been no response to our ad. for an asst manager for the assn.

4. Since receipts exceeded payments during 1981 the cash balance c/f to 1982 should be greater than the cash bal. b/f in the beginning of 1981.

**Exercise 270** **Type the following memorandum, using today's date and the reference FLPT/M/80/3. (Part of LCCI examination paper LC/53/M/Sp80 - Higher.)**

M E M O R A N D U M

| | | |
|---|---|---|
| To | Personnel Manager | Ref |
| From | Director | Date |

SELECTION OF EXECUTIVES

modern

Following our discussion last week about [redacted] replacements
[redacted] in several departments and [redacted] extra
UC/ staff needed in the business machines sector, I have been
considering the question of all our advertising, [redacted]
particularly with regard to the appointment of [redacted] senior
NP/ executives. I do not wish to follow the practice of having
outside consultants find our executives but there is scope
for a new approach to our press advertisements. The old
tradition of offering "a responsible position with good
prospects for men of drive and initiative" is fading, [redacted]
largely because such advertisements have brought a flood
trs/ of enquiries from unqualified or unsuitable [redacted] men.

Accordingly, I feel that we must define in detail what our
executives will be expected to do and to measure future
responsibilities of posts more accurately.

Furthermore, we must be prepared to allot [redacted]
far more time to candidates' interviews and arrange [redacted]
tests which will enable us more easily to measure a man's
total make-up against the demands of a particular job. Once
we have [redacted] described and evaluated a particular job it
should be simple enough to draft an appropriate advertisement
for display.

future

I would like you to prepare a draft for discussion.

## Exercise 199

Set margin at 10(12) and tab stops at 35(42) and 57(68). Centre the heading.

SIMPLE ABBREVIATIONS - II

| | | | | | |
|---|---|---|---|---|---|
| C/N | Credit Note | Contg | Containing | Dept | Department |
| Dis. | Discount | D/N | Debit Note | Enc. | Enclosure |
| Folg | Following | Fwd | Forward | Inst. | Instant |
| Inv. | Invoice | L/C | Letter of Credit | M.O. | Money Order |

## Exercise 200

Type the following sentences rendering in full all abbreviated words. Left-hand margin 15(20).

1 Since we have not received the L/C from your Bank we should suggest that you pay us by M.O.

2 We should fwd a D/N as soon as possible, in order to correct the undercharge on the inv. we issued on 15 inst.

3 We wish to apologise on behalf of the Packing Dept for rendering you a case contg defective shirts. For their value you will find a C/N among the encs. We have decided to give you a special 5% dis on the first 20 boxes you may purchase during the folg month.

## Exercise 201

Type the following manuscript in the blocked style, using double spacing. Centre heading over the page. Left-hand margin 15(25).

Good will letters

A good will letter – as its name implies – is not written for an order, or to answer an enquiry or to collect a bill. It is intended to pay for itself in another ~~a new~~ way by building good will. Businessmen would use letters of good will more often if there were some direct way of measuring their value but this is difficult. Surely it is worth something to you to have ~~pleased~~ your customers pleased with the feeling that they are getting a bit of extra attention. The trouble is that good will has always been difficult to evaluate.

## Exercise 202

Re-type the above passage in the indented style, using single-line spacing. Widen the left margin by five (six) spaces and centre heading over the lines.

## Exercise 269

**Type the following internal memorandum, using today's date. (Part of LCCI examination paper LC/53/Su78 - Higher.)**

INTERNAL MEMORANDUM

TO Planning Director

FROM Sales Manager

once quite a strong feature of the European industry.

NEW REGISTRATIONS OF NEW GOODS VEHICLES

I have managed to unearth some figures on this subject,
stet/ following our discussion meeting last Thursday, and these
have been prepared in tabular form for you. [redacted] From a
stet/ study of the figures list you will no doubt draw the same
conclusion as I have, namely, that the Japanese companies
seem to have continued to dominate pick-up manufacturing
on a world scale, Of course, where they have scored most
is in the United States where there is a large market for
open, these [redacted] vehicles. rugged

A NEW TECHNICAL APPROACH?

I feel that we must now give great attention to a new
technical approach. The penetration achieved by a fast,
lively vehicle which handles more like a car than a truck
and has been taken up by owner-drivers who spend a lot of
time in the van themselves, is something we should now bear [redacted]
in mind. The manufacturers of this particular [redacted] vehicle
have also [redacted] followed the path of so-called "value
engineering" and now produce cheap vehicles with no special claim to
longevity.

the Transit,

## Exercise 203

**Set margins and tab stops as in Exercise 199**

SIMPLE ABBREVIATIONS - III

| | | | | | |
|---|---|---|---|---|---|
| MS | Manuscript | MSS | Manuscripts | P & L | Profit & Loss |
| Pd | Paid | Pkg | Package | P.O. | Postal Order |
| p | Page | pp | Pages | Recd | Received |
| Regd | Registered | Shd | Should | Thrfr | Therefore |
| Thro | Through | Wd | Would | Yr | Your or year |

## Exercise 204

**Type the following sentences rendering in full all abbreviations. Left-hand margin 20(25).**

1. We have recd the pkg you sent by regd mail containing a MS of 300 pp.

2. We shd be obliged if you wd send us a P.O. for the amt we have pd to have yr MSS printed.

3. I have not read thro the report carefully; thrfr, I shd like to comment only on the P & L A/c on p. 15.

## Exercise 205

**Type the following manuscript in the blocked style, using double-line spacing. Margins: 20(30) spaces wide.**

The Right Diet → (Centre)

The right amts of the right foods at the right times of the day will give you the wonderful feeling of well-being. It is good to know that the normal daily diet shd include foods from each of four groups: Milk, meat, fruit vegetables and bread-cereal. These are the real building blocks of a good diet. Other foods, of course, will come in to round them out: Butter and other fats and oils, sugars, seasonings and flavourings, and refined bread and cereal products.

## Exercise 206

**Re-type the above passage in the indented style, using single-line spacing. Left-hand margin 20 spaces, right-hand 10. Centre heading over the lines.**

**Exercise 268** Type a copy of the following memorandum. The main part is to be typed in single-line spacing. Insert today's date. (Part of LCCI examination paper LC/54/S/Sp77 - Intermediate.)

M E M O R A N D U M

---

To Finance Director

From Chief Accountant Date

OFFSHORE CENTRES

I have now ascertained some facts for your information.

Singapore has ~~made even more sure of~~ consolidated its lead as the major local financial centre in the Far East. However, The advancement of the Asian dollar market has slowed ~~rather a lot~~ considerably. It now amounts to S$11 billion. This sum is still small when compared with the Euromarket's size.

uc trs lc Twnety-one licences have been issued since 1973, During 1975 the Royal Bank of Canada, Morgan Guaranty and the Swiss Bank Corporation were among those granted off-shore licences. For the first time in 1975, Singapore dollar certificates of deposit were issued. Since then a number of money brokers have opened offices.

## Exercise 207

Type the following with the indented method, using double-line spacing. Remember that the indentation of the first line requires five pica or six elite spaces. Margin stops 15-67 (20-77).

TERMS OF PAYMENT

Many firms lay down definite terms of payment and they expect their customers to abide by these them; terms but special arrangements may be made in certain cases. The purchaser should, however, pay his accounts at whatever due date is arranged. It is unwise to gain a reputation for slow payment, as this makes it more difficult to obtain consideration when actual need to delay payment for a time arises.

**Check the typescript before removing it from the machine.**
**Ensure that spelling is correct, particularly that of unfamiliar words.**

## Exercise 208

**Use the blocked method. Allow double-line spacing. When you finish the passage correct the mistakes, using the established correction signs, and re-type in single-line spacing. Margin stops at 10-75 (15-85).**

Early Rising (Spaced Caps)

Much has been written on the subject of early rising. from bed. Even more has been said about it but that had better be skipped. We all know that scattered through the land there exists a small and dwindling race of super men and women who moved by some strange odd impulse, spring lightly out of their warm beds, and at some zero hour, even upon the darkest and coldest of winter mornings, without so much as giving a thought to shivering or showing the least desire to yawn.

Some of these stalwarts even find a noisy and persistent alarm clock placed well out of reach quite an unnecessary spur to their activity. How they manage to wake up awaken without warning is a great mystery; but how, immediately on awakening, they can leap from their snug beds into the morning chilly air, is an even greater one.

## Exercise 266

**Type the following memorandum using reference EL/KN/81. Use a different style of layout from that used in the previous memo.**

To: all Employees. From: General Manager. Date: . . . . .
Subject: Staff Canteen Prices. I am pleased to be able to tell you that we have managed to keep down the price of set meals in the Staff Canteen. The standard charge will remain at 35p, though we cannot promise to maintain this figure in the face of continually
N.P./ rising costs. [Bon appetit!

## Exercise 267

**On A4 paper type the following two memos and then halve the sheet. Both memos are being sent today by the General Manager to all the Firm's employees. Use different styles of layout.**

(1) Subject: Christmas Bonus In appreciation of the hard work done by you during the past year the Board of Directors have decided to award a Christmas Bonus as follows:

| | | |
|---|---|---|
| Service up to 5 years | | £50 |
| " 5 to ~~ten~~ 10 | " | £100 |
| " over ~~ten~~ 10 | " | £150 |

I would like to take this opportunity of wishing you a ~~Prosp~~ Happy Xmas.

(2) FUEL SHORTAGE Because of the shortage of fuel, staff are asked to do
N.P./ their best to economize. [Hot water should be used sparingly, and staff should make sure that taps are fully turned off. Please switch off heating and lights in rooms not in use during the day. Windows must be shut before staff leave at night, in order to conserve heat.
Any money saved by these economies will be used to improve the facilities in the staff rest room.

## Exercise 209

**Type on A5 paper, portrait, in indented style. One-and-a-half-line spacing. Margins 15(18) and 70(85).**

Body Exercise

Exercise is essential if sound sleep is to be enjoyed. Much attention is wisely given by some ~~people~~ to indoor exercises, such as those for (moulding or reducing) the figure. What ever their nature, exercises should be done before an open window, or better still, in the open air. (N.P.) The best exercise is ~~the one~~ that taken out of doors in the form of play or work. A man with a ~~sexde~~ sedentary occupation will do well to spend each evening at least half an hour in the garden. Walking also is an excellent form of exercise. It should be a walk brisk enough to make the heart beat faster and the lungs breathe more freely.

## Exercise 210

**Type on A5 paper (landscape), in blocked style. Double-line spacing. Margins at 10-75 (15-85).**

Correcting the boss's grammar → Centre

A question that often bothers secretaries and shorthand-typists is whether or not they ~~must~~ should change the grammar in a letter that the boss has dictated. When an error is so glaring that the boss himself will wonder how he could ever have made such a slip, it should be ~~caught~~ spotted and corrected by the person who transcribes the dictation. (N.P.) Even when an error is not very serious, but can be changed easily without disturbing the rest of the sentence a secretary will see that the change is made. However, if this slight change will involve rewriting a sentence, or perhaps a paragraph, the better course would be to let it go. For one thing, there is the danger of changing the ~~meaning~~ sense of the dictation, and for another thing, the boss will probably be disturbed when he reads this letter just before signing it and does not recognize his own dictation.

## Exercise 264

**POINTS TO NOTE:**

Typed in fully-blocked style with **memorandum** placed at left-hand margin.
**Reference** initials are typed at the end of memo.
**Signature** is also inserted - although this is an uncommon practice.

(When addressee is mentioned by name then the sender's name should also be used.)

MEMORANDUM

Mr E Sullivan
Publicity Manager

15 August 198-

PUBLICITY T-SHIRTS

It has been decided that a T-shirt featuring our logo and a suitable slogan might boost sales considerably at this particular juncture. Your main aim should be to be eye-catching but at the same time we want something tasteful.

Please start the ball rolling as soon as possible.

J B Sullivan

J B Sullivan
General Manager

JBS/KN/Sec 2

## Exercise 265

**Type the following memorandum using single-line spacing. Insert today's date and the reference JG/KN/80.**

Memorandum

To: Chief Editor
From: Personnel Manager

Subject: Press Party

A press party to launch the new edition of the Pocket Dictionary is on the cards and I should like to have your thoughts on the subject. For instance, do you think it a good idea to hold it in the dictionary building? And should all dictionary staff and spouses be invited? Let me know when we can discuss this further.

## Exercise 211

**Type a copy of the following information in double-line spacing. Leave a top margin of 2.5 cm. (Part of LCCI examination paper LC/54/M2/Sp79 - Intermediate.)**

GENERAL INFORMATION ON SOME OF THE SPORTING FACILITIES

From the Chairman of the Tennis Section

uc In recent years tennis has not been a main feature of the club. ~~Recently~~ However, some members have now formed a ~~[illegible]~~ committee, ~~Their~~ whose objects are to create conditions which would ensure reasonable facilities. There are three green all-weather courts which are in first-class condition. Regular club sessions will take place from April to October on Wednesday evenings and Sunday afternoons.

subject to weather ~~conditions~~ and the state of the courts

From the Chairman of the Croquet Section

There are 28 playing members. The season opens on the first Saturday in April. Coaching for beginners will be on Monday afternoons and evenings. Anyone is welcome to partake in these sessions. In June there will be an Open Afternoon to attract new members.

From the Chairman of the Golf Section

uc The club has two championship golf courses designed by one of Britain's

stet most distinguished course ~~architects~~ planners. The second course was officially opened in November and the new Captain will 'drive' him/herself in on

uc the second Saturday of May each year. The professional will be pleased to give lessons from Tuesdays to Fridays. Members may bring guests for an additional green fee.

From the Chairman of the Billiards Section

The table may be booked, except on Wednesday afternoons, for one hour at a time. The bookings' ~~book~~ diary is at Reception. On Wednesday afternoons no

trs booking can be made between 1045 hours and 1730 hours. Members are encouraged to come and meet other members ~~to mix in and play~~ informally for two-a-side snooker.

## Exercise 262

MEMORANDUM

FROM Personnel Manager | TO Music Editor

OUR REF: FWB/81/2 YOUR REF: | DATE 2 May 198-

COMPANY FLATS

Two company flats have now fallen vacant and I should be obliged if you would bring this to the notice of your staff.

Please stress that the flats are available for only one year and prospective tenants must be prepared to leave at the end of that period.

Priority will be given to cases of special hardship.

**POINTS TO NOTE:**

Typed in the blocked style.
**Memorandum** is typed in closed capitals and underscored.
**Reference** Nos are typed on same line.
Dividing line between Subject and text is omitted.

(When addressee is addressed only by title the sender should also use his title - not his name.)

## Exercise 263

M E M O R A N D U M

TO Head of Accounts Dept. | FROM Managing Director

SUBJECT Pay Slips | DATE 5 November 198-

Several members of staff have been complaining of not receiving their pay slips on time. Something would appear to have gone wrong with the computer system. Any chance of fixing it before the end of the month? Much obliged.

cc Cashier

**POINTS TO NOTE:**

The whole text is indented 5(6) spaces from margin.
**Memorandum** is typed in spaced capitals.
**To, from, date, subject** are typed in capital letters.
The text being very short is typed in 1.5 line spacing.
Note the **c.c.** (copy circulated to) line.

(If a printed form is used the words should be typed a little above the dotted lines.)

**Exercise 212** Type a copy of the following passage in double-line spacing. (Part of LCCI examination paper LC/54/S/Sp78 - Intermediate.)

WORD PROCESSING

The savings effected by the ~~advent~~ introduction of word processing systems are now being appreciated in the United Kingdom and Europe. ~~The~~ It is time ~~has come when~~ that business houses in this country ~~should~~ also become aware of these systems. The cost of producing a typewritten letter ~~which has been typed~~ in the United Kingdom is £4.00, while on the Continent of ~~Eupe~~ Europe it can be as much as £6.00 - the equivalent of $25.00.

In the more advanced systems the machines are linked to a company's computer files, where the use of word processors may merge with that of a computer terminal.

~~Antagonism towards~~ Resistance to the word processing systems may be because of the vagueness of the term. Some employers ~~fear~~ are afraid that personal contact with their ~~typists~~ secretaries will be lost through ~~the~~ their replacement ~~of~~ by a robot system. Others may be confused as to ~~what the system can do.~~ the exact capabilities of the system. Whatever the reasons, sales for word processors during 1976 were sluggish in the extreme, despite the fact that there are more than 20 companies ~~selling~~ marketing the ~~cheaper~~ less expensive machines. However, during the first quarter of 1977 there was an upward trend in sales which has continued.

Basically, a word processor has the ability to drive an electric printer or typewriter automatically from a pre-recorded memory. In their simplest form, ~~W~~word processors produce standard documents which can appear personal, as names can be inserted manually. This means the secretary is relieved of the drudgery of lengthy copying and the employer receives documents of accuracy produced at great speed.

## Exercise 260

M E M O R A N D U M

To: All Employees    Date: 2 January 198-

From: General Manager

---

SUBJECT: Late arrivals, early departures

It has come to my notice that certain members of staff have taken to arriving late every morning and leaving before work is officially over.

Discontinuation of this practice will help me to avoid any unnecessary unpleasantness.

**POINTS TO NOTE:**

This memorandum is typed in the blocked style.
**Memorandum** is typed in spaced capitals and underscored.
**To, from** and **date** are typed in lower case.
**Subject** is typed in capitals.
Addressee and sender are aligned under each other.

## Exercise 261

MEMORANDUM

To: All Employees    5 September 198-

From: Personnel Manager

---

Staggered Hours

As you know, the increasing traffic in the city area is making it daily more difficult to get to and from work. The only solution seems to be staggered working hours, but management would like to hear your views before any decisions are taken.

A meeting to this purpose will be held in the General Assembly Hall on Friday at 2.00 p.m. sharp.

**POINTS TO NOTE:**

Typed in the indented style.
**Memorandum** is typed in closed capitals.
Words **date** and **subject** are omitted.
**Subject** is centred over text, typed in lower case, and underscored.

## Exercise 213

**Type a copy of the following particulars in the order as numbered. Do not type the numbers. All cities typed in capitals in the script are to be typed in capital letters by the candidate. Leave a 2.5 cm top margin. (Part of LCCI examination paper LC/54/M2/Sp80 - Intermediate.)**

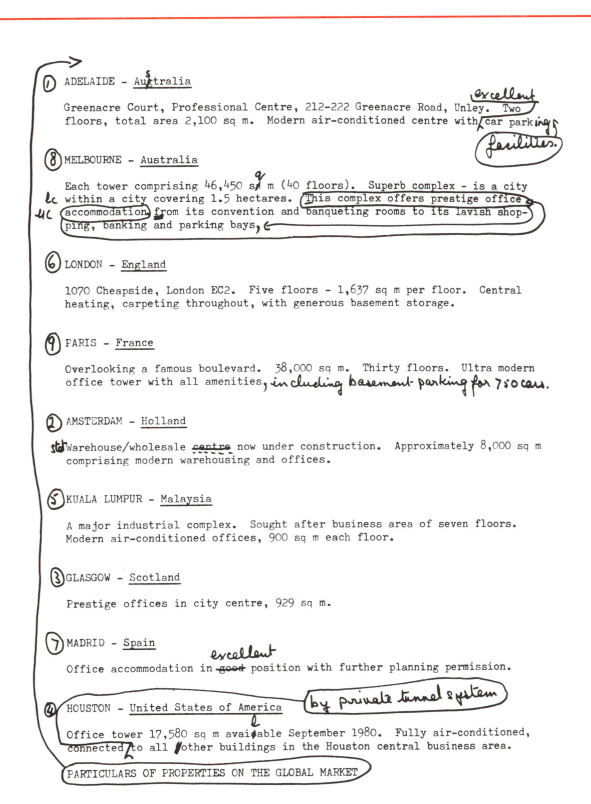

① ADELAIDE - Australia

Greenacre Court, Professional Centre, 212-222 Greenacre Road, Unley. Two floors, total area 2,100 sq m. Modern air-conditioned centre with excellent car parking facilities.

⑧ MELBOURNE - Australia

Each tower comprising 46,450 sq m (40 floors). Superb complex - is a city within a city covering 1.5 hectares. This complex offers prestige office accommodation from its convention and banqueting rooms to its lavish shopping, banking and parking bays,

⑥ LONDON - England

1070 Cheapside, London EC2. Five floors - 1,637 sq m per floor. Central heating, carpeting throughout, with generous basement storage.

⑨ PARIS - France

Overlooking a famous boulevard. 38,000 sq m. Thirty floors. Ultra modern office tower with all amenities, including basement parking for 750 cars.

② AMSTERDAM - Holland

Warehouse/wholesale centre now under construction. Approximately 8,000 sq m comprising modern warehousing and offices.

⑤ KUALA LUMPUR - Malaysia

A major industrial complex. Sought after business area of seven floors. Modern air-conditioned offices, 900 sq m each floor.

③ GLASGOW - Scotland

Prestige offices in city centre, 929 sq m.

⑦ MADRID - Spain

Office accommodation in ~~good~~ excellent position with further planning permission.

④ HOUSTON - United States of America

Office tower 17,580 sq m available September 1980. Fully air-conditioned, connected by private tunnel system to all other buildings in the Houston central business area.

PARTICULARS OF PROPERTIES ON THE GLOBAL MARKET

# Memorandums

MEMORANDUMS (or MEMOS) are messages exchanged between departments, branches or representatives of the same organization. They are much simpler and shorter than formal letters and, therefore, quicker to type.

For the typing of memos some firms use their own printed forms while others use plain paper.

The main features of memos are the following:

1. They are typed on A5 paper, landscape. Longer memos can be typed on 2/3 A4, or even on full-size A4.
2. The word «MEMORANDUM», printed or typed, is centred two lines above or below the letterhead; if the paper is plain, four lines are allowed from top of sheet.
3. The inside address, salutation and complimentary close are omitted. Usually, the signature is also omitted.
4. Essential information appearing on a memo is: TO WHOM it is addressed; FROM WHOM it is sent; DATE of despatch; SUBJECT to which the text refers; and, occasionally, a file reference.
5. The side margins are usually one inch wide, and paragraphs may be blocked or indented.
6. The body of a memo is typed in single-line spacing, with double space between paragraphs.
7. Below the message a space is left for the initials or signature of the sender - if these are used.

M E M O R A N D U M

TO: .................... DATE: ..................

FROM: .................... REF: ..................

---

SUBJECT xxxxxxxxxxxxxxxxxx

xxxxxxxxxxxxxxxxxxxxxxxxxxxxxxxxxxxxxxxxxxxxxxxxxxxxxxxxxxxxxxxxxxxxxxxxxxx
xxxxxxxxxxxxxxxxxxxxxxxxxxxxxxxxxxxxxxxxxxxxxxxxxxxxxxxxxxxxxxxxxxxxxxxxxxx
xxxxxxxxxxxxxxxxxxxxxxxxxxxx

xxxxxxxxxxxxxxxxxxxxxxxxxxxxxxxxxxxxxxxxxxxxxxxxxxxxxxxxxxxxxxxxxxxxxxxxxxx
xxxxxxxxxxxxxxxxxxxxxxxxxxxxxxxxxxxxxxxxxxxxxxxxxxxxxxxxxxxxxxxxxxxxxxxxxxx
xxxxxxxxxxxxxxxxxxxxxxxxxxxxxxxxxxxxxxxxxxxxxxxxxxxxxxxxxxxx

Main features of a memo

**Memorandums do not follow a standard form of layout. The examples that follow are typical of present-day practice.**

## Exercise 214

**Type a copy of the following passage in double-line spacing except where the script is typed in single-line spacing. Start typing the passage 2.5 cm from the top of the page. (Part of LCCI examination paper LC/54/MI/Sp78 - Intermediate.)**

MECHANICAL HANDLING - GUIDE TO CORRECTIVE ACTION

Recently a report was published [by the Department of Industry] in London. It has really made [manufacturers and] producers of raw materials realise that the return from investment in improving the handling of materials is ~~important~~ [well worth consideration]. Researchers for the report were able to show that in some industries about S$369 million could be saved ~~each year~~ [annually] by improvements in storage and materials handling, and this did not take into account the benefits derived from better materials flow. Any company ~~or firm~~ wishing to cost and re-assess its materials handling methods will find details in the report called "Materials Hnadling Costs - A New Look at Manufacture". The report is obtainable from HMSO, London for S$8.30.

The report of the Department of Industry ~~puts forward~~ [gives] several reasons why Companies ~~do nothing~~ [take no action] to reduce their materials handling costs. The three most important ones are given below.

1 Companies ~~are unaware~~ [~~do not know~~] of the costs of materials handling and factors contributing towards them.

2 Some copanies have poor organisation. Some have no programmes for training staff in the use of systems design and materials handling techniques.

3 ~~There was little~~ [A lack of any] strategic plans for site and method development, including financial planning, was apparent.

The report gives producers an opportunity to identify the main causes for high costs - the three main areas being

(a) Poor Layout planning
(b) Poor utilisation of space
(c) high labour costs.

The latter is a direct result of poor [~~to~~ layout] planning, complex movement and shortage of handling equipment.

# Part 6

## Contents

**Exercise 215** Type a corrected copy of the following in double line spacing. (Part of LCCI examination paper LC/53/W/78 - Higher.)

D I G I T A L [redacted] WATCHES

in Great Britain

Nearly a year ago the quartz watch followed the price-cutting lead of
the electronic calculator and broke the £10 barrier. The manufacturer
δ/ of this particular watch forecast that sales of it would double in the
first year and he was ~~indeed~~ right. Sales have soared as prices have
tumbled and nearly one and a half million watches [redacted] sold in [redacted]
have been United
[redacted] Britain, [redacted]
run on/ However, several well-known retailers have reported that "bewildered
customers simply do not understand the difference between the various
NP/ types and they often buy rubbish". There is no doubt that quartz
watches have revolutionised [redacted] watch-making. While some [redacted]
[redacted] traditional firms have talked about a "passing fad" sales
stet/ throughout the world have swept ~~upwards~~ onwards. The main Japanese
manufacturer [redacted] that over sixty per cent of its sales in the States
are now of quartz and in Britain they are approaching fifty per cent.
[redacted]
NP/ [redacted]. One of the
the
biggest changes in this field has been [redacted] marketing: many of the
sales in the past two years have been by mail order and discount
who bypass
houses [redacted] the jeweller. [redacted]

traditional

claims

proving that even the Swiss are not shock-proof

## 14

Target time 15'

**Blocked style, open punctuation**

1 June 19-- MHM/LCSsL/79 The Office Manager, Butler & Company Limited, 16th Floor Shing Kwan House, 414 Shenton Way, Singapore 1 Dear Sir ELECTRIC TYPEWRITERS Thank you for your letter of 28 May 19--. (NP) We are agents for Adler, Triumph, Imperial, Olivetti, Olympia and IBM typewriters. We should point out that IBM do not make any manual or portable machines. (NP) As you will appreciate, covering such a wide range of manufacturers, we can supply typewriters to meet most business requirements. We carry a certain stock of manual machines as there is a call for them in the event of power cuts and other mechanical failures. (NP) In answer to your query about British typewriters - there are none. When Adler/Triumph acquired Imperial in 1975 the last of the British typewriter manufacturers disappeared. Both Olivetti and Olympia manufacture machines in the United Kingdom, but these are mostly manual machines. The greater number of typewriters bought in this country are imported from Germany and Italy. IBM's European bases for manufacturing typewriters are in Berlin and Amsterdam. (NP) The two basic types of electric machine are the 'type basket' and the 'single element' machine. The latter is better known as the 'golfball' machine, about which your secretary was talking the other morning. This works on the principle of a single globe of about 2.5 cm in diameter with all the standard characters in relief on it. Yours faithfully INTERNATIONAL EQUIPMENT LIMITED, SALES MANAGER

## 15

Target time: 20'

**Semi-blocked style, open punctuation**
**Carbon copy and envelope required**

Ref:REK/EB 20th June 19-- Mrs D. A. V. Hutchinson, Head of Secretarial Department, Gateway College, Lawn Avenue, Belsize Park, LONDON N6 4BP Dear Mrs Hutchinson SECRETARIAL APPOINTMENTS. I am writing to you as we have two vacancies which may be of interest to students completing a secretarial course this summer. We are a company which supplies a very wide range of office equipment and software. Although the Head Office is five minutes' walk from Victoria Station both appointments will be in our Sales Department and it is anticipated that this Department will move to the Strand towards the end of the year. (NP) We require secretaries to fulfil the following roles:- (i) Personal secretary to one District Manager and three assistants. (ii) Personal secretary to one Area Manager and three assistants. The tasks involved will cover the full range of secretarial skills, shorthand and/or audio, dealing with customers both when they are calling in the office or telephoning, assistance with general office work, ie making travel arrangements, filing etc and generally contributing to the efficient running of the office. (NP) By the nature of the work, sales staff spend much time out of the office and we would expect a secretary to be prepared to share the workload with her colleagues when the occasion arises. (NP) Working conditions are good and the atmosphere is friendly; we offer four weeks' holiday per year (in addition to the usual public holidays) and an annual salary of £4,500 plus bonus. This year's holiday arrangements will be honoured. (NP) Should any of your students be interested in either of these posts they should, in the first instance, contact me to arrange an appointment. Yours sincerely, Mary Kenny (Mrs), Personnel Director

## 16

Target time: 13'

**Indented style, closed punctuation**

28 May 19-- FLPT/S/79/2 Miss S. Yeo, 375 Orchard Road, Singapore Dear Miss Yeo Thank you for your letter of 24 May 1979. I have pleasure in sending you a copy of our 1979 brochure which gives full details of the European holidays organised by this company. (NP) I notice from your letter that you are particularly keen on booking a holiday in Spain. Unfortunately, this year we have been forced to cancel a number of our tours to this country owing to problems of accommodation. There might well be other organisations which are operating tours to Spain, but we found that we could not offer our usual high standard of accommodation for the price or guarantee that a customer would not be caught up in a 'double booking' situation. We could have arranged to use the most expensive hotels in each town, of course, but the overall cost of such a holiday would have been prohibitive. (NP) If you are interested in any other tours shown in the brochure I suggest you contact us as soon as possible, as we cannot guarantee that bookings will be available for long. (NP) Should you require any further information please do not hesitate to get in touch with us. Yours sincerely, Tours Manager Enclosure

**Exercise 216** Type a corrected copy of the following advertisement in single-line spacing. The heading and the paragraph below it must be centred. (Part of LCCI examination paper LC/53/M/Sp80 - Higher.)

FURAMA IMPORT-EXPORT CORPORATION

QUALIFIED PERSONNEL REQUIRED to take up employment on 1 August 1980. All applications must [redacted] be [redacted] addressed to the Director to arrive by 12 June at the latest.

SHIPPING CONTROLLER    have proven administrative skill

Our company is now trading worldwide in sundry machines and
uc/ is appointing a senior man in the shipping department. The successful applicant will be mature, have had at least ten years' experience in shipping, and will be able to organise and control all aspects of the import and export of sundry goods including such matters as chartering, insurance, invoicing, documentation, and have a trader's ability to negotiate rates.

This is an exacting post, commanding high remuneration. Please write confidentially, giving details of experience and current position.    freight and haulage

SALES EXECUTIVE    highly successful

domestic    in

An experienced man needed with a record of selling machines. The successful candidate will play a leading role in the development of the sales and marketing function [redacted] the country. It is important that the person appointed be highly self-motivated and able to contribute in full to the development of the Corporation's interests.    further

In addition to an attractive salary, a commission will be paid on resultant sales or contracts.    as a whole

PLANNING OFFICER    for advising the Director

The successful candidate for this new post will have full responsibility and is likely to have previous knowledge of the policy of a progressive import-export company. He will be expected to develop a wide range of contacts with retail outlets
NP/ and overseas suppliers. [Applicants should have appropriate qualification in planning or business studies.

AUDIO VISUAL SENIOR TECHNICIAN

Versatile person to join a [redacted] small team. Responsibility will include the setting up, operating, and first-line maintenance of a wide range of equipment. Some experience of working with audio visual equipment essential.    imported projection, audio and video

MAGAZINE EDITOR

Man with sound knowledge of photographic industry and its [redacted] terminology required, to edit a new trade magazine which will have a section devoted to photographic equipment, particularly from Japan. The post will call for an ability to present [redacted]
trs/ technical and scientific topics in text and picture form [redacted] suitable for lay readership.    stamped

(All applications to include addressed envelope and sent to the Corporation at Jalan Tuanka Abdul Rahman, Kuala Lumpur.)

## 11

Target: 10'

**Indented style, closed punctuation**
**Envelope required**

KN/LI 7th June 19-- Messrs. Burns & Glover, P.O.Box 458, Calcutta, India Dear Sirs Referring to your letter of 3rd June 19-- regarding «Mascot» radios, please find enclosed two leaflets describing some of our models for the period 1982-3. We are also sending you our Norwegian brochure picturing the same models in colour. (NP) We are in a position to offer you our Mascot sets at the following prices: Mascot 44 AM FOB N.cr. 220, Mascot 44 FM FOB N.cr. 270, Mascot 61 FM FOB N.cr. 380. (NP) The above-mentioned prices are offered on condition that payment will be effected by Irrevocable Letter of Credit. (NP) Our portable radios have acquired a world-wide reputation. When introduced in your market we are confident that we will soon be very successful and get a very satisfactory turnover. Yours faithfully, OSTFOLD RADIO A/S, Export Manager Enc Leaflets

## 12

Target time: 20'

**Blocked style, open puncuation**

FLPT/M/80/2 3 April 198- The Freight Manager, Eastern Airfreight Company, 72 Chester Close, London, SWIX 7BQ Dear Sir We have been giving a good deal of thought to the proposals you made last month. The force of each point you made about the advantages of our arranging for goods to be sent by air has not been lost upon us but, as I mentioned earlier, current agreements with a number of shipping lines must remain in force for several months. It is, therefore, quite impossible for us to recommend to our suppliers both in Europe and North America and in the Pacific area, a changeover to your air services for the time being. (NP) I have recently returned from an interesting foreign tour when I was looking at the prospects for new suppliers in a wide range of goods. As a result I have little doubt that we shall soon be opening up new outlets for re-exportation and new lines for our importation. When we have decided our policy in regard to new suppliers and customers we shall be in a better position to negotiate an agreement with your company, although you will appreciate that this will call for an approach from your side to individual suppliers in respective countries. (NP) You will not deny that the cost of air freight for heavy goods is far greater than sending goods by sea. This extra cost will be worth our while only if it can be shown that far quicker delivery is an advantage to us and to our customers and, more importantly, if the customer is willing to bear the increased cost. We had this question of air freight in mind when talking to our possible new suppliers, but in few cases were they willing to move very much on their stated prices. (NP) Of course, for our part we must keep in mind the important fact that there is much less risk of breakages in the case of goods sent by air. Insurance charges are very heavy when sending goods by sea as there is a considerable loss of goods through damage and this may be a major factor in making a decision to export our goods by air through your company. (NP) As soon as we have some definite information about our new export and import sources I shall write to you again. Yours faithfully, Sales Director

## 13

Target time: 15'

**Blocked style, open punctuation**

GAP/SCG 13th June 19-- Mr. Oliver Greenwood, Greenwood Associates (UK) Limited, 135 Elmfield Road, LONDON WIS 3BD Dear Mr Greenwood I was very pleased to hear from you again and I can assure you that the Agency can offer the accommodation and secretarial services which your visitor from abroad will need. (NP) The office, which can be hired on a weekly basis, will be available in the week commencing Monday 25th June. As we already have a provisional enquiry for the following week please let me know as soon as possible if you think your visitor will require additional time. (NP) If you would like to make an appointment to visit us I should be pleased to show you the offices which have been recently re-decorated and are equipped with modern furniture and up-to-date office machinery. The main room is large enough to accommodate fifteen people. A smaller room is specially designed for interviewing and a third room is suitable for use by a secretary. Full details and a list of charges are enclosed. (NP) I can obtain the services of a highly qualified and very experienced temporary secretary for this period. Miss Anita Brooks, aged 28 years, has a pleasant personality. She is an excellent typist, a high-speed shorthand writer and a competent audio typist. Miss Brooks is used to working at executive level and handling confidential work. (NP) Please telephone my secretary when you have made a decision. You can be assured that our Agency will give your colleague all the help he needs. Yours sincerely, Gerald A Parker, Director Encs

**Exercise 217** **Type a copy of the following manuscript in single-line spacing. (Part of LCCI examination paper LC/53/S/Sp79 - Higher.)**

THE RENT-A-CAR SERVICE (particularly in America and Europe)

budget-economy

Many plans for the renting of cars/ are designed to provide flexibility. The idea of a 'Rent it here - Leave it there' system is to [redacted] ensure that the traveller enjoys convenience from the start to the end of his [redacted] trip. One can choose from more than twenty different models of car in a/ time and mileage arrangement, or an

NP/ unlimited mileage [redacted] privilege plan. [Car rental allows the traveller to see more during a foreign visit without any [redacted]/ costs. Cars can be picked up in one country and [redacted] left in another. You can/ start in Stockholm if you wish and end in Rome/ with no back-tracking, no scenic repetition and no drop-off charges.

add-on

, for example,

(a distance of nearly 2000 miles)

Usually, all rental prices are based on the official currency at the place of rental. Rentals from one ~~country to another are quoted~~ at the rate for the country from which the car is rented. For/ rentals a payment equal to the estimated value of the rental is payable upon pick-up of car. Any excess payments will be refunded at the termination of the rental. [redacted]

cash

Excess charges will also be due at that time.

Government

Travellers have to face/ taxes in almost all the countries our company deals with but partial waiving of this tax is possible for cars rented in Germany, France, Holland, Belgium or Luxembourg if the car is/ driven [redacted] outside of these countries during part of the rental period. At the main rental offices of these countries, validation papers are available on request. Properly completed documentation must be submitted at the completion of the rental.

to be

NP/ [The question of repair bills is often raised by [redacted] those people [redacted] who are thinking of foreign car rental but there is no real cause for concern. Repairs up to 100 American dollars/ may be obtained without [redacted] authorisation. Expenses over that amount must be authorised by the

trs/ nearest Rent-a-Car office. All expenses approved thus will be reimbursed when the car is returned, providing that appropriate bills and receipts are presented. If a replacement car is required, it will be handled by the nearest company office.

([redacted] or the equivalent)

**8** **Target Time: 15'**

**Indented style, closed punctuation**
**Carbon copy required**

KOS/rd. 30th June 198-. The Shoe Manufacturing Co., 198 Goldsmiths Road, Djakarta, Indonesia. Gentlemen We have noticed your advertisement in the U.S.A. bulletin 'Foreign Trade Opportunities' and we wish to offer you our products. (NP) We work as distributors for several large U.S. manufacturers who give us especially advantageous prices which enable us to offer their products at prices, lower than those of our competitors. (NP) To give you an idea of the products, we are enclosing our price-list No.120/AB and samples of a few articles. Under separate cover, we are also sending you a sample of a plastic heel for ladies shoes, the price of which is 98¢ a pair F.A.S. New York or Boston. (NP) We can supply more than a hundred different styles in various colours, such as white patent (lustrous finish), white calf, red calf, black, beige, blue (dull finish), or any other colour desired. We can also supply the heels with nylon toplifts. (NP) Please study the attached price-list and let us know your requirements. (NP) We look forward to hearing from you. Very truly yours, THE MANHATTAN FOREIGN SALES COMPANY, (G. J. Browning) Enc.

**9** **Target time: 20'**

**Blocked style, open punctuation**
**Carbon copy and envelope required**

EM/SCG. 15th June 198-. Mr James Osborne, 85 Bromley Road, Hayes, Kent, BR4 9EJ. Dear Mr Osborne Following your enquiry to the London and Provincial Building Society I have pleasure in enclosing illustrations showing the three different methods of mortgage protection. (NP) Plan 1 - Decreasing Term Assurance This contract will pay off the outstanding debt should either your wife or yourself die during the mortgage term. (NP) Plan 2 - Mortgage Protection Plan Without Profits This contract will pay an agreed sum if either your wife or yourself should die during the mortgage term, irrespective of the amount owing at the time of death. If you both survive the mortgage term you will receive an agreed amount tax free. (NP) Plan 3 - Mortgage Protection Plan With Profits As in Plan 2 above but the return will be calculated to include the profits as at that time. (NP) Specimen illustrations are given on the attached leaflet. (NP) I strongly recommend Plans 2 or 3 not only because the cover does not reduce and you receive a cash sum, but, in the event of a further mortgage, the Policy can easily be modified to fall in line with the new mortgage details. Premiums already paid are taken into account when calculating the new premium. This does not happen with Plan 1 - you simply cancel and start all over again. (NP) If there are any points which require clarification please telephone or write. My colleague Mr Shaw will be able to help you should I be out of the office. (NP) I also enclose a proposal form for completion together with a pre-paid envelope and as soon as I receive this form completed the Society can proceed with the underwriting. The Policy would not commence until nearer exchange of contracts. Yours sincerely, R. Mackie, Area Manager Encs.

**10** **Target time: 15'**

**Blocked style, open punctuation**

MHM/LCS2/78 1 June 19-- Mr P. S. Koh, Office Supplies Limited, Straits Building, 12th Floor, 191 Battery Road, Singapore Dear Sir TYPING POOL LOAD AT A GLANCE Further to our discussion at your office on 27 May with regard to equipping your Secretarial Services Department, you may be interested in the following information. (NP) The latest centralised dictation system - called 'Thought Tank System 2000' - gives accurate control over all work output, typing output and workload distribution. The new system uses the same recording and playback typing principles as the system we demonstrated to you, but the equipment has the added facility known as an electronic word controller. It is, in effect a console for the supervisor, having one instrument panel per station of work plus an electronic workload graph. (NP) The average speed of each typist is keyed in by the supervisor. When someone wishing to dictate picks up the telephone to do so, the word controller electronically compares each typist's backlog of work with the speed at which she types and automatically routes the dictator to the typist able to type his work soonest. As you will appreciate, the typing turn around time is kept to a minimum. The supervisor is able to up-date the typist's speeds continuously by using the data, obtained from the typist's counter, giving the total amount of work done over any measured period. (NP) We hope to have this system installed shortly in our showroom. Before placing your order, you may care to inspect the system. Yours faithfully, P. LEE, Office Manager

**Exercise 218** Type the following attractively. (Part of LCCI examination paper LC/53/M/Sp77 - Higher.)

1. POWER RESOURCES IN 1977

therefore,
For power generation, Malaysia continues to depend primarily on imported fuel oil.

trs/ The power resources of Malaysia include peat, coal, wood, petroleum and hydro-electricity. [illegible] Although ~~there are~~ some reserves ~~[illegible]~~ of coal and peat exist, they are by no means economic to mine and therefore remain only of ~~possible~~ potential use.

run on/ traditional
For many, many years wood and charcoal have been ~~the~~ fuels, but in the ~~[illegible]~~ urban areas they have rapidly been displaced by gas. bottled

(on the Perak River)

NP/ No hydro-electric power is generated in East Malaysia, but, as on the peninsula, the abundant rainfall and steep gradients of the rivers in the interior highlands offer a good hydro-electric potential. ~~[illegible]~~ The main hydro-electric schemes in operation in West Malaysia are at Cameron Highlands, at Batang Padang, and at Chenderoh; in addition there are small plants at Ulu Langat, Sempang and Rahman. The ~~oil~~ petroleum resources of Sarawak do not constitute a major source of fuel oil.

2. NATIONAL INCOME RESOURCES IN 1977

Fishing,
The most important sector of the Malaysian economy will continue to be constituted by Agriculture, Forestry and Mining. They contribute no less than 90 per cent of the value of all exports. More than half the working population of West Malaysia and three-quarters of that of Sabah will continue to be engaged in agriculture, fishing, forestry and mining.

will

and Sarawak

## 4

Target time: 10'

**Semi-blocked style, closed punctuation**
**Envelope required**

BTU/SEW. 25 July 198-. Electric Instruments, Ltd., P.O.B. No. 78, Riyad, Saudi Arabia. Attention Mr. R. Osman Dear Sirs re: Cash Registers. Thank you for your letter of 16 July 198-. (NP) We are very sorry to inform you that the manufacture of the Model 29 range has ceased and has been replaced by our Model 7AR range which we have been recommending to all our customers. (NP) For your reference, we are enclosing our price-list together with the relevant leaflets. In case you are interested in this new range would you order one cash register from each of the most representative models in order to investigate the actual possibilities of the machine in your market. (NP) We look forward to receiving your news. Yours truly, TOKYO CASH REGISTER MFG CO., LTD., H. Somei Director Enc.

## 5

Target time: 10'

**Indented Style, closed punctuation**

NC/KN 15th August 198-. J. B. Montgomery, Esq., 75 Milton Ave., Kuala Lumpur, Malaysia. Dear Sir We have received your letter of yesterday's date and in reply we regret to inform you that bells of the size and weight you specify are not at present in stock. These, however, will be available for sale in about 15 days. (NP) For your information, we quote below the rates at which we sell our bells, including cost of installation: Bells over 50 kilos, £19.50 per kilo. Bells over 80 kilos, £17.40 per kilo. Bells over 100 kilos, £16.25 per kilo. Bells over 150 kilos, £15 per kilo. (NP) Please note that we guarantee our products for two years and that we allow a discount of 5% for prompt payment. (NP) We shall be glad to receive your instructions at an early date so that we may manufacture and despatch the bell you desire as soon as possible. Yours faithfully, B. Brown, Manager

## 6

Target time: 25'

**Indented style, closed punctuation**
**Carbon copy and envelope required**

FLPT/M/78/6 April 198-. Boyle & Sons, 320 Western Avenue, Glasgow, G3 4JD. Dear Sir We were interested to learn that your company is considering a move to Malaysia within the next few years. Your concern to know something of the country is understandable and perhaps in this letter I can give you some idea of what Malaysia now offers. (NP) Living in Malaysia is pleasant and stimulating. Every modern convenience for the good life is available - homes, supermarkets, hospitals, schools, expressways, hotels and recreational facilities provide the necessary utilities. (NP) Kuala Lumpur, the capital and nerve centre of the country, is a modern and healthy city bustling with life. It is here that many of Malaysia's companies and banks have their headquarters. Facilities for relaxation abound. Time out for leisure can be a trip to the beaches of Penang or Port Dickson or to the various island resorts in the country. Here holiday makers can go fishing, swimming, water skiing, skin diving or shell-collecting in Malaysia's warm tropical waters. People can also enjoy the cool clean air of Malaysia's many hill resorts like Cameron Highlands, Penang Hill or Genting Highlands. Many of our hill resorts have hotels and golf courses of international standard. Malaysia also has ample facilities for bowling, horse racing, motor racing and night-clubbing. (NP) Living in Malaysia is also easy and inexpensive. Shopping is cheap and convenient and domestic help is easy to obtain at low cost. There is a hospital in every town, and an impressive teaching medical complex in the University of Malaya, equipped with some of the most advanced medical equipment in the world. Finally (and this will be of especial importance for you), there are several private schools in the capital serving the needs of European and American children. Yours faithfully

## 7

Target time: 10'

**Blocked style, open punctuation**

Our ref: LP/SCG 5th June 19-- Mr P. J. Baxter, Personnel Officer, The Lapwing Group, London Road, WOLVERHAMPTON, WV2 9LD. Dear Mr. Baxter I have read with great interest your letter of 1st June 19-- about the difficulties of training staff in organisations such as your own which comprise many small units scattered over a wide area. (NP) Our Training Division has been investigating the use of audio visual equipment and we believe that this has great potential in the kind of situation you describe. (NP) Our Training Adviser, Mr Denis Fordham, and I, would welcome the opportunity to call on you to discuss this equipment. We should like to show you some examples of programmes which have been devised by the Training Division. (NP) If you would like us to visit you, please telephone me on extension 246 so that we can arrange a convenient date. Yours sincerely, Anne Peterfield (Mrs), Sales Director

## Part 5

# Contents

# Production Typing

Production typing is the *speedy and quality* typing of letters, statements, tables and other complicated documents *under realistic conditions* as these prevail in a demanding office.

Production typing is, in fact, the criterion by which the efficient typist is judged; for it involves not only the mastery of correct typewriting techniques but also intelligence, decision making and an artistic taste in the display of the various typewritten tasks.

In addition, production typing involves a well-planned and orderly arrangement on the typist's desk of all necessary stationery (letter paper, carbon sheets, flimsies, etc) so that no valuable time is wasted. Office lighting, the comfort offered by suitable furniture, environment, and the typist's personal moods are also important factors contributing to productivity.

The 16 letters that follow are to be 'productively' typed within the target time and according to the instructions given for each one of them. "(NP)" indicates a new paragraph.

Use plain sheets of A4 and A5 paper and allow at the top a reasonable number of blank lines for the printed heading. Correct errors carefully as you type, remembering that any work which contains numerous erasures or corrections is not mailable copy and it is rejected.

*Except for letters 1, 3, 4, 5, 8, and 11, all others have been taken from LCCI's examination papers.*

**1** **Target time: 8'**

**Indented style, closed punctuation**
**Carbon copy required**

LR/BMW. 1st July 198-. Messrs. Tang Fun Manufacturing Co. Ltd., 320 Fuk Tsun Street, Kowloon, Hong Kong. Dear Sirs Thank you very much for your letter of 20th June with enclosed Proforma Invoice for 440 doz. No. 90 Batteries. (NP) We are enclosing herewith our cheque on the Commercial Bank No. I/1262 for £199 which covers the cost of only 88 doz. batteries and shall be pleased if you hasten the dispatch of our orders TF-439 and SK-63/1/9. (NP) With our best thanks, Yours faithfully, S. PHILLIPS CO., Manager Enc.

**2** **Target Time 12'**

**Blocked style, open punctuation**

SG/TI 9 June 19-- Charles Carter Esq., Secretary, Society of Travel Agents Limited, 17 Robertson Street, LIVERPOOL L21 IBU Dear Mr Carter Today I spoke to your secretary with regard to the Centenary Celebrations later this year for Travellers-Fare to discuss plans for extensive promotions for the remainder of the year. At a preliminary discussion with Mr Peter Miles, their Marketing Manager, it was suggested that an approach should be made to you with regard to your Travel Agents' Award. Travellers-Fare are naturally very interested in areas where they can spread the message and encourage those parts of the market which could be regular users of their wares. I have been asked to enquire whether you would be interested in being associated with the Centenary Celebrations. Mr. Miles thought that Travellers-Fare could donate a Special Travel Agents' trophy and might offer 100 agents a commemorative meal on board the special Centenary train which will be touring Britain. (NP) If this idea appeals to you and you would like to know more about the Celebrations, I should be happy to visit you in Liverpool. Perhaps our secretaries could fix a mutually convenient date. Yours sincerely, M. FARNWORTH Managing Director.

**3** **Target time: 8'**

**Blocked style, closed punctuation**
**Carbon copy and envelope required**

STR/Spt-95. 2 April 198-. The Crown Enterprises, Ltd., The Crown Estates, Manila, Philippines. Dear Sirs Subject: Extension of Guarantee. We regret to inform you that owing to a shortage of steamers bound to your port we shall be unable to effect shipment as stated in our letter of 15 March. (NP) We should suggest, therefore, that you kindly extend your Irrevocable Guarantee No. 7/35D to the end of the month. (NP) With warm thanks for your kind co-operation, Yours faithfully, TAN FUN MANUFACTURING CO., LTD., Director

# Letters

Letters are a form of communication between businesses and their customers as well as with citizens and public authorities.

Being *ambassadors* of their senders, letters are expected to represent them as efficiently and successfully as possible. To do so they should be typed on good quality paper, have an elegant appearance, and be written in good and simple language.

Letters are classified into three kinds: **BUSINESS, PERSONAL,** and **CIVIL SERVICE.** Business letters are being dealt with on pages 105–153, Personal letters on pages 172–173 and Civil Service letters on pages 174–175.

## The Business Letter

Business letters, depending on their length, can be typed on three sizes of paper: A4 for ordinary-length letters, A5 for small-length letters, and two-thirds A4 for medium-length.

### Styles of display

Business letters can be displayed in any one of the following styles:

**The Blocked, the Semi-blocked and the Indented.**

Of these the 'blocked' is the most popular owing to its simplicity, since all lines of the letter start at the left-hand margin, thereby saving valuable time. *(This is the style chosen for the instructions that follow below; the other two styles are being dealt with in later pages.)*

### Parts of the letter

The business letter is composed of the following seven basic parts: (1) Printed heading, (2) Date, (3) Inside name and address, (4) Salutation, (5) Body of letter, (6) Complimentary close, (7) Signature.

Other parts which may appear in a letter are: (1) Reference initials, (2) 'Subject' line, (3) 'Attention' line, (4) 'Enclosure' line, (5) 'Copy circulated to' line, (6) Postscript, (7) Special notations.

## MAIN PARTS OF THE BUSINESS LETTER

#### PRINTED HEADING

Business letters are typed on paper bearing a printed heading which contains the name of the organization, the nature of its business, postal address, telephone and telex numbers, telegraphic address, names of directors, etc.

*EEC legislation requires also place and number of registration of a Company, reference to 'Limited Liability', and the amount of paid-up capital, where the share capital is mentioned.*

#### REFERENCE INITIALS

Type the Reference initials two lines below the printed heading (unless a special place is provided for them in the heading); if using plain note paper, allow two inches (12 line spaces) from the top. These are the initials of the dictator of the letter and of the typist, separated by a solidus; e.g. PRT/md. (Large concerns often use a code representing the department and a file number, e.g. Reg/982.)

Where both firms use Reference initials courtesy demands those of the addressee first and those of the sender second.

THIS SPACE IS RESERVED
FOR THE PRINTED HEADING

If using plain paper allow two inches (12 line spaces) from top of paper before typing *reference initials.*

SB/KN

**Printed heading and Reference initials.**

# Typing Letters in Foreign Languages

**Typing in a foreign language is not an easy task for it requires absolute concentration on the keyboard. You will now have to substitute «letter-response» for «word-response» typing; i.e. you should think each separate letter as you strike it. Accents, if any, should be inserted neatly; and as they are fitted on 'dead' keys they should be struck before the letters over which they are to appear. If, however, accents are not available on the keyboard add them in ink of the same colour.**

**The letter below has been written in (a) English, (b) French, (c) German and (d) Spanish. Type the English one today and complete the rest within the next three or four lessons.**

**(a)**

Dear Mr Greenwood

I was very pleased to hear from you again and I can assure you that the Agency can offer the accommodation and secretarial services which your visitor from abroad will need.

The office, which can be hired on a weekly basis, will be available in the week commencing Monday 25th June. As we already have a provisional enquiry for the following week please let me know as soon as possible if you think your visitor will require additional time.

If you would like to make an appointment to visit us I should be pleased to show you the offices which have been recently re-decorated and are equipped with modern furniture and up-to-date office machinery. Full details and a list of charges are enclosed.

I can obtain the services of a highly qualified secretary for this period. Miss Anita Brooks, aged 28 years, has a pleasant personality, she is an excellent shorthand-typist, and is used to working at executive level and handling confidential work.

Please telephone my secretary when you have made a decision. You can be assured that our Agency will give your colleague all the help he needs.

Yours sincerely

Encs

**(b)**

Monsieur

J'étais très heureux d'avoir de vos nouvelles et puis vous assurer que l'Agence veillera à l'installation de votre visiteur étranger et mettra à sa disposition les services de son secrétariat.

Le bureau, qui peut être loué sur une base hebdomadaire, sera disponible à partir du Lundi 25 Juin. Comme nous avons déjà une demande provisoire pour la semaine suivante, nous vous prions de nous faire savoir si votre client aura besoin d'une prolongation de séjour.

Si vous désirez prendre rendez-vous pour visiter notre firme, je serai heureux de vous montrer nos bureaux qui ont été récemment redécorés et réaménagés d'équipement moderne. Vous trouverez ci-joint tous les détails et une liste de prix.

Pour cette période, je peux obtenir les services d'une secrétaire hautement qualifiée. Mademoiselle Anita Brooks, âgée de 28 ans, de caractère agréable, est une excellente sténo-dactylo de direction qui a l'habitude du travail confidentiel.

Veuillez téléphoner à ma secrétaire pour lui faire part de votre décision. Vous pouvez être certain que notre Agence donnera à votre collègue toute l'aide dont il aura besoin.

Veuillez agréer, Monsieur, l'expression de mes sentiments les plus sincères.

Pièces jointes

**(c)**

Sehr geehrter Herr Greenwood

Ich war erfreut, von Ihnen zu hören und kann Ihnen versichern, dass die Agentur Ihrem Besucher aus dem Ausland die erforderliche Unterkunft sowie Bürodienste bieten kann.

Das Büro, das auf Wochenbasis vermietet werden kann, steht ab Montag, dem 25.Juni für eine Woche zur Verfügung. Da wir bereits Bestellungen für die folgende Woche erhalten haben, möchte ich Sie bitten, dass Sie mich recht bald wissen lassen, ob Ihr Besucher unsere Büroräume für längere Zeit beanspruchen will.

Falls Sie also einen Besuchstermin mit uns vereinbaren wollen, wäre ich gern bereit, Ihnen unsere Büroräume zu zeigen, die vor kurzem neu dekoriert und mit modernen Möbeln sowie Büromaschinen ausgestattet worden sind. Weitere Einzelheiten sowie eine Preisliste werden beigelegt.

Des weiteren kann ich Ihnen die Dienste einer hochqualifizierten Sekretärin anbieten. Fräulein Anita Brooks, 28 Jahre alt, verfügt über ausgezeichnete Kenntnisse in Stenographie und Schreibmaschine. Sie ist spezialisiert für die Leitungstätigkeit und die Bearbeitung vertraulicher Materialien.

Falls Sie eine Entscheidung getroffen haben, rufen Sie meine Sekretärin an. Sie können sicher sein, dass unsere Agentur Ihrem Kollegen jede benötigte Unterstützung gewähren wird.

Hochachtungsvoll

**(d)**

Estimado señor Greenwood

Es con gran placer que he vuelto a escuchar de Ud., y le puedo asegurar que la Agencia está en condiciones de ofrecer ayuda y los servicios secretariales que su visitante del extranjero necesitará.

La oficina, que puede ser alquilada en base a un arreglo semanal, estará disponible en la semana que comienza el 25 de junio. Como ya hemos peticiones provisorias para las próximas semanas, le rogaría me hiciera saber, lo más rápido posible, si usted piensa que su huésped necesitará tiempo adicional.

Si desea cerrar una cita a fin de visitarnos, estaría encantado de mostrarle las oficinas, que han sido recientemente redecoradas y están equipadas con modernos muebles y modernas máquinas de oficina. Más detalles y una lista de precios, van incluidos aquí.

Para este período podría obtener los servicios de una secretaria altamente calificada. La señorita Anita Brooks, 28 años de edad, es una persona encantadora, es una excelente estenógrafa, y está acostumbrada a trabajar a nivel ejecutivo, así como a manejar materiales confidenciales.

Por favor, llame a mi secretaria cuando haya tomado una decisión. Usted puede estar seguro de que su colega recibirá, de parte de nuestra Agencia, toda la ayuda necesaria.

Sinceramente suyo

## DATE

Type the date two lines below the Reference in one of the following forms:

15 September 1982
15th September 1982
September 15, 1982

Some international firms use: year, month, day, as 1982 09 15.

## INSIDE ADDRESS

Place the inside address two or three lines below the date (always in single spacing) in the following order: Name of recipient, number and street name, town (in capitals), county, if needed, and Post Office code number; e.g.

Mr John D Anderson
56 Churchill Road
DERBY
DE2 9ZL

If a letter is to be sent abroad, the country should be added either after the town, separated with a comma, or below it. The name of the country may be typed in lower case, but when the address is repeated on the envelope it should be typed in capitals; e.g.

Mr John D Anderson
56 Churchill Road
DERBY, England
DE2 9ZL

The postcode, wherever possible, should be typed on the final line, with a single space separating its two parts. It could, however, be typed on the same line as the county or town but it must be separated by six spaces.

The words 'Street', 'Road' and 'Avenue' should not be abbreviated.

Personal titles, such as 'Messrs', precede the name; official titles, such as 'Manager', are typed on the second line of the address; e.g.

Mr Robert F Taylor
Assistant Manager
The Hubbart Supply Co
530 Highgate Avenue
MANCHESTER
34BZ 1UV

Where window envelopes are used the inside address is placed above the 'reference initials' in the position indicated by a ruled box or short right angles; this makes the address visible through the 'window' of the envelope; e.g.

Mr. James Carter
12 Park Avenue
PORT CREDIT, CANADA
L5G 4M3

## SALUTATION

Type the salutation two or three lines below the inside address. Common forms of salutations are: Dear Sir, Dear Madam, Dear Mr Brown, Dear Miss Brown, Dear Ms Brown.

**COMLON INTERNATIONAL LIMITED**

COMLON HOUSE
WEST STREET
LONDON SW1Y 2AR
Tel: 01 920 0261 Telex: Comlond 888941 Telegrams: Comlond London SW1

If using plain paper allow two inches (12 line spaces) from top of paper before typing *reference initials.*

SB/KN

15 March 1982

**Printed heading, Reference initials and Date.**

**COMLON INTERNATIONAL LIMITED**

COMLON HOUSE
WEST STREET
LONDON SW1Y 2AR
Tel: 01 920 0261 Telex: Comlond 888941 Telegrams: Comlond London SW1

If using plain paper allow two inches (12 line spaces) from top of paper before typing *reference initials.*

SB/KN

15 March 1982

Messrs Tang Trading Co
75 Victoria Street
KOWLOON
Hong Kong

**Printed heading, Reference initials, Date and Inside address.**

**COMLON INTERNATIONAL LIMITED**

COMLON HOUSE
WEST STREET
LONDON SW1Y 2AR
Tel: 01 920 0261 Telex: Comlond 888941 Telegrams: Comlond London SW1

If using plain paper allow two inches (12 line spaces) from top of paper before typing *reference initials.*

SB/KN

15 March 1982

Messrs Tang Trading Co
75 Victoria Street
KOWLOON
Hong Kong

Dear Sirs

**Printed heading, Reference initials, Date, Inside address and Salutation.**

## Exercise 258

**Type the following circular letter.**

| | |
|---|---|
| **Size of paper:** | **A4** |
| **Size of letters:** | **elite** |
| **Style of layout:** | **blocked** |
| **Punctuation:** | **open** |
| **Left-hand margin:** | **12** |
| **Allow for heading:** | **12 lines** |

To All Shareholders

Dear Sir or Madam

PROPOSED RECONSTRUCTION - History

In December 1978 the Board of EH announced that it was considering the possibility of reorganising the Group's capital structure, thus affording shareholders the opportunity to obtain a direct interest in a company owning the Group's assets situated in Malaysia.  This would represent a step in conformity with the guide lines laid down in the Malaysian Government's New Economic Policy.

It was announced in October 1979 that MEB, a Malaysian public company, had acquired 11,783,998 ordinary shares in EH at a price of 64p per share.  Since MEB already owned a fair proportion of ordinary shares in EH, it was required, under the provisions of the City Code on Takeovers and Mergers, to extend an offer of 64p per share to the remaining shareholders of EH.  This offer closed in December 1979 and MEB now owns a total of 64.4% of EH's issued and fully paid share capital.

MEB, which has many Malaysian shareholders, invests in companies which have property and plantation interests in Malaysia and also runs a co-operative society formed to benefit the less privileged members of the community.

In November the Board of EH announced that, notwithstanding the outcome of the offer, it was intended as soon as practicable to submit to shareholders detailed proposals to give effect to the reconstruction of the company referred to above.

Whether or not you are able to attend the meeting convened for 29 June 1980, you are requested to complete and return the enclosed form of proxy.

Yours faithfully
ESTATES HOLDINGS LIMITED

N BURNS
Accountant

Enclosure

JUNE 1980

Another method of dating the copies of a circular letter that are not to be mailed simultaneously is to type only the **month** and the **year** either in the usual date place or at the bottom of the letter.

If the signature cannot be satisfactorily reproduced, type ONLY the signatory's name.

## BODY OF THE LETTER

Start the body of the letter two lines below the salutation. Use single spacing, unless the letter is short, when one-and-a-half or even double spacing may be used.

Between paragraphs of a letter typed in blocked style leave an extra line over and above the set spacing; i.e.

*For single-line spacing leave 2 spaces between paragraphs*
*For one-and-a-half spacing leave 2 1/2 spaces*
*For double-line spacing leave 3 spaces.*

Between paragraphs of an indented style letter, however, do not allow an extra line unless the text is single-spaced.

When several subjects are dealt with in a letter use either ***shoulder* or *paragraph*** headings as described on pages 88 and 89.

## COMPLIMENTARY CLOSE

Type the complimentary close two or three lines below the last line of the letter. Most common forms are: 'Yours truly' and 'Yours faithfully'. If, however, the addressee's name is mentioned in the salutation, as ***Dear Mr Brown,*** use the less formal 'Yours sincerely'.

The Company name - when used - is typed in closed capitals one line below the complimentary close; e.g.

Yours faithfully
D WILLIAMSON & CO LTD

**PD Paterson & Co Ltd**

Riverside Way, Southampton, England SU48 1XX

If using plain paper allow two inches (12 line spaces) from top of paper before typing *reference initials.*

SB/KN

15 March 1982

Messrs Tang Trading Co
75 Victoria Street
KOWLOON
Hong Kong

Dear Sirs

Please send us at your earliest convenience a Certificate of Origin, to be issued by the Government of Hong Kong with respect to our latest order No AS/44.

The combined Certificate of Value and Origin despatched to us together with all other documents cannot, unfortunately, be accepted by the Customs at this end.

Yours faithfully
P D PATERSON & CO LTD

S Burns
Manager

**Printed heading, Reference initials, Date, Inside address, Salutation, Body of letter, Complimentary close and Signature.**

## SIGNATURE

A letter is signed in ink after it is removed from the typewriter. Below the signature, on the fourth or fifth line space from the complimentary close (or the company name, if given), type the signatory's name, followed underneath by his designation; e.g.

Yours faithfully
D WILLIAMSON & CO LTD

T S Arnold
Director

If the signatory is a woman it is usual to type in full both her first name and her surname. If she is married, the title (Mrs) - enclosed in brackets - should follow her name; e.g.

Yours faithfully
D WILLIAMSON & CO LTD

Mary L Jones (Mrs)
Secretary

## MARGINS

The normal width for the margins of a letter is 15 pica (20 elite) on either side; the minimum can be 10 pica (15 elite); and the maximum 20 pica (24 elite). The right-hand margin may be less wide than the left-hand but it can never be wider.

## PUNCTUATION

With the 'blocked' and the 'semi-blocked' style of letters use open punctuation, i.e. omit punctuation marks (mainly commas at line ends and full tops) in Reference, Date, Inside address, Salutation, Complimentary close and Signature. Punctuate normally in the main body of the letter.

With the 'indented' style of letters use the traditional method of punctuation throughout the whole letter.

*More details on letter typing appear in colour on the specimen letters that follow.*

## Exercise 257 **Type in the indented style.**

If the copies of a circular letter are to be mailed over a number of days do not type any date but the words **Date as postmark.**

Reference initials are sometimes omitted from circular letters.

| | |
|---|---|
| **Size of paper:** | **A4** |
| **Size of letters:** | **elite** |
| **Style of layout:** | **blocked** |
| **Punctuation:** | **closed** |
| **Left-hand margin:** | **20** |
| **Allow for heading:** | **17 lines** |

Date as postmark

Dear Sir or Madam,

We are pleased to despatch your copy of the new 'Ways to English' catalogue. In it, you will find details of a great number of new publications for the teaching of English.

During the year we shall be producing more information on these in the form of prospectuses, newsletters, specimen materials and sample copies. Your name is on our mailing list at present and we think we know the levels and types of ELT materials that you are interested in.

However, we are sure that some of our addresses are now out-of-date and perhaps we are sending materials to people who no longer want them. So we are now revising our lists completely and would be grateful for your help.

If you wish to continue receiving catalogues and other information on our 'Ways to English' publications may I ask you to complete the
... enclosed card (within the next two weeks, if possible) and return it to me.

Many thanks for your help.

Yours faithfully,

Mark Ellis

Mark Ellis
Promotion Executive

An enclosure may be indicated by three full stops or hyphens in the left-hand margin against the line where the enclosure is mentioned.

PS Please remember to let us know if you change your address at any time.

# Specimen Letterheads

**MULTIFOOD LTD.**

Länggassstrasse 51
CH-3012 Berne/Switzerland
Mail address:
P.O. Box 1974
3001 Berne/Switzerland
Telephone: (031) 24 44 22
Telex: 33554 (Answer back: muf ch)
Cables: multifood berne

*Cloetta*

SVENSKA CHOKLADFABRIKS AKTIEBOLAGET

THEOBROMA CACAO

TELEGRAMS & CABLES:
BOLSOKEMIC, LONDON-WC1

TELEPHONE:
01-636 8080 (10 LINES)

**INTERNATIONAL CHEMICAL COMPANY LIMITED**

FOREIGN AND EXPORT DIVISION

CHENIES STREET, LONDON, WC1E 7ET

# Circular Letters

Circular letters contain exactly the same text; therefore, the required number are produced by duplicating, printing or photocopying.

If the number of copies required are few, insert individual inside addresses carefully, using the same type and colour to match those of the copies; for a large number of copies, however, omit the addresses.

Salutations used in circular letters are: **Dear Sir, Dear Madam, Dear Sir/Madam** or **Dear Sir and Madam.**

**Exercise 256** **Type the following circular letter, using the blocked style of layout.**

| | |
|---|---|
| Size of paper: | A5 |
| Size of letters: | elite |
| Style of layout: | indented |
| Punctuation: | closed |
| Left-hand margin: | 12 |
| Allow for heading: | 8 lines |

**THE UNIVERSITY OF LEEDS**

*THE INSTITUTE OF EDUCATION*

WHW/EM/512/82 19th June, 1982

Dear Sir or Madam,

I write to let you know that the Ceremony for the presentation of Certificates and Diplomas to Institute students will be held this year on Tuesday, 1st July at 5.00 p.m. in the Rupert Beckett Lecture Theatre in the New Arts Block of the University.

Full academic dress will be worn by those entitled to do so. A seat will be reserved for one relative or friend of each diplomand who attends.

The Ceremony will be followed by a Reception at which the Vice-Chancellor will preside.

I should be grateful if you would let me know by Thursday, 26th June (a) whether you will be present; (b) whether anyone will attend with you.

Yours very truly,

B Atkins

Assistant Secretary

## Exercise 219

Size of paper: A5
Size of letters: pica
Style of layout: blocked
Punctuation: open
Left hand margin: 10
Allow for heading: 14 lines

# PD Paterson & Co Ltd

Riverside Way, Southampton, England SU48 1XX

If using plain paper allow two inches (12 line spaces) from top of paper before typing *reference initials.*

SB/KN

15 March 1982

Messrs Tang Trading Co
75 Victoria Street
KOWLOON
Hong Kong

Dear Sirs

Please send us at your earliest convenience a Certificate of Origin, to be issued by the Government of Hong Kong with respect to our latest order No AS/44.

The combined Certificate of Value and Origin despatched to us together with all other documents cannot, unfortunately, be accepted by the Customs at this end.

Yours faithfully
P D PATERSON & CO LTD

S Burns
Manager

A short letter; hence, A5 paper is used.

With blocked letters the left-hand margin is usually in line with the letter heading.

All lines begin at the left-hand margin.

**Exercise 255** Type a copy of the following letter to Mr Cheung Man Tat, 501, Jalan, Gladstone, Penang, Malaysia, using today's date and the reference FLPT/M/79/2. (Part of LCCI examination paper LC/53/M/Sp79 - Higher.) *Take a carbon copy and prepare an envelope.*

Dear Mr Cheung

the services

u.c./ In reply to your letter about private treaty sales, I am pleased to give you full particulars of our unique service. We feel that it will pay you to sell by Private

l.c./ Treaty through this Company for the following reasons.

1 In return for a small commission you obtain [redacted] of professional philately valuers - each an expert in his field - whose interests are best served by selling your [redacted] at the highest price.

possible

collection

It pays to have our company on your side!

collection

2 We are prepared to visit you within 72 hours - anywhere in the country - to arrange the sale of your [redacted] subject to our assessment of its size and value. There is [redacted] no obligation [redacted] and [redacted] no charge. extra

3 We give you a written valuation telling you exactly how much we can obtain for your collection. The valuation is given free of any charge or obligation.

4 [redacted] sale will be completed quickly and as soon as you have approved our valuation we will advance you - by cash or cheque - fifty per cent of the valuation, and we guarantee the balance within one month.

The

our valuation

5 If you refuse you owe us nothing except

trs/ return transport or postage charges.

unlimited

Stamps of the

should

We [redacted] remind you that currently the greatest demand is for older, high-quality British Commonwealth [redacted] (particularly Australia and its States, Canada and New Zealand), Japan, Western Europe, United States and, of course, Great Britain. We can obtain very high prices for specialised collections, postal history material and postcards. Naturally, larger [redacted] are the best sellers as international buyers with funds [redacted]

collections

NP/ will be interested. [Almost everyone connected with stamps has something which is no longer required and can be turned into cash. We know that you have been a discerning buyer over the years and we look forward to hearing from you. You can either send your material to us by mail or call at our office here. If you call please ask for the writer or one of our valuation staff.

registered

Time and again we have proved that the extra money obtained for clients far outweighs the commission charged.

Yours sincerely

Publicity Manager

# Exercise 220

**COMLON INTERNATIONAL LIMITED**

COMLON HOUSE
WEST STREET
LONDON SW1Y 2AR

Tel: 01 920 0261 Telex: Comlond 888941 Telegrams: Comlond London SW1

| | |
|---|---|
| **Size of paper:** | **A4** |
| **Size of letters:** | **elite** |
| **Style of layout:** | **blocked** |
| **Punctuation:** | **open** |
| **Left-hand margin:** | **18** |
| **Allow for heading:** | **16 lines** |

Ref: REK/EB

20th June 1980

Mr A W Dolphin
Dolphin and Dolphin Limited
Stream House
Brook Road
LONDON      SE2 2PD

Dear Mr Dolphin

Thank you for your letter of 18th June and kind invitation to the Energy Research and Technology Symposium which you are arranging. Unfortunately both our Managing Director and I are committed to a Board meeting on 10th August and therefore regret that we shall be unable to attend.

However, if acceptable to you, we should like our Research Director, Dr J Smith, and our Works Manager, Mr A Cottam, to attend. They have very considerable background and interest in the subjects which are being presented and are directly concerned with Energy Conservation within our Company. They will, I feel, therefore, be able to offer a valuable contribution to what I am sure will be a very useful symposium.

Yours sincerely
COMLON INTERNATIONAL LIMITED

M E Kenny

Mary E Kenny (Mrs)

Town and postcode, when typed on same line, should be separated by six spaces.

In a letter dates should be expressed with consistency; either all cardinal numbers (1, 2, 3) should be used or all ordinal numbers (1st, 2nd, 3rd).

**Exercise 254** Type the following letter in single-line spacing. Use today's date and the reference LCC/MHM/Sp77. Address it to The Manager, United Overseas Banking Group, 1007 Lombard Street, London, EC4 1WW. (Part of LCCI examination paper LC/54/S/Sp77 - Intermediate.)

Dear Sir

We are pleased to give you the following ~~Herewith some~~ information ~~about~~ which you requested ~~we were speaking~~ when you visited us last month.

As you know ~~are aware~~, the next ~~a~~ major development in the banking scene here will be the formalisation of the Monetary Authority of Singapore's de facto central bank status. In the meantime ~~At present~~, Singapore's Banking Institute is setting about up-grading local banking officers' skills to match the rapid expansion and diversification of Singapore's financial centre.

lc The Institute has 131 members. These comprise

#

| | |
|---|---|
| 37 full banks | 12 restricted banks |
| 16 off-shore banks | 2 representative banks |
| 20 merchant banks | 35 finance companies |
| 4 discount houses | 3 money-brokers |

the Monetary Authority of Singapore
the Post Office Savings Bank.

The members pay subscriptions in proportion ~~according~~ to the size of their establishments and the operational requirements of the Institute.

NP The Government is most interested in the Institute. [There are about 800 students attending courses ranging from foreign exchange to customer relations and management. It is hoped that it will be declared a proper Institute of Higher Education shortly.

NP [You stressed the need for the universities and the banking industry to work closely together. In fact this is proving to be the case - I am sure you will be pleased to hear this.

Yours faithfully
INTERNATIONAL BANKING COMPANY (SINGAPORE)

CHIEF ACCOUNTANT

NP [Under the directorship of the former deputy director of the local Adult Education Board, and an officer seconded from the local branch of the First National City Bank,

# Exercise 221

| | |
|---|---|
| **Size of paper:** | **A4** |
| **Size of letters:** | **pica** |
| **Style of layout:** | **blocked** |
| **Punctuation:** | **open** |
| **Left-hand margin:** | **10** |
| **Allow for heading:** | **15 lines** |

*Allow two inches from top of paper for the printed heading.*

---

7 June 1980

Peter Lewis Esq
Headmaster
Willow Green School
CROYDON
CR8 9Z0

Dear Mr Lewis

It has given me much pleasure to make your acquaintance in connection with the seminar on Microelectronics and to have the opportunity to discuss with you the problem of recruiting the right calibre of young person into engineering and technology generally.

As I am sure you are well aware, the Finniston report earlier this year acknowledged that the formation of prospective young engineers begins at school. Indeed, the report suggested changes in school curricula aimed at increasing the proportion of pupils wishing to become engineers and at generating a proper understanding of engineering and industry.

With this in mind, I should like to discuss with you the possibility of an interchange between some of your staff and senior pupils and staff representatives from one or two Comlon divisions, the products of which rely heavily on microelectronics during the manufacturing stages; our Food Processing Machinery Division is one notable example. If you are interested in this proposal, may I suggest that your secretary gets in touch with mine to fix a convenient date for a meeting here at West Street.

Yours sincerely

Anna Davidson (Mrs)
Director

AD/TI

The **reference initials** are occasionally typed at the bottom , two or three lines below the signature.

Note: **Mr** precedes a name, **Esq** follows it.

Postcode is here typed below the town — a preferred method.

*This is the continuation sheet of the letter started on the previous page.*

Allow six blank lines from top of paper and type the **page number,** the **addressee,** and the **date** in single, one-and-a-half, or double spacing. Allow five to six more blank lines below the heading details and continue the letter.

NB A continuation sheet should contain at least three lines of text, in addition to the closing lines.

Page 2

Trevor Taylor Esq

9 June 1979

7 Payments due to you will be made monthly in arrears, without deductions of tax, except for expenses which will be paid on receipt of the appropriate claim.

This agreement does not constitute a contract of employment and, with the exception of the items listed above, does not grant or imply any other benefit from Comlon.

Will you please sign one copy of this letter to signify your agreement and return it to me.

Yours sincerely

Managing Director

Enc

**With the semi-blocked style of layout the details would be set out as follows:**

Page 2

Trevor Taylor Esq                                        9 June 1979

**With the indented (traditional) style:**

Trevor Taylor, Esq.                    -2-                    9th June, 1979

## Exercise 222

# COMLON INTERNATIONAL LIMITED

COMLON HOUSE
WEST STREET
LONDON SW1Y 2AR

Tel: 01 920 0261 Telex: Comlond 888941 Telegrams: Comlond London SW1

**Size of paper:** A4
**Size of letters:** pica
**Style of layout:** blocked
**Punctuation:** open
**Left-hand margin:** 10
**Allow for heading:** 20 lines

Our ref LP/SCG

9 June 1983

Mr M Venables
Office Manager
Hyde Communications Limited
Neverton Industrial Estate
COVENTRY
CV4 2AS

Dear Mr Venables

I am sorry to learn from your letter of 4 June 1983 that you are having some difficulty with the Mark 3 machine recently delivered to you. From your description it seems that both the siting of the machine and the inexperience of the operators may be contributing to the trouble.

I have arranged for Peter Goodrich, our representative for your area, to call on you on Monday next, 13 June 1983. He will bring an installation engineer with him. I am sure they will be able to overcome the difficulty and advise you on a training programme for your operators.

Yours sincerely

Mary Peterfield

Mary Peterfield (Mrs)
Assistant Sales Director

The signatory's marital status **(Mrs)** is typed after the name - not before it.

# Exercise 253

## TWO-PAGE LETTERS

If a letter is too long for an A4 page use a continuation sheet. This should be plain, i.e. without a printed letterhead; but, of the same quality and colour as the letterhead paper.

Stop the text of the letter at about the fifth line from the end of the paper, seeing that the last line of the page (a) is not the first or the penultimate of the paragraph, and (b) does not end in an abbreviated or hyphenated word.

Note: Some typists add at the end the catchword «Cont'd» (continued) or «PTO» (please turn over) to show that there is a continuation sheet - should the next sheet have been inadvertently omitted.

SG/TI

9 June 1979

CONFIDENTIAL

Trevor Taylor Esq
17 Ross Walk Rise
Pen End
LONDON NW12 9RO

Dear Mr Taylor

CONSULTANCY SERVICES

Following your retirement on 30 September 1979, Comlon International Limited is willing to use your services as a Design Consultant on the following basis.

1 The period of agreement will commence on 1 October 1979 and last until 30 September 1980 with a possibility of extension.

2 The work you would be called on to undertake would normally be in respect of advice on design matters.

3 Comlon will pay you £1,200.00 fee for the year 1 October 1979 to 30 September 1980 (payable monthly in arrears), irrespective of the number of days you work for Comlon, provided you are available to work for Comlon a minimum of one day a week. The days you are required to work will be decided by Comlon in the light of the circumstances prevailing but will not exceed one day a week unless by agreement with you. If circumstances require, however, it may be necessary for you to work several days in one or more weeks, again by mutual agreement.

4 In respect of each of the first 50 days worked, you will be paid a fee of £70. For each day worked in excess of 50 days you will be paid £90 a day.

5 This agreement does not constitute an undertaking to employ you for any specific number of days a year.

6 You agree that you are willing to travel abroad on Comlon's behalf, if requested. You will be entitled to reasonable expenses incurred during the course of Comlon business.

| | |
|---|---|
| Size of paper: | A4 |
| Size of letters: | pica |
| Style of layout: | blocked |
| Punctuation: | open |
| Left-hand margin: | 10 |
| Allow for heading: | 18 lines |

# Exercise 223

| | |
|---|---|
| Size of paper: | A5 |
| Size of letters: | elite |
| Style of layout: | semi-blocked |
| Punctuation: | open |
| Left-hand margin: | 12 |
| Allow for heading: | 10 lines |

*Set a tab stop at about the centre of the typing line and use it for positioning reference lines, date and complimentary close.*

Your ref BC/rb
Our ref  KN/GF

12 February 1982

Messrs H Shields & Co
38 Greenwood Road
LEEDS, Yorkshire
DR2 7SF

Dear Sirs

The goods listed on invoice of 20 January arrived yesterday in excellent condition, and were found to be satisfactory in all respects.

We especially appreciate the good judgement you displayed in selecting styles and patterns suitable for our market and we are indeed thankful.

Yours faithfully
QUALITY GOODS LIMITED

L. R. Larsen

L R Larsen
Manager

**Exercise 252** Type a copy of this letter in single-line spacing, using the reference MHM/LCMI/78 and today's date. Be sure to leave sufficient room for the signature. (Part of LCCI examination paper LC/54/M1/Sp78 - Intermediate.)

Dear Mr Forrest

Thank [redacted] (you) for your letter of (8th May) regarding the range of marine insurance work covered by our organisation.

NP/ [We [redacted] (should) like to print out that the Group has been a leader (and innovator) in the field of marine insurance since 1833. No matter what the problem in

ꝺ/ this field, we can help you solve it ~~more~~ efficiently, economically and quickly.

NP/ [Apparently, the questions which motivated your original inquiry were those of claim settlements

stet/ abroad, and reinsurance. We have over 530 ~~500~~ claims settling agents, all over the world. [redacted] So important is the business of [redacted] reinsurance that we have now transferred (Mr Sinclair Dawson) from the General Claims Department to handle it. [redacted] His skills and service as a member of (the experienced team from) this Group are recognised by an increasing number of

l.c./ Shipowners, who appreciate his inventiveness.

NP/ [We [redacted] (should) like you to call us so that we can arrange preliminary discussions (on general problems) before you take up specific questions with Mr Dawson personally. [redacted] Perhaps we can arrange a date towards the end of the month.

Yours sincerely

General Manager

Mr R. Forrest
59 Grangemouth Road
[redacted] HULL HU6 3EE

# Exercise 224

| | |
|---|---|
| **Size of paper:** | **A4** |
| **Size of letters:** | **elite** |
| **Style of layout:** | **blocked** |
| **Punctuation:** | **open** |
| **Left-hand margin:** | **15** |
| **Allow for heading:** | **15 lines** |

FLPT/A/78/1

21 November 1978

Mrs G Perry
55 Springbank Road
CROYDON
CR7 3BX

Dear Mrs Perry

I have received your letter about the servicing of our H371 refrigerator and suggest that some simple checks may save you trouble and expense.

1 If the motor is apparently not operating, check that the plug is firmly fixed in the wall socket; check that there is an electricity supply to the socket by plugging in another appliance; if the plug is fused, replace the fuse, plug in and switch on.

2 If the motor runs but the cabinet is not cold enough, check the setting of the thermostat; carry out a de-frosting, re-start and check that it is freezing satisfactorily.

It is possible, of course, that if the motor runs too much, the door has been left ajar, or warm foodstuffs have been put in the refrigerator. I must remind you that you should not pack your shelves so tightly as to obstruct the free circulation of air.

Yours truly

(Service Manager)

For the indentation of the two numbered paragraphs set tabs **and remember to use them.** Alternatively, re-set margins for the indented portions, using the left-hand margin release to return to the original margin for the numbers.

# Exercise 251

Notations such as **Confidential, Personal, Private,** etc. are positioned two or three lines below the date. Type them either in closed capitals or in lower case and underscored.

| | |
|---|---|
| **Size of paper:** | **A4** |
| **Size of letters:** | **elite** |
| **Style of layout:** | **blocked** |
| **Punctuation:** | **open** |
| **Left-hand margin:** | **15** |
| **Allow for heading:** | **15 lines** |

MHM/LCM1/78

5 April 1978

CONFIDENTIAL

Mr K Lee
Chairman
Group Rubber Estates Limited
Jalan Raja Chulan
Kuala Lumpur 005-100

Dear Mr Lee

I enclose a copy of a letter which I am thinking of sending to Mr Peter Bullen, Managing Director of Gutherie Estates.

Bearing in mind the possibility of a merger between our two companies, I thought it was advisable to write to him in general terms. However, you may prefer to meet him rather than have a letter sent. Please let me know your preference.

I shall be away for ten days from Monday, 24 April, visiting our estates. At the beginning of May I shall be in the UK negotiating a further contract with Lewis Frozen Foods. While I am in the UK, I shall be looking at Bagnall-Lansing's new mechanical handling equipment. An extract from their brochure about this is enclosed.

Yours sincerely

pp W T WEBSTER
Group Manager

(Dictated by Mr W T Webster
and signed in his absence)

Enclosures

## Exercise 225

Letters not long enough for A4 paper are sometimes typed on two-thirds A4.

Note the omission of the question mark at the end of the second paragraph; this is because the sentence is a simple request disguised as a question.

| | |
|---|---|
| Size of paper: | 2/3 A4 |
| Size of letters: | pica |
| Style of layout: | blocked |
| Punctuation: | open |
| Left-hand margin: | 12 |
| Allow for heading: | 12 lines |

---

**COMLON INTERNATIONAL LIMITED**

COMLON HOUSE
WEST STREET
LONDON SW1Y 2AR

Tel: 01 920 0261   Telex: Comlond 888941   Telegrams: Comlond London SW1

AD/TI

7 June 1980

Mr P Villiers
Secretary
Association of Electronic Engineers
95 Drury Lane
EAST MOLESEY, Surrey
KT13 0AY

Dear Mr Villiers

Mrs Davidson has asked me to let you know that, unfortunately, because of a business engagement out of town on the same date, she will not be able to attend the next Committee Meeting called for Tuesday, 24 June.

Would you please convey Mrs Davidson's apologies for absence to the Chairman and members of the Committee.

Yours sincerely

Secretary to
Mrs Anna Davidson

**Exercise 250** **Type a corrected copy of the following letter in single-line spacing and address it to Mr. G. A. Sung, 489 Jalan Ladang, Kota Kinabalu, Sabah. Use today's date and the reference FLPT/M/77/2. (Part of LCCI examination paper LC/53/M/Sp77 - Higher.)**

Dear Mr Sung,

Sociological Problems of the Far East

I have been looking through your manuscript on the topic ~~subject~~ above-named before

uc/ passing it on to our reader on the subject, for his professional

appraisal of its worth.

run on/ I feel that you have closely followed the synopsis [redacted] which you submitted to us last year, and I am very impressed by your layout and the detailed cross-referencing.

As a former student myself of educational problems in this country, third

I venture to suggest that a short [redacted] table inserted in the paragraph of your chapter entitled "Education and Health" would add to its real value. The following are the appropriate figures for last year:

| | Schools | Teachers | Students |
|---|---|---|---|
| Primary (age 6 to 11) | 6,632 | 54,033 | 1,714,185 |
| Secondary (age 12 to 18) | 1,088 | 22,475 | 602,174 |
| Teacher training: Vocational | 105 | 1,003 | 21,622 |
| Higher | - | ~~970~~ 938 | ~~14,955~~ 14,935 |

Your paragraph on literacy in the country is most interestingly composed and I had not realised that there has been a significant improvement since 1970 when the figures for West Malaysia, Sabah and Sarawak were much lower.

NP/ [I do hope that our Reader will feel able to recommend the manuscript as I feel that there is a ~~real~~ need for a work on the subject.

Yours sincerely,

General Manager

# How to Use Certain Courtesy Titles

## IN THE OPEN PUNCTUATED STYLE

1. For personal titles before names:

Mr - for a man
Messrs - for two or more men
Mrs - for a married woman
Mesdames - for two or more women
Miss - for an unmarried woman
Misses - for two or more unmarried women
Ms - for a married or unmarried woman
Esq - old fashioned for a gentleman; it follows a name; as, B Davies Esq

2. Use 'Messrs':

When addressing partnerships, except when the trade name begins with 'The' or a title:

Messrs R Lincoln & Sons; *but*
The Lincoln Trading Co
Sir Isaac Pitman & Sons Ltd

3. 'Dr' is abbreviated only before a name:

Dr Brown is in the Hospital; *but*
The doctor is in the Hospital

4. Decorations and honours, educational qualifications and professional titles should be typed in order of importance:

Mr R Reynolds, VC, MC, DSO, CBE
Mr R Reynolds, PhD, MA, BA, BSc
Mr R Reynolds, FRCS, FRSA, ACA
Mr R Reynolds, VC, MA, FRSA, MP

*(MP for Member of Parliament is placed last because it is a temporary title.)*

5. Such abbreviations as Sen, Jun or Snr, Jnr or Sr, Jr (for Senior, Junior) and I, II, III etc (for First, Second, Third etc) are used after a full name; not with the surname alone:

Queen Elizabeth II
Chris Christopher, Snr, Esq.
Mr Chris Christopher, Sr

6. Address unmarried sisters as follows:

The Misses B & R Browning; or

Miss B and Miss R Browning

7. Address a young boy under eighteen by his first name and surname:

Basil Winterton; or

Master Basil Winterton *(less popular)*

8. Abbreviate civil, military, professional, or religious titles before *full* names:

Sen. D Alex Westinghouse
Gov. Nelson A Rockefeller
Brig. Gen. John McArthur
Prof. Albert Einstein

But type them in full if followed by *surnames* only:

Senator Westinghouse
Governor Rockefeller
General McArthur
Professor Einstein

9. 'Reverend' and 'Honourable' are typed in full when preceded by 'The':

The Honourable John Richard
The Reverend Dr Hammond; *but*
Hon. John Richard
Rev. Dr Hammond

These titles, abbreviated or not, are used only with a person's full name or with a surname preceded by Mr or Dr; never with a surname alone:

Hon. John Richard
Rev. Dr Hammond
The Reverend Dr Hammond
Rev. Henry Hammond
*but not:* Rev. Hammond

## Exercise 249

**This letter is sent by the Malastamp Company. Type a corrected copy of it to Mr J Hallows, 593 Grosvenor Road, London, SE13 6SF using today's date and the reference FLPT M 79 1. (Part of LCCI examination paper LC 53 M Sp79 - Higher.)** *Make a blind carbon copy for the information of Mr Adam Smith.*

**Blind carbon copies** are used when the addressee should not know that copies have been sent to other persons. *How to make them:* Insert a piece of paper between ribbon and top copy and type **bcc** (blind carbon copy) followed by the names of recipients.

---

Dear Sir

development of the

Thank you for your letter regarding the literary side of our business. As a matter of fact we have been [redacted]

stet/ considering for some time months the proposition that booklets on philatelic milestones would have a [redacted] wide appeal to members of societies and unconnected enthusiasts.

certain

Enquiries that we have [redacted] made in foreign centres suggest

dates that the following have the greatest support and we would like to hear your views on them:

#/

| | |
|---|---|
| 1635 | CharlesI in Britain establishes the post as a monopoly (royal) |
| 1836 | The system of postal rates based on weight [redacted] suggested by Hill in Britain (Rowland) |
| 1840 | Introduction of the world's first postage stamps, in Britain, and [redacted] adoption by Mauritius, Brazil and the United States |
| 1874 | Formation of the Postal Union, demonstrating the adoption of Hill's system all over the world. (Universal) |

trs/

Two members of our staff have already indicated their wish to be associated with the project and in all [redacted]

NP/ we shall ask them to start work [redacted] within a couple of months. Meanwhile, I hope you will [redacted] express your views on the dates that have been proposed.

Yours faithfully

, Mr Chung Lee Lim and Miss Lily Wong,

Publicity Manager

probability

**Exercise 226** **You are typist to the General Manager of Information Services (Malaysia). Type a corrected copy of the following letter in single-line spacing, and address it to Mr E. Baker, 277 George Street, Wolverhampton WV2 5DF. Use today's date and the reference FLPT/M/78/1. (Part of LCCI examination paper LC/53/M/Sp78 - Higher.)**

Dear Mr Baker

Thank you for your [redacted] letter asking for information about the various aspects of life in Malaysia. [redacted] Having considered your request, may I suggest you try to obtain a copy of the booklet entitled [redacted] "Malaysia: Your Profit Centre in Asia" by the [redacted] Federal Industrial Development Authority?

run on/ This publication not only has short articles on the land, country, and the people, but also devotes space to such topics as the economy, the road to industrialisation, investment, [redacted] trs/ tax incentives, sites for industry, and markets for products.

NP/ This lavishly illustrated booklet [redacted] ends with an UC/ invitation from the chairman of the Federal Industrial Development Authority to all those who are seriously considering the whole question of investment. Your own particular [redacted] interest - transport - is covered in a [redacted] special section devoted to both sea and air [redacted] services. I wonder if you are aware that the air cargo rates from Kuala to the major cities of the world are among [redacted] the lowest in the world? There are daily air cargo flights from the capital.

Yours sincerely

of 2 April

industrial and social

Lumpur

, of course,

issued a few years ago

# Exercise 248

| | |
|---|---|
| **Size of paper:** | **A4** |
| **Size of letters:** | **elite** |
| **Style of layout:** | **blocked** |
| **Punctuation:** | **open** |
| **Left-hand margin:** | **15** |
| **Allow for heading:** | **12 lines** |

FLPT/M/80/1

3 April 1980

The Manager
Kuantan Tours
108 Jalan Ampang
Kuala Lumpur

Dear Sir

We thank you for your enquiry of 31 March and very much appreciate your remarks about our equipment. We feel certain that our latest imports in each department (particularly those from Germany and the United States) have few equals.

We can supply you with a modern filing system which will meet all your requirements. The following special features should be noted:

1 Red bars indicate the start of each section

2 Titles are indicated on the top surface of the coupling bars, as well as on the folders

3 'Removal' folders are marked by special blue 'out' cards and show the present location of each missing folder

4 A wide range of colours is available for folders for those firms which ask for the service.

The price of the cabinets (all A4 size), complete with one hundred folders, are as follows:

| | |
|---|---|
| One-drawer cabinet | M$ 720 |
| Two-drawer " | M$ 875 |
| Three-drawer " | M$1080. |

Delivery can be made upon receipt of order. If you will let us know of a convenient day and time, our Mr Koh will be happy to call and discuss your requirements in detail.

Yours faithfully

Sales Director

cc Mr R Adams
Mr T Stevens

Second paragraph of letter. Note that full stops are omitted at the end of the numbered lines, except the last one.

The names of two or more recipients of carbon copies are typed in alphabetical order, each starting on a new line at the same point. (The name of the person for whom each copy is intended is ticked at the side.)

**Exercise 227** You are typist to the Tours Manager of Explorer Travel Company of Singapore. Type the following letter in single-line spacing, using today's date and the reference FLPT/S/79/1. Address the letter to Mr Ong Bang Lee, 400 North Bridge Road, Singapore. (Part of LCCI examination paper LC/53/S/Sp79 - Higher.)

Dear Sir (first) (matter)

Thank you for your letter acknowledging receipt of [redacted]
the batch of travel documents covering part of your
NP/ trip to the United States. [redacted] [We believe that
the remaining tickets and reservations will be ready
soon after receiving your cheque and these will [redacted]
NP/ be arranged in a special folder [[Your failure to
understand our quotations for air movements between
the American cities is appreciated and we regret
that this [was not made clear in our last letter.
ʃ/ We must ~~again~~ emphasise that [redacted]
UC/ discount air tickets for internal flights must be
purchased ~~wi~~ prior to or within thirty days
after your arrival in the United States.]
run on/ [A minimum of three stopovers must be made
between the point of origin and the [redacted] final
destination shown on the ticket. Travel must be
completed not later than the 45th day after [redacted]
UC/ travel from the gateway city.
Upon receipt of your cheque for S$2600 we shall
be able to ~~with~~ prepare this set of tickets and
let you have them within a few days.

Yours faithfully

Tours Manager

(in which we urge you to place the documents in the appropriate sections.)

# Exercise 247

| | |
|---|---|
| **Size of paper:** | **A4** |
| **Size of letters:** | **elite** |
| **Style of layout:** | **blocked** |
| **Punctuation:** | **open** |
| **Left-hand margin:** | **12** |
| **Allow for heading:** | **12 lines** |

MHM/LC1(2)78

5 April 1978

Mr Peter Bullen
Managing Director
Gutherie Estates Limited
3232 St Mary at Hill
LONDON
EC3R 8DH

Dear Sir

ALTERNATIVE CROP FOR PLANTATIONS

It was a great pleasure having you as the guest of our Company during your stay in Malaysia last month. You asked us to let you have some detailed information on the production of palm oil as an alternative crop to rubber - which we give below.

You may be surprised to learn that our Company started planting oil palms 50 years ago. It was, however, only in the mid-sixties that oil palms were planted in any quantity in Malaysia. One of the main reasons for our production of palm oil, alongside rubber production, was that an oil palm reaches maturity within three years whereas a rubber tree takes twice as long.

The other two reasons possibly added impetus to the surge of planting oil palms recently. The first reason is that the world market is larger and more widespread than for rubber and the demand for vegetable oils is on the increase. The second is that rubber companies, such as ourselves, were trying to achieve a balance to offset the cyclical market in rubber.

Over the years we have tried to achieve a 50-50 split between the two crops (so maybe our Company name is misleading).

Looking to the future, we may consider what next to cultivate. A third crop would, we think, increase stability of profits and offset any over-supply problem of which there is a danger.

Yours faithfully
GROUP RUBBER ESTATES LIMITED

C Godfrey

GENERAL MANAGER

cc Mr K Lee

When a carbon copy is to be sent to persons other than the addressee type at the foot of the letter **cc** (meaning 'copy circulated to' or 'carbon copy to') followed by the name of the additional recipient(s).

NB Errors should be carefully corrected both in the top and the carbon copies.

## Exercise 228

# COMLON INTERNATIONAL LIMITED

COMLON HOUSE
WEST STREET
LONDON SW1Y 2AR

Tel: 01 920 0261    Telex: Comlond 888941    Telegrams: Comlond London SW1

| | |
|---|---|
| **Size of paper:** | **A4** |
| **Size of letters:** | **elite** |
| **Style of layout:** | **blocked** |
| **Punctuation:** | **open** |
| **Left-hand margin:** | **20** |
| **Allow for heading:** | **15 lines** |

DJ/MW

12 June 1980

Mr B Hilton
23 Northcotes Avenue
DURHAM      DH5 7DW

Dear Mr Hilton

Thank you for your letter of 8 June from which I note that you will be taking up an appointment in Reading on 1 August and that you would like to find a property within a 30 mile radius of the town.

I have arranged for your name to be added to our mailing list and you will automatically receive our weekly property schedule which is published every Friday.

With regard to rented property you will appreciate that it is almost impossible to acquire a short term lease on anything in this area and our leasehold manager informs me that we have nothing on our books at the moment.

If you will let me know when you propose to come down, I shall be happy to take you to view any properties in which you are interested.

Yours sincerely
COMLON INTERNATIONAL LIMITED

Joyce Deacon
Residential Property Manager

Enc

The **Enclosure** notation is typed two or three lines below the signature, and is indicated in one of the following ways: **Enclosure, Enc, enc, ENC.**

The postcode is here typed in a different way; compare it with the preferred style shown on page 115.

# Carbon Copies

## TO TAKE A CARBON COPY:

1. Place the flimsy (thin paper used for copies) on the desk. On top of it place a sheet of carbon paper, ***with carbon side facing the flimsy;*** and on top of both of them place the sheet for the original, ***with the typing side up.*** (Use one carbon and one flimsy for each copy required.)

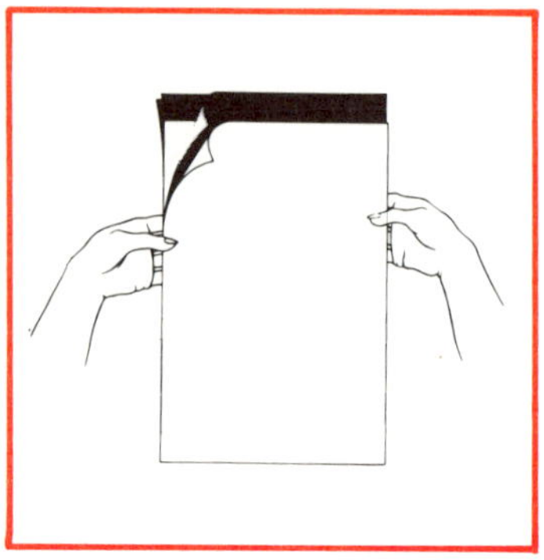

2. Pick up the papers, *with top edge facing down,* tap them gently to straighten, and insert pack into the typewriter *with the carbon side towards you.*

3. To insert the sheets into typewriter, hold them firmly to prevent slipping. Hold the pack with your left hand and turn platen with your right hand. ***To avoid any possible wrinkles of the sheets, insert pack into typewriter with paper-release lever pulled forward; reset this immediately, and turn the pack into the machine.***

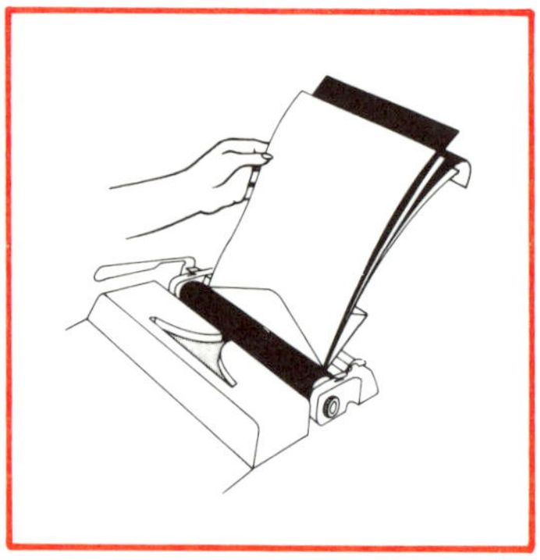

4. If many copies are to be taken, you can place the pack in a sheet with a folded end (or under the flap of an envelope), in order to help keep the edges straight in line.

POINTS TO OBSERVE: (1) To produce clear copies, clean the type faces and use good quality carbon sheets. (2) For large numbers of copies - up to eight - use a hard platen *if possible,* and strike keys with more force - especially letters 'm', 'a', 'w', 'g' and all the fractions. (The punctuation marks require a light stroke.)

## TO CORRECT CARBON COPIES

To correct errors neatly, i.e. without smudges appearing on the carbon copy: insert a slip of paper behind the sheet of carbon *at the point of error*; erase on the copy, with a soft (pencil) eraser.

To make corrections to a carbon copy after you have removed it from the typewriter: place a piece of carbon paper between the ribbon and the paper; this will secure uniformity in the appearance of the copy.

If you have to type a note on the carbon copies *which should not appear on the original,* insert a piece of paper between the ribbon and the paper at the printing point. Conversely, if you have to type something on the original but *not on the copies,* insert a slip of paper behind each carbon.

# Exercise 229

INDENTED STYLE OF LAYOUT: (1) Indent paragraphs 5 spaces for pica, 6 for elite. (2) Punctuate fully the whole letter. (3) Type **date** opposite to reference and finish it at the same point with right-hand margin. (4) Start **complimentary close** and **signature** at about the centre of typing line, centralizing all their lines vertically with one another. (5) In **date** use ordinal number, as 1st, 2nd, 3rd, etc.

LWC/DJB                                        7th October 1980

| | |
|---|---|
| **Size of paper:** | **A4** |
| **Size of letters:** | **pica** |
| **Style of layout:** | **Indented** |
| **Punctuation:** | **closed** |
| **Left-hand margin:** | **18** |
| **Allow for heading:** | **18 lines** |

Mrs. E. N. Nichols,
217 Lowther Hill,
LONDON, SE23 1PZ

Dear Madam,

As Export Agents for Messrs. Jonathan Stevens, 467C Regent Street, London W1, we have pleasure in enclosing our Invoice No. EX 779, together with official receipt for your payment of £708, in connection with the Dyed Marmot Coat and Natural Blue Fox Stole which you purchased from them on the 3rd instant.

In accordance with your instructions the two furs, packed in one parcel, will be delivered c/o B.A. Flight B/A 638, which is scheduled to leave from London Airport for Athens/Nicosia/Beirut on the 9th October 1980 at 2115 hrs.

We sincerely hope that the furs give you complete satisfaction.

Yours faithfully,
C. ROSS & CO. SUCCESSORS LTD.

H. White

EXPORT DEPARTMENT

Enclosure

NB If an enclosure is smaller in size than the letter, it is attached above the letter; if larger, it is attached under it.

## Exercise 246

The abbreviation **PS**, meaning **postscript**, is typed at least two line spaces below the last item at the end of the letter and is initialled by the signatory.

The letters **PS** (or **P.S.**) may be omitted.

KN/ew 2nd April, 1982

Messrs. Milling & Gamon,
72 Richmond Road,
CAMBRIDGE,
PB2 6EF

Dear Sirs,

We are sorry that we cannot grant the request made in your letter of 28th March to allow you an additional discount on the goods invoiced to you on 13th February. You will note that the terms distinctly state that goods may not be returned or allowances made for them for any cause after five days from delivery.

We have sold over a thousand pieces of this cloth and yours is the first complaint we have received. You will remember that our usual terms of thirty days were extended in your case at your earnest request. Now, nearly two months after the receipt of the goods, you are seeking an additional allowance because of the quality.

If you have any of this cloth on hand you may return it to us and pay merely for the amount used. Otherwise, we shall expect from you on 13th April, when your account falls due, a cheque for £911.20.

Yours truly,
THE LINEN MANUFACTURING CO., LTD.

Alice D. Blake

Alice D. Blake (Miss)
Sales Manager

PS Our Mr. Brooks will soon be in your area. If you would like him to call on you please let us know.

ADB.

**Size of paper:** A4
**Size of letters:** pica
**Style of layout:** indented
**Punctuation:** closed
**Left-hand margin:** 15
**Allow for heading:** 15 lines

## Exercise 230

| | |
|---|---|
| Size of paper: | A4 |
| Size of letters: | pica |
| Style of layout: | indented |
| Punctuation: | closed |
| Left-hand margin: | 15 |
| Allow for heading: | 15 lines |

# COMLON LTD.

5 BISHOPSGATE WAY,
LONDON EC4T 9AW

12th May, 1979

Mr. John Lisgo, M.A., B.Com.,
Head of Department of Commerce,
Midvale Technical College,
High Hill Way,
Midvale.

Dear Mr. Lisgo,

Thank you for your letter of the 8th May. It would give us great pleasure to arrange for twenty of your students to visit our offices. I attach a suggested programme for the visit and hope you will find it suitable for the kind of students you propose to bring. We frequently have visits from technical students but this is the first such visit by students from the commercial stream.

I suggest that the visit should take place on either Tuesday 6th June or Thursday 8th June. Will you please confirm which would be the most convenient date for you?

I would also appreciate a list of names of the students and staff who will be coming, so that I may arrange the preparation of suitable name-tags for each person: this is normal procedure for all visitors, as a security measure.

I look forward to hearing from you as soon as possible confirming these arrangements.

Yours sincerely,

B. Foster

Enc. Draft programme

With the indented style of layout, left-hand margin need not be in line with printed heading, as the latter is usually centred on page.

The **enclosure** notation is sometimes followed by a description of enclosed document.

**Exercise 245** Type this letter in single-line spacing. Use today's date and the reference MHM/A78/LCI and address it to Jones & Robinson & Co Ltd, Palace Chambers, New Bond Street, LONDON, WC1 5CC. (Part of LCCI examination paper LC/54/A78 - Intermediate.)

FOR THE ATTENTION OF MR G K ROSEBERRY

Dear Sirs

Thank you for your letter of ~~9~~ 16 November. on future trends of relocation

After reading the enclosed article, you will appreciate how difficult it is for us to give you advice on your problem. However, we shall be happy to meet Mr Roseberry early next week to discuss any plans you ~~have~~ may have in detail, and to give you all the help we can.

In the ~~interim~~ meantime we would point out that in times of recession, the ~~removal~~ costs of moving premises are high, which can offset the advantages of slightly lower rates and rents. Another fact to bear in mind is that in the present property market it

stet is possible that ~~vacating~~ leaving premises could well lead to a company having to pay a reverse premium to its successor.

It is ~~little~~ not widely known that the Greater London Council ~~are~~ is so concerned with the steady depopulation of central London that it is giving serious consideration to a location policy for office development in the Greater London Plan. ~~which~~

uc we can discuss this at our meeting. Among its recommendations it is suggested that office development must be ~~in~~ confined to areas which are served by first class public transport facilities, and preference be given to those sectors where the ratio of office jobs to resident office workers is low.

Yours faithfully
BOURNE & BRUTON

R ELLIS (Miss)

Enclosure

# Exercise 231

| | |
|---|---|
| **Size of paper:** | **A4** |
| **Size of letters:** | **pica** |
| **Style of layout:** | **indented** |
| **Punctuation:** | **open** |
| **Left-hand margin:** | **15** |
| **Allow for heading:** | **12 lines** |

Your ref JFT/ds
Our ref Adv/156

19 March 1981

Messrs B Alexander & Co
P O Box 5467
NICOSIA, Cyprus

Dear Sirs

We acknowledge receipt of your letter of 11 March, in which we note your interest in the importation and distribution of our toy items.

As requested, we have pleasure in enclosing one of our 1980 Catalogues which covers, except for two or three items, our complete range. As, however, the Catalogue is not exhaustive we will arrange to send you a few copies of the 1981 Catalogue as soon as these are received from the printers.

Toymaster toys originated in the USA some twenty-five years ago following suggestions put forward by the Gezell Institute of Child Welfare and, throughout the years, Toymaster Products have been manufacturing these items with great success. The tendency for children, nowadays, is to play with realistic child-size toys and you will find that our items are priced so that even the lower income groups can afford the cost of them.

We look forward to hearing from you in the very near future, and we wish to assure you that any orders you may place with us will receive our immediate attention.

Yours faithfully
TOYMASTER PRODUCTS LTD

J. F. Taylor

J F Taylor
Manager

Enc 1

An uncommon variation of indented style, whereby (a) open punctuation is used, and (b) all closing lines begin at the same point.

Some firms indicate the number of the documents enclosed; e.g. Encs 2. Others list the items enclosed on succeeding lines, indenting them three spaces from the left-hand margin; e.g.

ENCS
1. Invoice No. 342
2. Cheque for £600
3. Receipt for £290

# Exercise 244

The **attention** line is used when a letter addressed to a firm is to be dealt with by one particular person.

In a letter the **attention** line and the **subject** heading should be typed in similar style - either all in capitals or with initial capitals and underscored.

| | |
|---|---|
| **Size of paper:** | **A4** |
| **Size of letters:** | **elite** |
| **Style of layout:** | **blocked** |
| **Punctuation:** | **open** |
| **Left-hand margin:** | **20** |
| **Allow for heading:** | **15 lines** |

JD/MW

12 June 1980

Messrs Jackson Bright & Co
48 Wheeler Gate
NOTTINGHAM NG1 2CB

As the addressee is the Company, the salutation must be **Dear Sirs** - not Dear Sir or Dear Mr Jackson.

FOR THE ATTENTION OF MR L JACKSON

Dear Sirs

46 DALTON DRIVE WIMBLEDON COMMON

On behalf of my clients Mr and Mrs John James, I have now arranged a provisional sale of the above property to your clients, Mr and Mrs H Pearson of 127 High Road Bramcote Nottingham at an agreed price of £46 000 for the freehold with vacant possession on completion and subject to contract.

Your clients have agreed to exchange contracts on 18 July with completion on 15 August.

I have instructed my clients' solicitors to prepare and forward a contract for your approval.

Yours faithfully
COMLON INTERNATIONAL LIMITED

Joyce Deacon
Residential Property Manager

# Envelopes

The envelopes used for business letters are 11 x 22 cm in size and are known as C5/6 or DL. They take A4 letters folded into three or A5 folded once. Other International Paper Size envelopes are: C4, C5 (big), and C6, C7/6 (small).

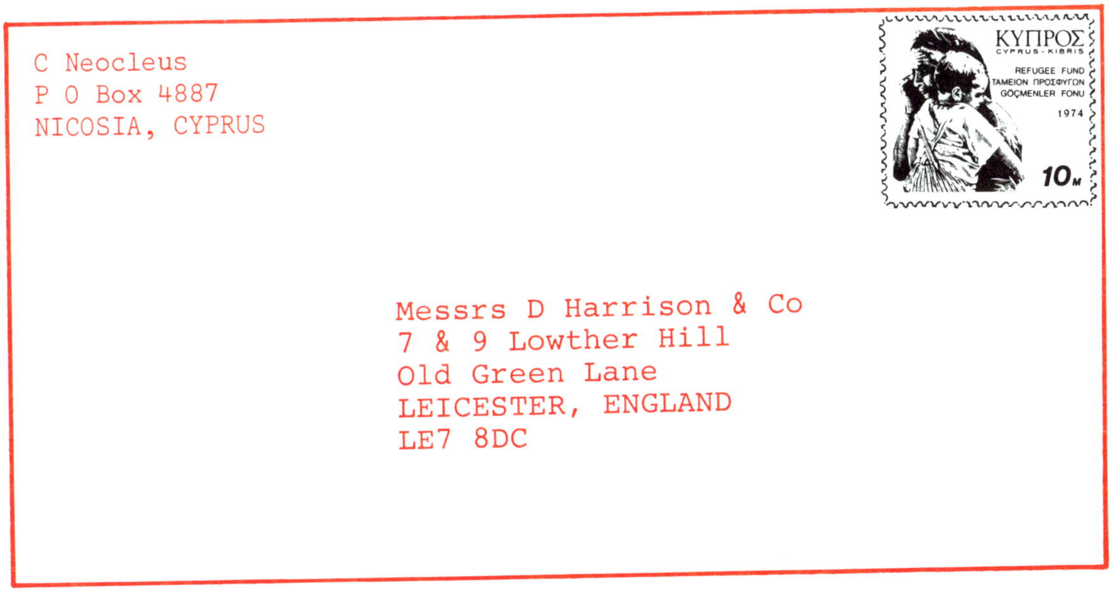


## HOW TO TYPE AN ENVELOPE

1. Insert envelope into machine with flap downward and facing you.
2. Start first line a little more than half-way down and about two-fifths of the way across.
3. Repeat name and address as they appear in the inside address of the letter.

Note: The postcode should always be the last item in an address. It is typed either on the final line by itself or, if the address is long, six spaces after the country, county or town, whichever comes last.

4. Depending upon the practice in your country, the return address should be typed as illustrated above, or centred on the back flap.

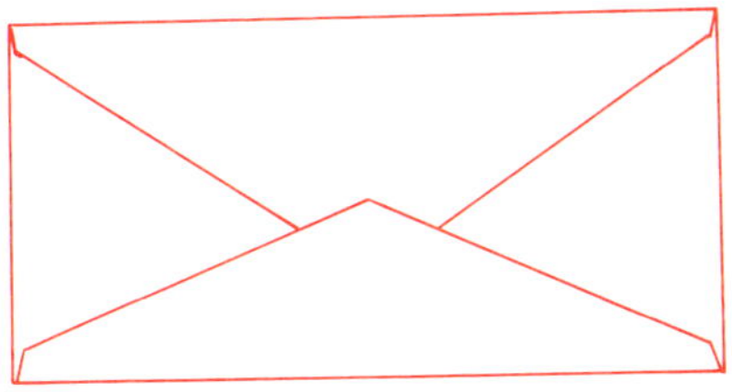

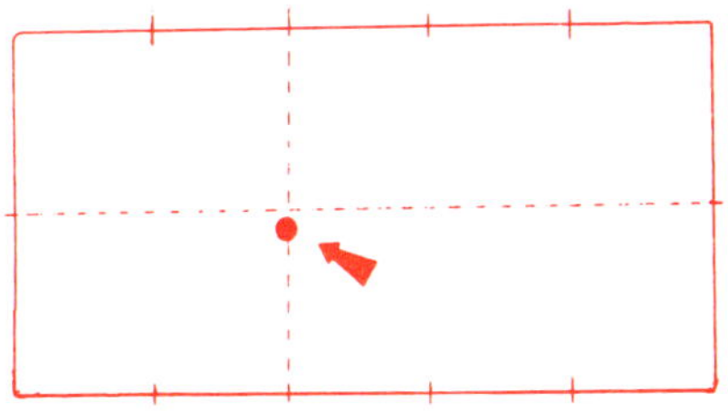

## SPECIAL POINTS

Where the address occupies four or more lines use single spacing. For fewer lines use one-and-a-half line spacing for the sake of more legibility.

Mr Peter Bullen
3232 St Mary at Hill
LONDON
EC3R 8DH

If the enclosed letter is in the blocked form use open punctuation on envelope; if in the indented use the traditional (closed) method. Use capitals for the town and the postcode; this will help the Post Office to sort and send the letters without delay.

Mr Peter Bullen

3232 St Mary at Hill

LONDON EC3R 8DH

# Exercise 243

**For space economy allow 1.5 spaces between paragraphs**

Type the **attention** line a double space below the inside address in one of the following ways:

(a) ATTENTION: MRS GILLIAN WALES

(b) ATTENTION OF MRS GILLIAN WALES

(c) FOR THE ATTENTION OF MRS GILLIAN WALES

(d) Any of the above styles in lower case and underscored, as in example below.

NB If a **window** envelope is used the **attention** line should be typed above the inside address, as Post Office regulations forbid anything below the Post Code.

Ref GD/urs

19 June 1980

Spencer Gilbert & Company Limited
Argyle House
158 East Street
PERTH
PH5 2RZ

Attention: Mrs Gillian Wales

Dear Sirs

At a meeting of the Directors last week it was decided to open a hairdressing salon in Perth, subject to our being able to obtain suitable premises. We should like to hear from you whether you have anything suitable on your books. For your information we require:

1 Ground or first-floor premises, preferably in the town centre.

2 The premises should comprise 4 rooms for use as salon, beauty room, staff room and stock room. We would consider an area large enough to meet these requirements provided partitions could be used.

3 A 10-year lease or satisfactory rental terms.

4 Private parking for a minimum of 10 cars.

We would like to open by the beginning of November at the latest so that we can establish ourselves in time to capture the Christmas trade.

In view of the distance from London I am instructing Mr Mark Lawson to carry out all preliminary enquiries and inspections on my behalf. He is at present the manager of our Edinburgh branch but it is our intention to move him to Perth. Mr Lawson is a highly experienced and knowledgeable person and we have absolute confidence in his judgement. I would appreciate it if you would deal directly with him for the time being. Correspondence should be addressed to him at 6 Fitzwilliam Square, Edinburgh EH2 6CL and his telephone number is 031-112 4999.

Our solicitors are Messrs Makepeace, Makepeace & Scott, Buckingham Chambers, Southampton Road, London WC3P 1AK, and our bankers are Messrs Watkinson, Grant, 240 Queen Street, London SW1K 5RS.

I hope you will be able to assist us.

Yours faithfully

G DCosta

Gina D'Costa (Mrs)
Managing Director Comlon Hairdressing

| | |
|---|---|
| **Size of paper:** | **A4** |
| **Size of letters:** | **elite** |
| **Style of layout:** | **blocked** |
| **Punctuation:** | **open** |
| **Left-hand margin:** | **12** |
| **Allow for heading:** | **12 lines** |

Such notations as URGENT, PERSONAL, FOR THE ATTENTION OF, CONFIDENTIAL etc. are typed two line spaces above the name of the addressee, either in capitals or underscored (see envelope opposite and addresses a, b and c below).

The notation BY HAND is typed in the stamps corner. This will prevent affixing stamps in error; also it will help covering the notation with stamps if it is decided later to mail the letter.

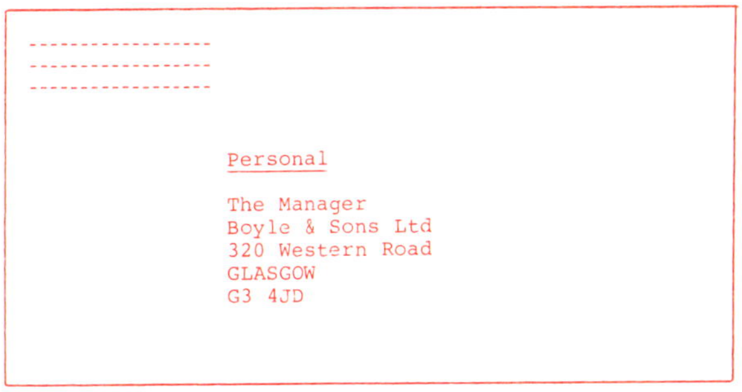


For small envelopes (C6 and C7/6) start the address at about one-third across the envelope (see envelope above). For large envelopes (C4 and C5) use one-and-a-half or double spacing, with lines either blocked or each one indented three spaces (see c below).

CONFIDENTIAL

Mr John D. Davies
Wild Acre
Old Green Lane
Camberley
SURREY GU15 4LG

**(a)**

FOR THE ATTENTION OF
MR A SIMONS

Messrs Lawson & Palmer
380 Riverside Drive (Apt 8)
NEW YORK N.Y. 10025
USA

**(b)**

<u>Urgent</u>

Mrs M. Irving,

40 Northwood Crescent

BRISTOL BS2 4BO

**(c)**

## WINDOW ENVELOPES

To save time from repeating the inside address on the envelope some firms use 'window' envelopes. The address is thus typed only on the letter in such a place and manner as to show through the transparent part of the envelope (see opposite).

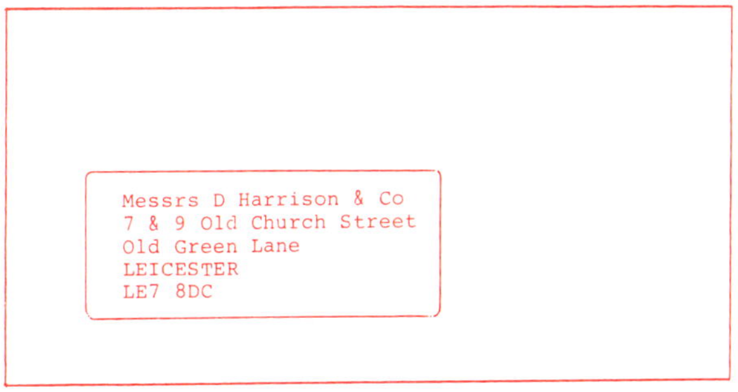


## HOW TO FOLD LETTERS

**Envelopes C5 / 6 (DL)**

**With letter face up, fold slightly less than 1/3 of sheet up towards top.**

**Fold down top of sheet to within 1/2 inch of bottom fold.**

**Insert letter into envelope with last crease towards bottom of envelope.**

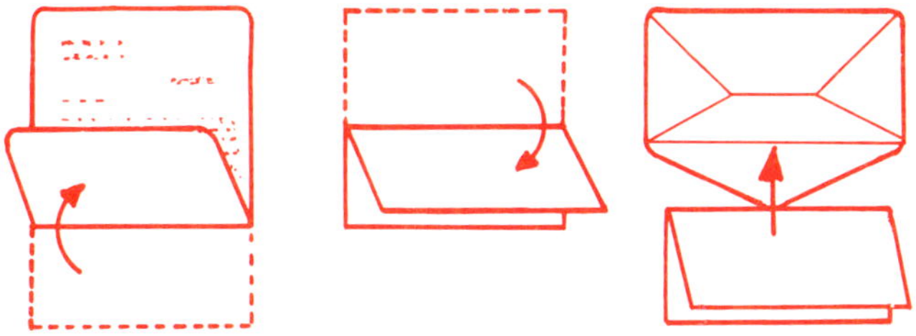

**Window Envelopes C5 / 6 (DL)**

**With sheet face down, top towards you, fold upper third down.**

**Fold lower third up so address is showing.**

**Insert paper into envelope with last crease at bottom.**

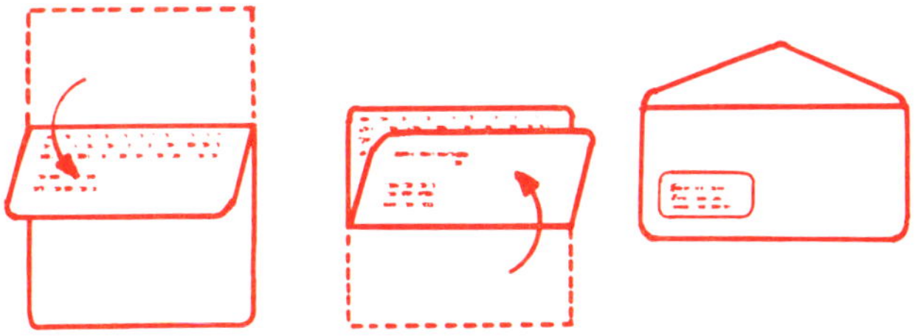

## Exercise 242

**Type a corrected copy of the following letter in single-line spacing, ready for signature for 1 May. Leave a top margin of 3 cm. Use the reference MHM/LGSpL/79 and address it to Mr T Murphy, Tyrone Farm, ORMEAU, BT6 9JJ. (Part of LCCI examination paper LC/54/Sp79 - Intermediate.)**

Dear Sir

Caps <u>Solar Dome Specification</u>

Thank you for your letter of ~~2 May~~ 27 April 1979. We have pleasure in giving you the following information on our latest Solar ~~dome~~ Dome, details of which are not yet published.

THE STRUCTURE - is made from galvanised tubular steel to British Standard specification. It is assembled with 8 mm diameter nuts and bolts.

GUTTERS - are made of non-corrosive aluminium. They are wide and strong enough to walk along. The water is discharged at the ends through a pvc rainwater pipe which ends at ground level.

FILM ANCHORAGE - There is a continuous film anchorage device incorporated in the gutters. This new device (which we hope to patent shortly) ensures that sheets of film are easily secured from inside the "dome" with a completely dry seal.

stet GABLE END FRAMES - are made in ~~timber~~ wood, shaped like goal posts, and secured firmly to the steel framework by fabricated steel brackets, making for strong connection.

uc DOOR OPENINGS - ~~To~~ every multi "dome" tunnel is fitted with one door, framed in timber, o/
stet ~~is given for~~ easy access. To single tunnels a draped curtain is supplied as an alternative to a door.

VENTILATION - A timber framed panel, covered in nylon mesh which is rot proof, is included in kit form, to be fitted to each gable end.

If you could spare the time to pay us a visit ~~soon~~ next month, we shall have our latest "domes" on show in Lincolnshire.

INSURANCE - All our products are insurable and, if you are interested, we shall be pleased to send you details.

Yours faithfully

G RICHARDS
Manager

## Exercise 232

You are typist to the Managing Director of Malaysian Construction Limited. Type a copy of the following letter in single-line spacing using tomorrow's date and reference MHM/LCM2L/80. Leave a 4 cm top margin and address it to The Ellis International Corporation, Hibiscus House, Highway Sydney, Australia. (Part of LCCI examination paper LC/54/M2/Sp80 - Intermediate.)

Dear Sirs

Thank you for your letter of ~~30 May~~ *27 March* with its enclosures.

We have some land in Penang which may be suitable for you~~r~~. ~~requirements.~~

*UC* ~~present~~ planning permission has been granted for a factory complex to be built close to the harbour. As you will see from the enclosed ~~drawings and~~ plans, there is some additional land available. The main production area in the plans covers 8,500 sq m.

*UC* ~~There is~~ a helicopter pad ~~being built which~~ *is under construction and* should be completed by August ~~and~~ *which* will make on-the-spot inspection of the site easy. It will also facilitate the frequent, necessary journeys once the building work starts. So far the hard core for the roads has been laid and water is being piped to the site. *stet* ~~Once~~ *When* the roads have been ~~completed~~ *laid* transport should present no problems and ~~there is~~ plenty of labour *is* available. Transport may have to be provided for *stet* some workers and, possibly, temporary ~~accommodation~~ *housing* found for others. Much of the materials for the construction may be found within a short distance of the site. *NP* [We have ~~contacted~~ an excellent firm of electrical engineers ~~who are~~ working out costs of labour and materials required and we should have their figures within the next ~~two weeks~~ *fortnight*. These electrical engineers have just completed work on a similar complex in Kota Bahru, ~~and so have first hand knowledge of what is required.~~ *know what is required as they*

We sugge~~r~~*s*t you send out a construction engineer so that he may judge the situation for himself. August will be the best time for his visit ~~and~~ *when* we shall be pleased to make any (reservations) (necessary) ~~for your engineer and his party.~~ We shall be happy to meet ~~them~~ *your party* on their arrival.

Yours faithfully

MANAGING DIRECTOR

Enclosures

## Exercise 241

Type a copy of the following letter in single-line spacing, leaving a top margin of 3 cm. Insert the reference MHM/Sp/79/M1/2 and today's date. Address the letter as well as an envelope to The Organising Secretary, Exhibition Hall, BIRMINGHAM, W11 7EP. (Part of LCCI examination paper LC/54/M1/Sp79 - Intermediate.)

Dear Sir

AUDIO/VISUAL AIDS EXHIBITION

We return herewith the plan of the Exhibition on which ~~has~~ [have] been marked the stands we wish to occupy.

As we shall be using ~~much~~ [a great deal of] equipment, we wonder if it is possible to have the platform on Stand 39 removed, thereby linking up with Stands 38 and 40. If this is possible, our Chief Technician, Mr Lim Keng Aun, will be pleased to visit you, at a time which is convenient, ~~to you,~~ to ~~advise you of~~ [explain] our requirements and to help with any movement of fittings.

[Mr Lim can leave for England at any time within the next 14 days.]

It would be helpful if the side upright of Stand 41/42 could have the acoustic panels fitted, as you suggested. ~~The~~ [We hope to have our] slide sequence display ~~will be~~ in that end of the stand. This will mean that spoken commentary and music will be more or less continuous in that area throughout the Exhibition.

The [furniture and] equipment we wish to hire from the Exhibition authorities are as follows

2 L-shaped oak desks
2 electric typewriters
2 manual typewriters.
lc 2 Typists' chairs
lc 6 Large armchairs
lc 4 Small occasional tables

stet We shall ~~need~~ require a rubber-backed mat measuring 2 m x 1.5 m on which to put a heavy cabinet which has drawers and will be in continual use. With a mat of this description, the cabinet should remain stationary.

Thank you for all ~~your~~ [the] help you have given us over the arrangements for the Exhibition.

Yours faithfully

DANIEL FISHER
Sales Manager

Enclosure

**Exercise 233** You are working for the Riverside Club. Type a corrected copy of the following letter in single spacing, leaving a top margin of 3 cm. Use the reference MHM/SP/79/M2/2 and insert today's date. Address the letter to Mr Wong Wai Lin, 2121 Jalan Melaka, KUALA LUMPUR Malaysia. (Part of LCCI examination paper LC/54/M2/Sp79 - Intermediate.)

Dear Mr Wong

Thank you for your letter of ~~2 April~~ [21 March] 1979.

[I have pleasure in enclosing] ~~Enclosed, please find~~ a short ~~account~~ [description] of this Club, which I hope you will find interesting.

On reading through your letter [and your family] it seems that the facilities we offer would be most suitable for you. I am also enclosing the list of membership subscriptions, an application form and a sheet of general information of the sporting facilities. The latter [is brief as it] is just to give you an idea of the wide variety of pastimes available. NP On most Saturdays there is some form of social function. The bedrooms in the Club are so situated that no music [or other noise] is transmitted to them. ~~So~~ [This means that] when members wish to be quiet the music for dancing does not disturb them.

Stet Many ~~excursions~~ [outings] are organised by the Club - shopping days in London; visits to the theatre both in London and the surrounding towns; parties to places of interest - to mention three. There is a Members' Cocktail Party on the third Thursday of every month so that new members may meet existing ones. (moved)

Should you join our Clιb [u], we shall be happy to help make your stay in the United Kingdom as enjoyable as possible. We can ~~make arrangements~~ [arrange] for a car [to bring you here] to meet you at the airport. If you wish to hire a car, while you are in this country, we can make arrangements for one to be made available. (moved)

I look forward to hearing from you again.

Yours sincerely

T L MARTIN
Secretary

Enclosures

# Exercise 240

| | |
|---|---|
| Size of paper: | A4 |
| Size of letters: | pica |
| Style of layout: | Indented |
| Punctuation: | closed |
| Left-hand margin: | 15 |
| Allow for heading: | 12 lines |

KJH/PID 1st October, 1982

Messrs. L. Stevens & Co.,
P.O.Box 2901,
NICOSIA.

Dear Sirs,

Credit No. 7/726 in favour of 'Cutlery Industrial Co., Hong Kong'

With reference to your Letter of Engagement of the 15th September 1982, instructing us to establish the above Credit we should like to inform you that we have paid to the accreditees through our Correspondent in Hong Kong the sum of £860 against delivery of the following documents:

Invoice in triplicate
Bill of Lading S/S "Sumida Maru"
Insurance Policy
Draft for £860
Certificate of Origin

Please note that we have debited you in a Provisional account, as follows:

| | £ |
|---|---|
| Amount paid | 860.00 |
| Correspondent's charges | 0.50 |
| Opening commission | 1.00 |
| Exchange comm. and postages | 0.81 |
| | £862.31 |

Kindly see that all the a/m Documents are withdrawn against payment of the above amount, plus interest as from 30th April 1983 in accordance with the terms of the said Letter of Engagement.

Yours faithfully,
THE NICOSIA COMMERCIAL BANK

Manager

With the indented style **subject** line and inset matter are centred to the typing line.

NB To create a double underscore (see money column above): type the underscore, roll the paper slightly (using the line finder) and repeat the underscore.

# Exercise 234

**COMLON INTERNATIONAL LIMITED**

COMLON HOUSE
WEST STREET
LONDON SW1Y 2AR

Tel: 01 920 0261    Telex: Comlond 888941    Telegrams: Comlond London SW1

| | |
|---|---|
| Size of paper: | A4 |
| Size of letters: | elite |
| Style of layout: | blocked |
| Punctuation: | open |
| Left hand margin: | 18 |
| Allow for heading: | 15 lines |

RM/SCG

15th June 1979

Mr J A Lennon JP
"Oakways"
The Grange
TUNBRIDGE WELLS
Kent
TN3 3AN

Dear John

Life Assurance Proposal

Thank you for the completed proposal form which is receiving my personal attention.

To enable further consideration to be given to this assurance it will be necessary for you to undergo a medical examination.

The appropriate instructions have today been sent to Dr J R Pickering of Cumberland Mews, Tunbridge Wells, telephone 722116. Will you please telephone his surgery to make an appointment for your examination? I thought you would not find this too difficult to arrange as Dr Pickering's surgery is in your locality. The Society will, of course, be responsible for payment of the Doctor's fee.

Yours sincerely

R McKie

R McKie
Area Manager

A **subject** heading is typed two lines below the salutation. It may be typed in lower case and underscored (as in above example), or in capitals without an underscore.

No full stop is put at the end of a **subject** line, unless the last word is abbreviated and traditional punctuation is used.

Note: **JP** after addressee's name stands for **Justice of the Peace.**

## Exercise 239

Size of paper: A5
Size of letters: elite
Style of layout: semi-blocked
Punctuation: open
Left-hand margin: 12
Allow for heading: 10 lines

# STAINLESS STEEL CO LTD

48 GLADIATOR DRIVE
LEEDS
YORKSHIRE
ENGLAND LE4 7BT

Your ref BR/TS
Our ref EN-771

12 July 1982

Messrs Black & White
Post Office Box 783
PORT SAID, Egypt

Dear Sirs

ORDER SO/78 DATED 2/7/82

We take pleasure in enclosing herewith our Invoice No ER-83 dated 17 June 1982, valued at $79.80, in respect of the despatch of one case of Stainless Steel goods per S/S VENUS. The relative documents under No 437/BT/R have been sent to your Bankers for collection.

We request you to pay the amount on presentation of the Documents and you will oblige us.

Yours faithfully
STAINLESS STEEL CO LTD

R Brooks
Sales Manager

Enc Invoice

Semi-blocked letter with **subject** line beginning at left-hand margin.

# Exercise 235

**Subject** line is here typed in capital letters, without an underscore or a full stop. (This method is more popular than the one used on previous page, as it is much quicker to type.)

Note that in complimentary close only the first word is capitalized.

| | |
|---|---|
| **Size of paper:** | **A4** |
| **Size of letters:** | **elite** |
| **Style of layout:** | **blocked** |
| **Punctuation:** | **open** |
| **Left-hand margin:** | **15** |
| **Allow for heading:** | **12 lines** |

MHM/LCS1/80

30 May 1980

Mr J R Thomas
Medico Services Limited
Barnett House
Barnett Street
LONDON
E11 9AA

Dear Mr Thomas

LICENSING AND REGISTRATION OF BUSINESS

Thank you for your letter of 20 May. We look forward to welcoming you and your wife here on 4 June. We have booked you both into the Hotel Miramar for your three week stay.

Generally there is no restriction on types of businesses that may be set up out here. However, businesses intending to manufacture certain goods have to obtain a special licence and this could apply to you, as we understand that once your construction contract is completed you may wish to set up a manufacturing concern specialising in producing drugs etc for the hospital complex. Every business out here must be registered with the Registry of Businesses or the Registry of Companies.

There are no set regulations for local equity participation in foreign businesses set up in Singapore. Potential foreign investors may discuss this aspect with the Economic Development Board or the Department of Trade. Plenty of local capital is available to help firms, such as yourselves, to get started in Singapore. There is a provision that such firms may eventually buy back all or a part of the Government's share.

To set up a representative office, Form A must be obtained from the Department of Trade which must be returned to the unit for processing. This takes about two weeks, and once approval has been given the company must be registered. We are enclosing some particulars with regard to foreign companies.

Yours sincerely

P. Turner

MANAGING DIRECTOR

Enclosure

# Exercise 238

**COMLON INTERNATIONAL LIMITED**

COMLON HOUSE
WEST STREET
LONDON SW1Y 2AR

Tel: 01 920 0261 Telex: Comlond 888941 Telegrams: Comlond London SW1

| | |
|---|---|
| **Size of paper:** | **A4** |
| **Size of letters:** | **elite** |
| **Style of layout:** | **blocked** |
| **Punctuation:** | **open** |
| **Left-hand margin:** | **17** |
| **Allow for heading:** | **15 lines** |

HM/SCG

23 September 1979

The Clearlight Glazing Company
19 High Street
SWINDON
Wiltshire
SN1 7KS

Dear Sirs

<u>OUR INSURED: David Bunting</u>

<u>POLICY NUMBER: S608/59/345</u>

<u>VEHICLE: Ford Cortina XL</u>

We are dealing with the claim arising from the accident involving our insured's vehicle and the van owned by you and driven by Mr Timothy Roach. The accident took place on 10 September at the junction of Connaught Street and the Market Place in Marlborough at approximately 1100 hours.

On completion of our investigations we may have to hold you responsible for all loss or damage sustained and would advise you to forward this letter to your Insurance Company so that they can contact us.

Yours faithfully
COMLON INTERNATIONAL LTD

S. Smith

pp R McKie
Area Manager

The **subject** is divided into three headings, separated from one another by double spacing.

**pp** in front of signatory's name stands for the Latin 'per procurationem' meaning 'on behalf of', and is used to indicate that some other official is signing the letter - not the one mentioned.

## Exercise 236 (LC/53/M/Sp77)

Size of paper: A4
Size of letters: elite
Style of layout: blocked
Punctuation: open
Left-hand margin: 15
Allow for heading: 12 lines

FLPT/M/77/1

7 April 1977

Mr W L Kee
199 Temple Street
Kuching
Sarawak

Dear Mr Kee

Telecommunication Installation in Sarawak

I believe that Mr White has spoken to you on this matter and I would like to acknowledge receipt of the contracts which he sent to us on Monday last. I have not been able to reply previously as we were awaiting survey reports on the premises but I am glad to say that we sent the contracts for the purchase of the lease to our solicitors yesterday and they should be completed shortly.

As you know, the internal telephone contracts run to 31 December 1979 whereas the lease of this building terminates on 31 December 1978. We are prepared to accept the transfer of the internal telephone contracts subject to an undertaking by your company that, in the event of payments becoming due under the 'termination in special cases' clauses of these contracts, your company would reimburse us, or any subsequent assignee of the contracts and lease of that portion of such payments which relates to the period from 1 January to 31 December 1979. The contracts referred to in this paragraph will be sent to you under separate cover, tomorrow.

If you would send us a letter giving the undertaking set out in my last paragraph, signed on behalf of your Company by one of your Directors, and
--- would also sign and return the enclosed transfer agreement we shall complete the latter and send it to the requisite Authority.

Please telephone me if there is anything you would like to discuss further; otherwise we look forward to receiving all these papers within the next week or two.

Yours sincerely

H Williams

Enclosure

**Subject** heading is here centred to the typing line despite the blocked form employed.

An alternative (or complementary) method to indicate an enclosure is to type three hyphens or full stops in the left-hand margin against the line where the enclosure is mentioned.

# Exercise 237

**COMLON INTERNATIONAL LIMITED**

COMLON HOUSE
WEST STREET
LONDON SW1Y 2AR

Tel: 01 920 0261  Telex: Comlond 888941  Telegrams: Comlond London SW1

| | |
|---|---|
| **Size of paper:** | **A4** |
| **Size of letters:** | **elite** |
| **Style of layout:** | **blocked** |
| **Punctuation:** | **open** |
| **Left-hand margin:** | **15** |
| **Allow for heading:** | **14 lines** |

JD/MW

12 June 1980

Mr & Mrs M Hughes-Junes
18 Cathedral Close
CANTERBURY
CT2 3CG

Dear Mr and Mrs Hughes-Junes

24 MEWS COTTAGES PETERSHAM PLACE SW7

Following your instructions regarding this property, I now present my report and valuation as follows:

SITUATION AND DESCRIPTION

The property comprises a small terraced house built at the turn of the century in a quiet cul-de-sac. It has been well modernised and maintained by previous owners and is well situated for public transport and local shopping facilities.

CONDITION

I have not carried out a full structural survey of the property but I can report that it has obviously been cared for and kept in excellent repair. The modernisation has been carefully planned to maintain its original charm and character.

VALUATION

In view of its excellent condition I would value this property at £58 000.

If you require any further assistance please do not hesitate to contact me.

Yours sincerely
COMLON INTERNATIONAL LIMITED

Joyce Deacon

Joyce Deacon (Mrs)
Chartered Surveyor

In addition to the subject heading this letter also has paragraph headings for each separate part of the main subject.

In the sum **£58 000** note the omission of the comma.